AN ROINN COMHSHAOIL

sustainable development

A Strategy for Ireland

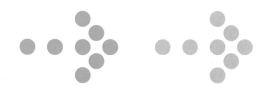

Printed on recycled paper

DEPARTMENT OF THE
ENVIRONMENT

© Government of Ireland 1997

ISBN 0706 3850-X

Le ceannach díreach ón
OIFIG DHÍOLTA FOILSEACHÁN RIALTAIS,
TEACH SUN ALLIANCE,
SRÁID THEACH LAIGHEAN,
BAILE ÁTHA CLIATH 2.

Nó tríd an bpost ó
FOILSEACHÁIN RIALTAIS,
AN RANNÓG POST-TRÁCHTA,
4-5 BÓTHAR FHEARCHAIR,
BAILE ÁTHA CLIATH 2.

(Teil: 01-6613111, fó-líne 4040/4045;
Fax: 01-4752760)
no trí aon díoltóir leabhar

To be purchased directly from the
GOVERNMENT PUBLICATIONS SALE OFFICE,
SUN ALLIANCE HOUSE,
MOLESWORTH STREET,
DUBLIN 2.

or by mail order from
GOVERNMENT PUBLICATIONS,
POSTAL TRADE SECTION,
4-5 HARCOURT TOAD, DUBLIN 2.

(Tel: 01- 01-6613111, ext. 4040/4045;
Fax: 01-4752760)

or through any bookseller

Price £20.00

Contents

Foreword by Mr. Brendan Howlin, T.D., Minister for the Environment

 Sustainable development is one of the most universally endorsed aspirations of our time. It has been defined as development which meets the needs of the present generation without compromising the ability of future generations to meet their own needs.

Continued economic growth is essential to meet people's legitimate ambitions for a better life and to provide the resources for implementing environmental protection measures. But we should not tolerate development that is inefficient, that is excessive in its consumption of natural resources or that unduly pressurises the environment.

The Irish public already strongly support this assessment. In a recent EU commissioned attitude survey, only 9% of Irish people agreed that economic development was more important than environmental protection. The overwhelming majority, some 68%, wanted economic development to be progressed but the environment to be protected at the same time.

Sustainable development is also about solidarity: solidarity between the present and future generations, between various participants in our society and between different countries.

This National Sustainable Development Strategy is designed to apply considerations of sustainability more systematically to Irish economic policies and to integrate them into associated decision making processes. The EPA's *State of the Environment in Ireland* shows that Ireland's environment, while still generally of a high quality, is affected by a number of adverse trends and serious threats.

There are two ways of responding to these problems. First and immediately, we need where possible to establish specific counter-measures to mitigate adverse environmental effects. Regulation, improved environmental infrastructure and other targeted actions are all important in providing solutions of this kind.

But we must also get the fundamentals right. Environmentally adverse trends can only be radically reversed by having the main economic sectors pull with rather than against the environment.

We must do more with less. We must reduce the intensity of natural resource consumption associated with energy, industrial and agricultural production. We need more efficient and sparing use of transport and of consumer goods. Through changes of this kind, excessive waste generation and pressures on air, water and soil, are headed off at source. This is the meaning of sustainable development.

More sustainable approaches to economic activity will also be assisted by a better valuation and pricing of relevant products and services. The external polluting impact of products and services must be better factored into their costs so that consumers receive the right price signals to inform their market choices.

Sustainable development is not just a constraint on the economy. In the Irish situation, it offers many opportunities to enhance the marketing of key natural resource based industries and to exploit the fast growing world market for environmental goods and services. Adoption of sustainable policies is calculated to increase rather than threaten Irish employment.

This Government Strategy is important in providing a focus for the concept of sustainable development and a plan for its integration into key economic sectors. But achieving sustainable development is a continuing task; that is why the Strategy also puts in place mechanisms for monitoring and review. I intend that these will be actively deployed.

I am satisfied that this new Strategy reflects and takes forward Ireland's commitment to the principles and agenda for sustainable development agreed at the Earth Summit in Rio in 1992. It responds also to the EU Fifth Action Programme for the Environment, which was reviewed during the Irish Presidency of the European Union and in whose implementation Ireland is actively participating. The Strategy will assist Ireland's participation in the major UN review of *Agenda 21* which will take place at a Special Session of the General Assembly in June 1997.

Brendan Howlin T.D.
Minister for the Environment

Brollach leis an Aire Comhshaoil

Tá forbairt inmharthana mar cheann de na mianta dár linne lena réitítear go huilíoch. Sainmhíníotar í mar fhorbairt a riarann ar riachtanais na glúine seo gan chumas na nglúnta atá le teacht a gcás féin a riaradh a chur i gcontúirt.

Ní foláir fás eacnamaíochta leanúnach chun uaillmhianta dlisteanacha daoine ar saol níos fearr a shásamh, agus chun na hacmhainní a sholáthar chun bearta d'fhonn cosaint na timpeallachta a chur i gcrích. Ach ní chóir dúinn glacadh le forbairt atá neamhéifeachtach, a ídíonn achmainní nádúrtha go hiomarcach, nó a chuireann brú éagorach ar an dtimpeallacht.

Aontaíonn pobal na hÉireann go láidir leis an measúnú seo cheana féin. I suirbhé a iarraidh an CE le déanaí, níor aontaigh ach 9% de phobal na hÉireann go raibh forbairt eacnamaíochta níos tábhachtaí ná cosaint na timpeallachta. Theastaigh ón mórchuid millteanach, 68%, leanacht le forbairt eacnamaíochta ach an timpeallacht a chosaint ag an am céanna.

Tá dlúthpháirtíocht mar chuid d'fhorbairt inmharthana freisin: dlúthpháirtíocht idir an ghlúin atá anois ann agus dóibh siúd a bheas ann amach anseo, idir rannpháirtithe éagsúla an sochaí againne, agus idir tíortha éagsúla.

Ceaptar an Stráitéis Forbartha Inmharthana Náisiúnta seo chun cúrsaí cothabhála a chur i bhfeidhm ar bhealach níos struchtúrtha i bpolasaithe eacnamaíochta na hÉireann, agus chun iad a thabhairt isteach sna bproiséis cinnteoireachta a bhfuil bainteach leo. Taispeánann an Tuairisc ar Staid an Chomhshaoil (An Ghníomhaireacht um Chaomhnú Comhshaoil, 1996) go gcuireann treonna naimhdeacha agus bagartha chinniúnacha isteach ar timpeallacht na hÉireann, cé go bhfuil ard-chineál ar an dtimpeallacht sin go ginéarálta.

Is féidir diriú ar na fadhbanna seo i ndá shlí. I dtús báire, ní mór dúinn, áit ar féidir, frithbheartanna faoi leith a bhunú chun toraidh naimhdeacha comhshaoil a laghdú. Tá rialachán, infrastructúr feabhsaithe comhshaoil, agus gníomhaithe le cuspóirí eile go léir tábhachtach chun teacht ar réitigh den chineál seo.

Ach ní mór dúinn na bunphrionsabail cearta a aimsiú chomh maith. Ní féidir treonna naimhdeacha comhshaoil a aisiompú go fréamhaí gan na príomh-earnálacha eacnamaíochta a bheith ag obair ar son na timpeallachta, in áit ina coinne.

Caithfimid breis a dhéanamh le níos lú. Caithfimid tréine ídiú achmhainní nádúrtha, atá comhcheangailte le fuinnimh, táirgeadh tionsclaíoch agus talmhaíocht, a laghdú. Tá gá le húsáid níos éifeachtaigh agus níos coigiltí d'iompair agus d'earraí íditheora. Is tríd athruithe den chineál seo a sháraítear, ag an bhfoinse, táirgeadh truflaise iomarcach agus brúnna ar aer, uisce agus talamh. Seo is brí le forbairt inmharthana.

Rachfaidh luacháil agus meastóireacht níos fearr ar tháirgí agus ar sheirbhísí ábharthacha i gcabhair ar bhealaí níos inmharthanaí chuig gníomhaíocht eacnamaíochta. Ní mór turraing sálú imeallach de tháirgí agus seirbhísí a chur isteach ina gcostaisí, chun go mbeidh tuilleadh eolais ag íditheoirí ó chomharthaí praghsanna agus rogha margaidh á dhéanamh acu.

Ní iallach ar an eacnamaíocht í forbairt inmharthana. I gcás na hÉireann, cuireann sí go leor deiseanna ar fáil margaí méadaithe a bhaint amach do thionscail bunaithe ar achmhainní nádúrtha, agus sochar a bhaint as an margadh domhanda do tháirgí agus do sheirbhísí comhshaoil, atá ag fás go tapaidh. Is féidir le polasaí inmharthanachta fostaíocht in Éirinn a mhéadú, seachas a bheith mar bhagairt uirthi.

Tá an Stráitéis Rialtais seo tábhachtach chun fócas a thabhairt ar choincheap forbartha inmharthana agus ar phlean chun í a chur i ngníomh sna phríomh-earnálacha. Ach is saothar leanúnach í chun forbairt inmharthana a chur i gcrích; sin é an fáth go mbunaíonn an Stráitéis meicníochtaí le haghaidh monatóireacht agus athbhreithniú. Tá sé de chuspóir agam go mbainfí úsáid gníomhach astu siúd.

Táim sásta go dtaispeánann agus go gcuireann an Stráitéis seo le ceangal na hÉireann leis na prionsabail agus leis an gclár d'fhorbairt inmharthana a shocraíodh ag Cruinniú Mullaigh na Cruinne i Rio i 1992. Tugann sí freagra freisin ar an 5ú Clár Gníomhaíochta ar an dTimpeallacht den CE, a rinneadh athbhreithniú air le linn Uachtaránacht na hÉireann ar an gComhphobal Eorpach, agus ina a bhfuil Éire páirteach go fuinniúil ina chomhlíonadh. Cabhróidh an Stráitéis le rannpháirtíocht na hÉireann san mhór-athbhreithniú ar Chlár 21 ag Seisiún Speisialta de Thionól Ginéarálta na Náisiún Aontaithe i mí Mheithimh, 1997.

Breandán Ó hÚilín
Aire Comhshaoil

PART I - STRATEGIC PROGRAMME

I   Summary of Key Strategic Actions

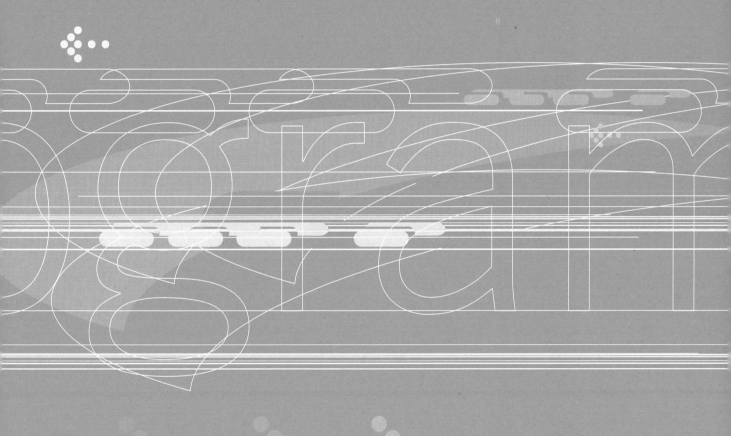

Key Strategic Actions

The principal purpose of the Strategy is to provide a comprehensive analysis and framework which will allow sustainable development to be taken forward more systematically in Ireland. This process cannot be completed by the Strategy document itself, but requires a continuing adaptation and review of policies, actions and lifestyles. It is not, therefore, intended that the main impact or contribution of the Strategy should consist in a series of discrete new initiatives. However, for ease of reference various specific initiatives indicated in the Strategy are set out below.

Securing Sustainable Development: Better Supporting Structures

- The Government will propose that the **Joint Oireachtas Committee on Sustainable Development** should become a standing Committee of the Oireachtas to oversee relevant policy development and the implementation of this Strategy.

- The Government will establish a **National Sustainable Development Council**, independently chaired and with wide representation from Social Partners and environmental NGOs to facilitate participation in the achievement of sustainable development and promote consultation and dialogue.

- Relevant Government Departments, and the EPA as appropriate, will be designated as **Task Managers** to lead in the development of the more detailed processes and measures necessary to give full effect to the Strategy. Their reports, and the National Sustainable Development Council's comments on them, will provide a basis for the periodic review of the Strategy by Government.

- Regional Authorities will have ongoing responsibility for the regionalisation of the Strategy. They will be asked to define regional sustainability priorities, recommend appropriate implementation mechanisms in the regions, and develop regional sustainability indicators. Regional Sustainability Fora will be held in 1997.

- An Eco-Management and Audit Scheme will be developed for local government.

- Local authorities have a key role as environment protection authorities and agents of sustainable development. All local authorities will be asked to complete a Local Agenda 21 for their areas by 1998.

- Sustainable development projects by local authorities and NGOs in partnership will be co-funded by a new **Environment Partnership Fund**.

- Government will bring forward proposals, within three years, to develop a **strategic environmental impact assessment (SEA)** system for major plans and programmes, in addition to supporting EU proposals for SEA of land use plans and programmes.

A Positive Impact on Enterprise and Employment

- In line with *Partnership 2000* Government will consider further streamlining of the planning system and the introduction of accelerated planning procedures for major projects involving significant employment and added value.

- Government will support a shift in tax burdens away from labour towards polluters.

- Government will develop suitable economic instruments to improve internalisation of external costs, including:
  - resource pricing;
  - green taxation measures; and
  - exploration of market-based instruments, such as emissions trading, offering flexibility to industry to achieve environmental improvements.

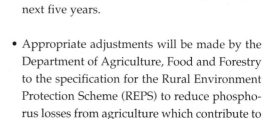

- Enterprise authorities will encourage and promote the development of environmental industry.

- Government will maintain a substantial environmental infrastructure investment programme to underpin sustainable economic and social development.

- Active labour market policies will be pursued to support the transition to cleaner production and extension of environmental management.

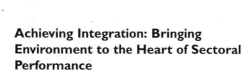

Achieving Integration: Bringing Environment to the Heart of Sectoral Performance

Agriculture

- The Government will extend environmental cross-compliance as a standard consideration in respect of agricultural support generally or in selected schemes.

- The *Code of Good Agricultural Practice to Protect Waters from Pollution by Nitrates*, launched in July 1996, and including recommended Nitrogen application rates, will be promoted by local authorities, Teagasc and farmer representative associations. The implementation of the Code will be closely monitored. Efforts to prevent build-up of nitrates in waters will maintain and, where necessary, improve on the quality of drinking water.

- The use of revised recommended application rates for phosphorus fertilisers for grassland (launched by Teagasc in December 1996) will be encouraged and promoted so as to reduce soil P levels, where excessive to crop require-

ments at present, down to the recommended levels over a period of five years. In particular, the Strategy targets a reduction of 10% *per annum* in artificial P fertiliser usage over the next five years.

- Appropriate adjustments will be made by the Department of Agriculture, Food and Forestry to the specification for the Rural Environment Protection Scheme (REPS) to reduce phosphorus losses from agriculture which contribute to eutrophication of rivers and lakes.

- The Department of Agriculture, Food and Forestry will produce comprehensive guidance and advice on agricultural practices for the purpose of protecting all environmental media and the ecosystems they support, and promoting sustainable agriculture.

- Nutrient Management Planning (as now statutorily provided for in the *Waste Management Act, 1996*), will be promoted mandatorily by local authorities in areas where the Environmental Protection Agency (EPA) water quality data identify agriculture as a significant contributor to eutrophication of rivers and lakes. Emphasis will be placed on such planning on an individual farms basis and in catchment and regional areas.

- Teagasc will continue to provide advice and educational services to farmers, including the promotion of awareness on the nutrient value of farm wastes and the achievement of a more sustainable balance between soil inputs and outputs. The services will be reviewed to allow greater targeting, in consultation with EPA, towards the catchments of eutrophic rivers and lakes.

- Intensive agriculture is a scheduled activity for the purposes of Integrated Pollution Control (IPC) licensing under the *Environmental Protection Agency Act, 1992*. IPC requirements for new activities were introduced in September 1996 and IPC requirements for existing activities will be phased in from 1998.

- To assist in maintaining an environmentally-sound farming sector, the Government is introducing, for a three-year period to 1999, improved capital allowances for targeted investment by farmers in pollution control measures.

- A system of environmental management of farming in proposed Natural Heritage Areas (NHAs), including sustainable stocking densities, will be elaborated between the Department of Agriculture, Food and Forestry, the Department of Arts, Culture and the Gaeltacht, Teagasc and REPS planning agencies, as well as environmental and farm organisations. Agreed conditions in this regard, correctly applied, will provide for sustainable farming systems in such areas, as well as placing restrictions on environmentally-damaging activities.

- The Department of Agriculture, Food and Forestry is seeking the approval of the European Commission to extend the application of REPS in overgrazed areas from 5 to 15 years. Measures will also be put in place to ensure that the environmental benefits achieved under REPS in designated commonage areas are not diminished by non-participants in the scheme.

- An uptake of 30% of farmers in REPS will be achieved by the year 1999.

- The National Biodiversity Plan, to be completed by end-1997, will identify the actions necessary to preserve biodiversity, including species and habitats, from human activities including the pressures of agriculture.

- The Department of the Environment will review the regulatory thresholds for environmental impact assessment of drainage works in 1997.

- The Department of Agriculture, Food and Forestry will coordinate action to improve information on the use of pesticides, and to reduce the environmental risks associated with their storage, use and disposal.

- The Department of Agriculture, Food and Forestry will continue its support for organic farming, including financial support for measures to improve marketing and public awareness of the environmental benefits of organic products.

- A farm plastic films recovery scheme, a voluntary initiative involving industry and farming operations, is commencing operation in 1997, and will contribute to national recycling targets.

- The need for precaution in the use of genetically modified organisms (GMOs) in food production is recognised. The new Food Safety Authority will be established in 1997, and will have responsibility for novel foods. Better labelling provisions in Community legislation are being sought for products containing GMOs.

Forestry

- The threshold at which planning permission and environmental impact assessment (EIA) is required for afforestation has been reduced with effect from 1 October, 1996, from 200 hectares to 70 hectares. In addition, planning permission and EIA will now be required for cumulative afforestation which results in a total area planted exceeding 70 hectares.

- The Minister for the Environment will take new powers in relation to forestry control in the next Local Government (Planning and Development) Bill to enable planning permission to be required for plantations which would not warrant EIA.

- Forestry legislation will be reviewed to reflect the principles of sustainable forestry development, as set out under the Helsinki process. As part of this process, Ireland will also develop a national sustainable forestry plan and national criteria and indicators by which progress can be measured, and the Department of Agriculture, Food and Forestry will develop a Code of Practice for sustainable forest management over the full forestry rotation period.

- The Department of Agriculture, Food and Forestry will implement a strategic plan for the forestry sector in Ireland, which will take account of sustainable development requirements.

- The Department of the Environment has issued draft consultation guidelines for planning authorities in relation to forestry and the need to protect views and scenic areas, landscape and water quality, and the natural and archaeological heritage and to avoid rural isolation. These guidelines will be finalised in 1997. In accordance with the guidelines, planning authorities will be entitled to designate areas which they consider to be sensitive to forestry development, and the Forest Service will notify these authorities of all proposed forestry developments, regardless of size, within such designated areas.

- The Department of Agriculture, Food and Forestry will regularly review its existing environmental controls, including its existing guidelines in relation to the landscape, fisheries and archaeology, and will introduce new guidelines on wildlife and habitat diversity, harvesting and clearfelling, use of chemicals and herbicides, and amenity and recreation. Particular attention will be paid to the planting of broadleaf trees on the margins of large coniferous plantations.

Marine resources

- Ireland will continue to support efforts, under the EU Common Fisheries Policy (CFP), to optimise the management and conservation of sea fisheries in the interests of sustainable and renewable use.

- In this context, Ireland will support the development within the CFP of further measures to reduce the catching of juvenile fish, through improvements in the selectivity of fishing gear and other technical conservation measures, and monitor and quantify the by-catch of cetacea in fishing gear, as required by the Habitats Directive.

- National measures will be maintained to conserve inshore fish-stocks of salmon, sea-trout and bass. A new salmon management strategy is being implemented on a phased basis.

- The Minister for the Marine has introduced proposed legislation to establish a new licensing and regulatory system for aquaculture. The new system will include an independent Appeals Board.

- The *Dumping at Sea Act, 1996*, will be implemented to prohibit waste dumping in the majority of situations and ensure rigorous control of residual disposals.

- Existing regulations for preventing pollution from port operations and ships in harbours will be reinforced by the express duty of port companies established by the *Harbours Act, 1996*, to have due regard to the consequences of their activities on the environment.

- Ireland will ratify the Convention for the Protection of the Marine Environment of the North-East Atlantic (OSPAR) in 1997.

- A Quality Status Report, required by the OSPAR Convention, is being prepared for the Irish and Celtic Sea and areas west of Ireland and Scotland in cooperation with the UK authorities.

- Cooperation with UK authorities on management and monitoring of the Beaufort's Dyke munitions dumpsite will be continued, and an inventory of other dumpsites will be developed in preparing the Quality Status Report under the OSPAR Convention.

- The Minister for the Environment will formulate a policy directive to planning authorities, An Bord Pleanála and the Environmental Protection Agency indicating that there should be a presumption against the location of new landfills adjacent to coasts or estuaries.

- The Framework Strategy for the development of the marine sector, to be published shortly by the Department of the Marine, will take full account of the requirements of sustainable development.

- The Department of the Marine, in consultation with the Department of Transport, Energy and Communications, is devising an updated and comprehensive strategy to ensure that offshore oil and gas exploration and development do not adversely affect the marine environment.

- The Government will continue to press in the appropriate international fora for the implementation of a strict new code governing the shipment of nuclear materials, and will seek to have the existing *Code on the Safe Carriage of Irradiated Nuclear Fuel, Plutonium and High-Level Radioactive Wastes in Flasks on Board Ships* made mandatory.

Energy

- Energy conservation and demand side management programmes will be encouraged and monitored. The Irish Energy Centre will continue to develop its energy conservation programme, including the promotion of energy efficiency in industry, the provision of technical advice, and information campaigns and support measures.

- Under the Department of Transport, Energy and Communication's *Renewable Energy Strategy*, installed electricity generating capacity from renewables will reach 10% of total installed capacity by the end of 1999; further growth under the strategy will increase this to 14% by 2010.

- The Minister for Finance, in consultation with the Minister for Transport, Energy and Communications, will introduce new incentives to encourage investment in renewable energies.

- For purposes of the UN climate change negotiations, Ireland has adopted an indicative national objective of limiting the growth in total emissions of carbon dioxide, methane and nitrous oxide up to the year 2010 to 15% above their 1990 levels.

- A study has been commissioned to evaluate the scope for intensifying (or introducing new) policies and measures to limit greenhouse gas emissions.

- Action will be continued to reduce emissions of sulphur dioxide and nitrogen oxides (NO_x) from power generation; these actions include fuel substitution, energy conservation and installation of low-NO_x burners in some power stations, supported as necessary by voluntary agreements with energy producers.

- Ireland will ratify the Second Sulphur Protocol (Oslo Protocol) in 1997.

- In relation to emissions of NO_x, Ireland will work towards achievement of the more stringent emission ceilings now being developed at UN ECE and EU level.

- Energy is a scheduled activity for the purposes of Integrated Pollution Control licensing under the *Environmental Protection Agency Act, 1992*, and IPC licensing requirements will come into operation for the sector by the end of the decade.

- The threshold at which peat extraction becomes liable to EIA will be reduced.

- The Government will continue to oppose any expansion of the international nuclear industry, and to avail of all opportunities at bilateral, EU and wider international level to advance its concerns in this regard. Closure of the Sellafield operations remains an objective and will be pursued through legal action should sufficient evidence of pollution or public health impact be obtained. Possibilities in this regard are being pursued in particular under the provisions of the Paris and OSPAR Conventions. Ireland has ratified the Nuclear Safety Convention, and is actively promoting a new Global Convention on Radioactive Waste Management, which is expected to be finalised in 1997.

Industry

- While legislation and regulation will continue to be important instruments for managing industrial impacts on the environment, a broader mix of instruments will be applied where environmental benefits are achievable as efficiently or more cost-effectively. This will include increasing the use of market-based instruments over time and using voluntary agreements with industry where appropriate.

- Integrated Pollution Control licensing is being extended on a phased basis by 1998 to most industries covered by the *Environmental Protection Agency Act, 1992* (the *EPA Act*).

- The *EPA Act* will be amended to give effect to the provisions of Council Directive 96/61/EC on Integrated Pollution Prevention and Control (IPPC).

- The *Waste Management Act, 1996*, will be rapidly implemented. This will increase the focus on waste prevention and minimisation and on recovering, rather than disposing of, the by-products and wastes arising from industrial processes, and of products themselves and their packaging.

- Producer responsibility initiatives (such as the REPAK scheme already mobilised) will be encouraged to increase reuse and recycling of wastes, with regulatory support to ensure fair competitive conditions for participating industries.

- A Pollution Emissions Register will be published by the EPA in 1997. Regulations will be introduced subsequently to establish by 1998 a more complete Toxics Release Inventory.

- Ireland will support international efforts to develop legally binding instruments for the reduction and/or elimination of emissions of persistent organic pollutants to the environment.

- The Department of Enterprise and Employment will review the coordination of cleaner production mechanisms to ensure maximum efficiency and value in the uptake and replication of initiatives, and as a basis for future targeting of supports to the SME sector.

- The extension of the EU Eco-Management and Audit Scheme (EMAS) to all major industrial sites will be actively promoted.

- Grant assistance for industrial development will remain conditional on compliance with environmental regulatory requirements.

- The EPA, in cooperation with the Central Statistics Office and the Department of Transport, Energy and Communications, will develop a materials and energy balance for industry to determine the full extent of industry's environmental/natural resource impacts and advise on targets for greater eco-efficiency.

- Forbairt and An Bord Tráchtála, with the support and assistance of the Marine Institute, as appropriate, will explore the opportunities for Irish industry in the growth area of environmental industry, including pollution control technology and equipment and environmental consultancy services.

- The Government has undertaken and will pursue a rapid mobilisation of new initiatives in the Science and Technology area, in line with the 1996 *White Paper on Science, Technology and Innovation.*

- Greater policy coordination at Departmental level in the areas of industry, environment and sustainability will be ensured through the development of the Green Network of Government Departments.

Transport

- Minimisation of potential growth in transport demand will be incorporated as a leading consideration in land use planning.

- Government policy and investment for road transport will support necessary economic growth. To this end, the roads programme will continue to target bottlenecks which represent inefficiencies in the infrastructural system.

- Increased efforts will be made to manage the existing roads network more efficiently.

- Government policy will continue to support and improve public transport systems and infrastructure with a view to increasing their market share. Efficient, cost-effective and customer focused development of the rail network will be supported for its economic, social, environmental and regional development benefits.

- The agencies concerned, led by the Department of the Environment and the Department of Transport, Energy and Communications, will work together to provide more sustainable and environmentally-acceptable alternatives to private car transport, including better facilities for non-motorised transport and, where feasible, improved public mass transport modes.

- Implementation of the Dublin Transportation Initiative will be intensified.

- Noise controls will be developed under roads (or other) legislation to limit permissible noise from road transport.

- Opportunities for non-motorised transport will be improved. This will include increased provision of cycle lanes and safer facilities for pedestrians.

- The Department of the Environment and appropriate agencies, such as the Dublin Transportation Office, will actively encourage greater public awareness of the unsustainable aspects of increasing use of vehicle transport.

- The Government will commission research to more accurately estimate the environmental externalities of road transport, and will make the results available both for public information and to the National Roads Authority (NRA) and local authorities. The NRA will be asked to amend various planning parameters to take greater account of these externalities and the cost benefits and viability of proposed major roads schemes will be assessed accordingly.

- The Government will support policy development at EU level and participate in measures towards internalising the external costs associated with transport.

- Ireland will strongly support the completion of EU proposals to reduce CO_2 emissions from motor vehicles and/or provide greater incentives for the use of fuel efficient vehicles. Pending full establishment of measures to reduce CO_2 emissions from motor vehicles, Irish vehicle tax provisions will be aligned more closely with this objective.

- Where allowable under EU law, consideration will be given to the application of tax incentives to encourage the placing of more efficient and less polluting vehicles on the market ahead of relevant EU deadlines.

- The scrappage scheme introduced in the 1995 Budget, which encourages the replacement of older cars with new, more efficient models, is being maintained for 1997 as a financial incentive to improve the age profile and efficiency standard of the vehicle fleet. Its effects will be monitored to ensure that it continues to meet this objective without creating other environmental problems, particularly in relation to disposal of vehicle waste. The Minister for the Environment is pursuing with the motor industry the development of more systematic voluntary arrangements for recycling vehicle materials.

- Ireland will support the EU Auto Oil programme as an appropriate means of addressing many of the environmental issues arising from transport emissions.

- Ireland will support the continued development at EU level of strict emission control standards for motor vehicles. In particular, Ireland will support a significant tightening of benzene and other limits in the context of the Auto Oil programme.

- The use of leaded petrol will be phased out by the year 2000.

- Vehicle testing will be extended to apply to private cars over four years old with effect from 1 January, 1998. Particular emphasis will be placed on adequate emission controls to reduce pollutants.

- Air transport is an increasing source of polluting emissions (particularly CO_2 and NO_x). Ireland is supporting the initiation of action by the EU to address this problem in a wider international context, with due regard to effects on national competitiveness.

Tourism

- Tourism development will be taken into account, as appropriate, by the Department of the Environment in the preparation of land use policy guidelines for planning authorities, developers and the public.

- Planning authorities will make provision in their development plans for sustainable tourism, and ensure through the planning process that over-development does not take place.

- Bord Fáilte will consider the implementation of a managed network of scenic landscapes by 1999.

- The Department of Tourism and Trade/Bord Fáilte will issue appropriate guidelines on good environmental management to the tourist accommodation sector.

- The Department of Arts, Culture and the Gaeltacht will implement good environmental management, including energy conservation, in historic properties and other tourist attractions under its care.

- The Department of Arts, Culture and the Gaeltacht will consider implementing collective transport, such as operates in Glenveagh, in other National Parks.

- The provisions of the Foreshore Acts in relation to preventing and penalising damage to beaches, sand dunes and seashore ecosystems will continue to be fully implemented.

- The Department of Arts, Culture and the Gaeltacht will ensure that all river cruisers licensed for hire are fitted with appropriate waste water storage and pumping facilities. Local authorities and the Department will ensure that the complementary shore pumping facilities are properly used and maintained.

- The Department of Arts, Culture and the Gaeltacht will develop appropriate management strategies to protect riverine archaeological monuments, which may be vulnerable to damage from cruising activities.

- Consideration will be given to the need for controls or restrictions on certain unsustainable leisure activities; the Department of the Environment, in consultation with the Department of Arts, Culture and the Gaeltacht, the Department of Tourism and Trade and the Department of the Marine, where appropriate, will provide suitable guidance for local authorities.

- Bord Fáilte, the Department of Tourism and Trade and the Marine Institute, where appropriate, will commission research on the "critical loads" of tourist destinations, including sensitive coastal or wilderness areas, to provide a firm basis for the establishment of sustainable tourist numbers.

- CERT, in conjunction with the education sector, will continue to provide suitable training emphasising the sustainable use of resources and highlighting natural products.

- Bord Fáilte, the Department of Tourism and Trade and the Department of Arts, Culture and the Gaeltacht will develop, and widely publicise, codes of conduct and practice to foster a greater awareness of the potential impact of tourist behaviour on sensitive areas and sites.

A Quality Environment: An Investment in the Future

Water resources

- An integrated catchment management initiative will reverse deteriorating quality trends in selected catchments.

- New regulations will be made under the *Waste Management Act, 1996,* to limit/prevent water pollution from waste disposal practices.

- New water quality standards will guide EPA and local authorities in devising and implementing management strategies to deal with diffuse pollution.

- The UN ECE Convention on Protection and Use of Transboundary Watercourses and International Lakes will be ratified in 1997.

- The *Fisheries (Amendment) Bill, 1996,* will be enacted to provide for the development of the aquaculture industry in accordance with high environmental standards.

- An updated methodology for the preparation of Water Quality Management Plans (WQMPs) will be developed by the EPA and will be used to review all WQMPs over the next five to ten years.

- EPA will, by end-1998, comprehensively review discharges to waters to assess discharges of nutrients and toxic/persistent substances.

- A national groundwater programme will be established under the coordination of the EPA to quantify resources, establish quality and make recommendations for protection/sustainable use.

- There will be continued implementation of the major programme of investment in water and sewage infrastructure to meet water quality standards and requirements, including nutrient reduction in the case of waste water discharges to waters subject to eutrophication. The programme will also ensure that Ireland's excellent record under the Blue Flags for Beaches scheme is maintained.

- Government will fund phased implementation of large-scale projects, including the Dublin Water Strategy.

- The Department of the Environment and local authorities will develop and implement a water conservation programme, including "water audits" for water supply capital projects, capital funding for water conservation projects and a commitment to long-term active leakage control.

- Pricing policies will be developed to promote conservation by major industrial and commercial water users.

The coastal zone

- A strategy document on coastal zone management will be published in 1997. Following public consultation, a national policy on coastal zone management will be determined and published.

Landscape and nature

- An amending Bill is being prepared to update the *Wildlife Act, 1976,* and provide a statutory basis for designated Natural Heritage Areas (NHAs).

- A National Parks and Heritage Bill will be published in 1997 to provide statutory recognition for national parks, national historic parks and national gardens.

- The National Biodiversity Plan will be published in 1997.

Waste management

- New Regulations under the *Waste Management Act, 1996,* will include:
  - EPA licensing of landfill sites, commencing on 1 May 1997;
  - management of packaging wastes; and
  - establishment by EPA of a Toxics Release Inventory.

- There will be a rapid implementation of improved planning and organisational arrangements under the *Waste Management Act, 1996*.

- Waste management policies will achieve:
  - stabilisation of municipal waste arisings by 1999, and their reduction by 20% by 2010;
  - diversion of 20% of municipal waste from landfill, by recycling, by 1999; and
  - an increase from 27% by 2001 to at least 50% in the recovery rate for packaging waste by 2005.

- There will be a continued improvement in the compilation of waste statistics to measure future performance.

- The use of economic instruments will be explored to reduce waste, promote reuse/recycling and increase management efficiency.

- A hazardous waste management plan will be completed by the EPA in 1998.

- Capital funding aid (EU co-financed) will be provided for hazardous waste facilities based on recovery or other specialist treatment systems.

Air quality

- Local air quality will be maintained and improved particularly in urban areas.

- Ireland will actively support international action on climate change, ozone depletion and transboundary air pollution.

- Ireland will participate in international actions to reduce low-level ozone precursor emissions from transport and power generation, and to develop acidification abatement strategies.

- Research will be undertaken on the impacts of acidifying depositions, in particular sulphur dioxide and nitrogen oxides.

- Ireland will support the development of stricter EU standards for air pollutants.

- EPA will prepare a national air quality monitoring programme.

Spatial planning

- Planning and Development legislation will be amended to require planning authorities to take account of sustainable development considerations in the elaboration of development plans.

- The Department of the Environment will conclude the current series of Land Use Guidelines.

- No State funding will be provided for infrastructure in the event of overzoning.

- Regional Authorities will be assigned a role (in line with *Better Local Government*) in setting out strategic planning guidelines for development planning by constituent local authorities.

- The relationship between a development plan and other forms of special designation, for example, NHAs, Special Protection Areas (SPAs), will be clarified in the forthcoming Bill to amend the *Wildlife Act, 1976*.

- Development exempted from development control will be reviewed.

- The UN Convention on Environmental Impact Assessment in a Transboundary Context will be ratified.

- Developments in regard to Strategic Environmental Assessment will be monitored - Ireland will take a constructive position on new EU proposals.

- There will be an ongoing review of the operation of complementary planning and Integrated Pollution Control procedures, with appropriate amendment, if required, to the *Environmental Protection Agency Act, 1992*.

• Planning authorities will be encouraged to take a more strategic view of settlement patterns, development needs and major infrastructural services, combining the statutory five-yearly review of the development plan with a coherent longer-term rolling plan.

Human Settlements are Shaped by their Environment

Built environment

• More sustainable urban development will be promoted by:
  - closer coordination between transport and land use planning;
  - the promotion of higher residential densities in appropriate locations;
  - emphasis in the proposed new Guidelines on Development Plans on clear demarcation between urban and rural land use; and
  - Local Agenda 21 initiatives by local authorities.

• Policies for achieving sustainable urban regeneration will have as key elements:
  - integrated strategic economic and social planning;
  - ecological principles;
  - improving accessibility;
  - environmental upgrading;
  - design flexibility;
  - open spaces;
  - mechanisms and resources to overcome critical barriers; and
  - a partnership approach.

• New legislation is being prepared along lines recommended in *Strengthening the Protection of the Architectural Heritage* (published in September 1996), and a package of administrative and financial measures will create a fully effective framework for protecting the built heritage.

• Under the Building Regulations since 1992, insulation standards are estimated to have increased by up to 50%, with a reduction of 20% in energy use in buildings. By 2000, the new standards will result in a 2% reduction in CO_2 emissions from buildings. Arising from a review of the Regulations, a further 5% saving in energy use for heating will be achieved.

• A new Energy Rating System for new houses is being introduced.

• The Government is committed to ensuring that its policies in relation to housing and the urban environment take full account of the provisions of the HABITAT Agenda, and will also work in this regard with EU partners to agree common approaches, where appropriate.

• Housing policies will continue to promote sustainable settlement formation, with greater social integration.

• The *Guidelines on Residential Development in the Designated Tax Incentive Areas* will be reviewed in the light of experience.

• Investment under the Urban and Village Renewal Sub-Programme of the *Local Urban and Rural Development Operational Programme, 1994-1999*, will continue to promote the rejuvenation of towns and villages, rehabilitate the built environment and restore and conserve important heritage buildings.

• The Department of the Environment will formally request the National Standards Authority of Ireland to revise the existing Irish Standard to make provision for a flush toilet water cistern involving substantially lower water consumption. Following consultation at national and EU level, the revised standard should be operational by end-1999.

Individual Action Counts....

- Government will ask the Director of Consumer Affairs to make recommendations for providing full and authoritative environmental information to consumers.

- The Office of Consumer Affairs will also be asked, in consultation with the Department of Enterprise and Employment and the Department of the Environment, to prepare a **Code of Practice** on green marketing.

- The *Access to Information on the Environment Regulations, 1996*, will be reviewed in the context of Freedom of Information legislation, and a **Code of Good Practice on Issuing Environmental Information** will be prepared for implementing authorities by the Department of the Environment.

- The detailed anti-litter provisions in the Litter Pollution Bill will be vigorously implemented.

- The role of ENFO will be further developed.

- The Department of Education will promote and improve the position of environmental education within the formal education system.

Global Sustainability requires Global Solidarity

Trade

- Trade policy will be examined to ensure compliance with the objectives of *Agenda 21* in relation to promoting an open, non-discriminatory and equitable trading system, taking particular account of the needs of developing countries.

- Ireland supports the EU consensus on the importance of upholding the validity of multilateral agreements (MEAs) designed to protect the environment and of ensuring the integration of sustainable development into world trade policies and practices.

- The Department of Arts, Culture and the Gaeltacht will make any amendments to legislation which may be necessary to enable Ireland to ratify the Convention on International Trade in Endangered Species of Wild Fauna and Flora (CITES) in 1997.

International actions

- Ireland will participate fully in UNGASS, the UN review of *Agenda 21*.

- The Government is committed to increasing Official Development Assistance by 0.05% each year to meet the UN target of 0.7% of GNP.

- Ireland will invite OECD environmental performance review for 1998.

- Ireland supports strengthening the Treaty on European Union to make sustainable development an explicit objective of the Union.

Measuring Progress Towards Sustainability

- A series of environmental quality indicators will be prepared by 1998.

- Sustainability indicators will also be developed and preparations advanced towards satellite green accounts.

PART 2 - STRATEGIC FRAMEWORK

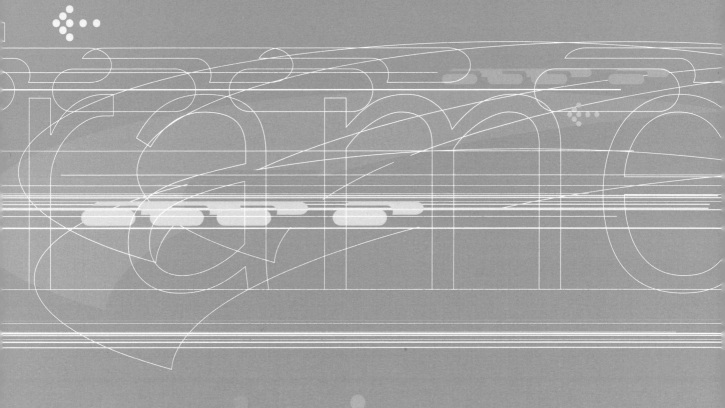

Chapter 2
Overview

Introduction

The quality of Ireland's environment, and the availability of abundant natural amenities, have traditionally been relied upon as important elements of the national resource base. Socio-economic progress, changed settlement patterns and changing lifestyles are however, in Ireland as elsewhere, leading to the transformation and transportation of increasing quantities of energy and materials; this is altering the balance between environment and society. A new strategic approach (together with policies and measures to realise it) is therefore necessary to establish a sound relationship between Ireland's economy and environment.

The *Policy Agreement for a Government of Renewal* (December 1994), committed Government to the preparation of a National Sustainable Development Strategy which

> "will address all areas of Government policy which impact on the environment and will contain detailed targets and a commitment to an annual review." [1]

This Strategy responds to that commitment. It addresses all areas of Government policy, and of economic and societal activity, which impact on the environment. It seeks to re-orientate policies as necessary to ensure that the strong growth Ireland enjoys and seeks to maintain will be environmentally sustainable. There is already evidence that traditional policies and controls have been inadequate in this regard. Despite improvements in some areas (e.g. drinking water quality), trends such as increasing water pollution, intensifying consumption/depletion of natural resources, growing waste production and energy consumption, and erosion of landscape quality are all symptoms of an ongoing and structural environmental deterioration. Some relevant indicators are shown in Fig. 2.1.

Fig 2.1 Some Recent Environmental Trends and Pressures in Ireland

Water
- there was a significant increase in 1991-1994 in slight to moderate water pollution, now up to 28% of measured river channel length
- 39% of lake surface area examined in 1991-1994 was moderately to seriously enriched

Natural resources/landscape
- 18% of flowering plant species and 18% of fauna are threatened with extinction
- important habitats for many upland bird species have been severely damaged by excessive sheep stocking in hill and mountain areas
- the remaining area of raised bog of conservation importance is now 6% of the original total area of raised bog

Waste
- overall waste generation in Ireland has been growing by some 4% per annum for at least a decade
- at least 100,000 tonnes of hazardous waste now arise each year

Energy
- total primary energy requirement increased by 24% between 1980 and 1993
- energy consumption *per capita* is increasing

Transport
- vehicle kilometres travelled *per capita* increased by 47% between 1986 and 1995

Source: DOE/Environmental Protection Agency [2]

Sustainable development policies focus on causes rather than on symptoms. They also consider the balance of present and longer-term needs - socio-economic and environmental - as well as the totality of resources available to meet those needs. Certain approaches essential to implement sustainable development are already being adopted in Ireland:

- economic and environment policy integration has begun;
- policy instruments and management tools are being broadened; and
- public appreciation of the need for lifestyle changes is increasing.

But a more concerted approach must now be adopted, involving Government, economic and voluntary organisations, and the public.

Meaning of Sustainable Development

Sustainable development is based on universal principles, relevant to all nations and peoples. It seeks an acceptable quality of life for present and future generations, recognising that the actions of the present affect the inheritance of future generations. In a sustainable world, human activity must not undermine the long-term productivity of supporting ecosystems.

"Humanity has the ability to make development sustainable - to ensure that it meets the needs of the present without compromising the ability of future generations to meet their own needs."

- World Commission on Environment and Development[3]

Sustainable development is increasingly recognised as the key to managing economic and environmental interdependence. It is neither a fixed concept nor a narrowly defined process, but an approach in which
- the exploitation of resources,
- the direction of investments,
- the orientation of technological development, and
- institutional change are made consistent with future as well as present needs. Of necessity, therefore, it involves difficult choices and depends on decisive political action.

In setting out this strategic framework, the Government looks to sustainable development as:

- a **dynamic** concept which must be given both practical and concrete expression in the present to generate a new development model for the future involving change in socio-economic and consumer behaviour;

- an **inclusive** concept bringing environment to the heart of economic growth and quality of life concerns, and requiring the active participation of economic operators and the public, as well as all levels of Government; and

- a **quality** concept which recognises that a clean environment and a conscientious approach by business to environmental protection are an advantage to, rather than a constraint on, successful economic performance.

This Strategy aims at securing the transition, over time, to an environmentally sustainable society and economy. While many of the measures and actions included will be undertaken in the short to medium term, the overall time horizon of the Strategy must, necessarily, be a long-term one, recognising that sustainable development is a continuing process which needs ongoing assessment and refinement.

International Recognition of Sustainable Development

Agenda 21[4], the main product of the UN Conference on Environment and Development (UNCED) held in Rio de Janeiro in 1992, the Treaty on European Union (the Maastricht Treaty)[5] and the EU's Fifth Environment Action Programme *Towards Sustainability*[6] all endorsed the concept of sustainable development. They underlined the fact that traditional policies must be replaced by an integrated approach to environment and development issues, if growth is to be achieved in parallel with, rather than at the expense of, environmental quality.

Agenda 21 was elaborated as a dynamic programme which would evolve over time in the light of changing needs and be carried out by

"the various actors according to the different situations, capacities and priorities of countries and regions in respect of all the principles contained in the Rio Declaration on Environment and Development."[7]

These principles recognise the rights of all States to exploit their own resources pursuant to their own environmental and developmental policies, but require, *inter alia,* that

- environmental protection should constitute an integral part of the development process,
- developed countries accept responsibility for their disproportionate pressure on the global environment,
- unsustainable patterns of production and consumption should be eliminated,
- effective environmental legislation should be enacted,
- access to environmental information and public awareness and participation in decision-making should be facilitated,
- the precautionary approach should be applied, environmental impact assessment should be undertaken for activities likely to have a significant environmental impact, and internalisation of environmental costs should be promoted, and
- the needs of the least developed countries should be given special priority.

The EU's Fifth Environment Action Programme was adopted in 1993 following the inclusion, as a principal objective, in the Maastricht Treaty of the promotion of sustainable growth respecting the environment.

The Programme

- focused on the agents and activities depleting natural resources and damaging the environment,
- sought to initiate changes in current detrimental trends and practices,
- aimed at achieving changes in behaviour through shared responsibility for the environment by all sectors of society, and
- proposed a significant broadening of the range of instruments to be used for environmental protection purposes.

In its 1995 report on the environment in the European Union, for purposes of the review of the Fifth Action Programme[8], the European Environment Agency (EEA) concluded that progress in reducing pressures on the environment was not enough to improve general quality and even less to progress towards sustainability. Without accelerated policies, the pressures observed would continue to lead to the exceedance of human health standards and environmental carrying capacity. Some successes, including the reduction of ozone depleting substances and emissions of heavy metals and sulphur dioxide, were noteworthy, but the European Union as a whole has not moved sufficiently from concept to realisation.

Recognising the need to revitalise and accelerate the Fifth Action Programme, the Council of Environment Ministers in December, 1996, reached political agreement on a Commission proposal for a co-decision by Council and the European Parliament on an action plan to intensify the implementation of the Programme.

Development of Irish Environment Policy

A high quality environment has been an assumed part of Irish national identity. For much of the 20th century, threats to the environment were not perceived as significant in view of Ireland's low population density, traditional agricultural practices and late industrialisation. But with economic growth in the 1960s came a new appreciation of the environment as a factor in development and a potential source of wealth creation.

Fig 2.2 Increased Environmental Pressures in the European Union

Ozone layer

- the ozone layer over Europe has been depleted by an average of 6-7% between 1979 and 1994
- levels of chlorine in the atmosphere have increased six fold since 1950

Acidification

- acid deposition exceeded critical loads for eco-loads in 34% of the total European area (with an even higher proportion in the EU)

Waste production

- municipal waste *per capita* has shown an increase of about 20% between 1985 and 1993; it will continue to grow, and is projected to increase by 30% by 2000 compared with 1985 levels

Transport

- over the period 1980-1990, passenger transport by road increased by almost 40%; projections for the period 1990-2010 are for a further increase of over 40%
- between 1980 and 1990, car ownership rose by 37%
- congestion problems are now being experienced regularly on 10% of the major roads within the EU

Agriculture

- while livestock trends indicate gradually declining numbers of cattle, sheep and laying hens, numbers of pigs and poultry are increasing

Energy

- electricity consumption increased almost continuously between 1974 and 1992, by an average of 2.7% *per annum.*
- an average growth in primary energy consumption of around 1.1% *per annum* is expected for the period 1990-2010

Tourism

- the number of tourist overnight stays in 1992 (840 million) represented an increase of 21.5% over 1980 levels

Source: European Environment Agency[9]

Environmental legislation distinct from the physical planning code began to develop in the 1970s, and in 1978 the Minister for the Environment was assigned general responsibility to promote the protection and improvement of the physical environment. Other Ministers of the Government were in parallel assigned responsibility for assessing the environmental implications of their policies, programmes and projects before taking decisions. But in practice, the need to achieve a balance between environment and development did not exert a strong influence on policy formation in many sectors during the 1980s.

An *Environment Action Programme*[10] was adopted by Government in 1990 against the background of growing world environmental concern. Good progress, reported on in 1991[11] and again in 1995[12], was made in its implementation, notably by:

- the establishment of the Environmental Protection Agency;
- the development of ENFO - a new information service of the Department of the Environment; and
- an increased investment programme in public environmental infrastructure.

Subsequent policy documents, such as the Culliton Report[13], and the *GREEN 2000 Advisory Group's Report*[14], clearly underscored the relationship between an unpolluted environment and social and economic well-being, and emphasised the importance of natural resource based economic activity linked to high environmental quality and standards.

The reform of the EU Structural Funds from 1989 provided a new growth opportunity for Ireland. By 1992 and 1993, the inflow of structural funds under Ireland's *Community Support Framework, 1989-93*, amounted to some 3.5% of GNP.[15] Influenced by the EU Fifth Environment Action Programme, the further reform of the Structural Funds in 1993 sought to promote sustainable development and better environmental integration in EU co-financing operations. The establishment of the Cohesion Fund[16] gave further impetus to the environmental dimension of EU policy and increased support to the promotion of sustainable development.

In addressing the new environmental requirements which emerged from the reform of the Structural Funds, the *National Development Plan, 1994-1999*[17], sought, as a fundamental strategic consideration, the integration of environmental and economic objectives in the interests of sustainable development. This was seen to be necessary, not only for the sake of the environment, but also for the continued efficiency of economic sectors interacting with the environment. The environmental profile of the National Development Plan was incorporated in the agreed *IRELAND - Community Support Framework, 1994-99*[18] (*CSF*), and reflected as appropriate in the more detailed approaches of relevant Operational Programmes now being implemented.

Environmental Strengths and Weaknesses

In considering how to make Irish national policies more sustainable, the following strengths are evident in the Irish situation:

- Ireland has retained, and can build on, a clean, attractive, environmental image. This is a key contributor to the quality of life, and a basis for economic advantage. Public concern about, and commitment to, environmental protection is high. Recognition by business of the range of opportunities presented by a quality environment is growing. There is a high level of investment in environmental protection by both the public and private sectors;

- Good policy foundations are in place at international and at national levels. A comprehensive, modern legislative code has been substantially completed with the enactment of the *Waste Management Act, 1996*. Management and organisational arrangements have been rationalised with the mobilisation of the Environmental Protection Agency;

- Regulatory arrangements for environmental protection enjoy wide public participation; both physical planning and environmental legislation provide for public involvement in decision-making on projects. Environment and development NGOs have been active and constructive in their engagement with environmental issues. Industry and business share responsibility through voluntary action as well as investment and legal compliance. There is a supportive environmental research and development network in the academic sector; and

- Information systems continue to improve, for example, through the activities of the EPA and ENFO, and the operation of the *Access to Information on the Environment Regulations, 1996.*

There are also significant weaknesses which must be addressed in formulating a framework for sustainable development:
- Structural conflicts still exist between environment and development objectives. This is a primary reason why, despite substantial investment and increasingly stringent legislative controls, environmental quality trends continue to disimprove in several respects;

- Although policy integration has been an objective for nearly two decades, mechanisms to achieve the necessary degree of integration have not been sufficient. While this is internationally recognised as a difficult issue, practical steps are now only beginning to be taken, and must be strengthened;

- Not enough has been done to value environmental resources, so as to promote proper internalisation of environmental costs in economic activities and to prevent environmental resources being used inefficiently, as free or undervalued goods;

- Effective action is in some respects hampered by administrative/organisational boundaries. In particular, there is a need to increase the implementation of catchment-based programmes for environmental protection;

- Although information systems are improving, substantial gaps remain. Overall, data collection is not yet adequate to allow a full evaluation of materials use and energy flows in the Irish economy. Their limitations mean that the definition and measurement of sustainable development indicators will remain tentative in the short-term.

Need for a New Approach

Over the past two decades national environment policy has developed in response to growing threats to, and growing public concern about, the quality of the environment. Organisational, legislative and voluntary initiatives have been undertaken. Information, awareness, public participation and investment in environmental protection have all increased. Some progress has been made in articulating an environmental dimension within economic, and to a much lesser extent fiscal, policy.

More is needed. The transition to sustainable development has been identified as the most important global transformation since the agricultural and industrial revolutions. The growth model of the 20th century, characterised by increases in the use of energy and raw materials and leading to over-exploitation of scarce environmental resources, cannot be sustained indefinitely into the 21st century.

At a global level, the UN Commission on Sustainable Development is seeking to develop and realise the policies and programmes of *Agenda 21*. Within the EU, the European Commission's 1994 White Paper on *Growth,*

Competitiveness, Employment[19] proposed ideas for a new development model for the European Union to reverse the negative relationships between environmental conditions, quality of life and economic prosperity. This Strategy has been framed to direct the impressive growth of the Irish economy, and the changes now being experienced in consumption and lifestyle patterns, towards a more sustainable course, having regard to international experience, and to national environmental, economic and social imperatives.

Chapter 3
Overall Goals and Priorities

Strategic Aims and Goals

The overall aim of this Strategy is

to ensure that economy and society in Ireland can develop to their full potential within a well protected environment, without compromising the quality of that environment, and with responsibility towards present and future generations and the wider international community.

Within this overall aim, the Government affirms that:

- Ireland's environment must be protected for its own intrinsic value;
- a well managed environment sustains a healthy economy and a good quality of life: environmental, economic and social policies must be mutually supportive;
- economic growth and social development cannot be to the detriment of environmental quality and must be within the limits set by nature; in particular, this must involve changes in production and consumption patterns;
- every person is entitled to enjoy a clean, healthy environment and shares with Government the duty to maintain that environment;
- environmentally sustainable development requires, and can only succeed with, the participation of the whole of society;
- Government and other public authorities must work to improve and protect the environment for all generations, exercising leadership and fostering partnerships with economic and social groups;
- a quality environment is the natural heritage of the whole of Ireland; where appropriate, conservation action and development in the interests of environmental excellence will be pursued in a coordinated manner North and South;
- meeting the needs of the present in a sustainable way involves equity in the access to and use of resources, as well as equitable opportunities to participate in decision-making and to achieve economic and social progress;
- responsibility towards future generations involves sustainable use of renewable resources, optimised use of non-renewable resources, and the free transfer of natural capital unburdened by pollution and waste; and
- the developed world bears a disproportionate responsibility for the depletion and degradation of the global environment and natural resources, and must demonstrate leadership in the implementation of sustainable development policies.

Concepts and Principles

Concepts

The concept of **sustainability**, which has informed Irish environmental policy over recent years and which underpins this Strategy, requires development to be within the capacity of the environment to support it without suffering lasting damage or depletion. **Carrying capacity** has provided the rationale for many environmental standards and land use planning and development controls. It may be expressed as

- the ability of the environment to sustain a particular form or intensity of development, or
- the ability of the environment to support bio-diversity or particular species, or
- the **critical load**[1] of a specified pollutant which an environmental medium may tolerate without lasting damage being experienced.

Where there is uncertainty in regard to the definition of carrying capacity and the limits or thresholds which it should imply for sustainable human activities, the precautionary principle must be applied; this has influenced global action, for example, in regard to the objective of stabilising CO_2 emissions to abate the threat of global warming. A further development from this is the concept of **appropriated carrying capacity**, which can be defined as the biophysical resource flows and waste assimilation capacity appropriated from global totals by a defined economy or population.

There is an increasing recognition of unsustainable development pressures on the earth's carrying capacity. These include:

- the intensive exploitation and depletion of natural resources;
- the growth in consumption and production;
- the unequal division of resources among the world's population; and
- the pressures on the developing world to match the living standards of more developed countries.

This recognition of unsustainable pressures has led to the development of new forms of measurement and analysis which can make these pressures more clearly understandable and communicable.

Fig 3.1 Increased Pressures
on the Global Environment

- world population has more than doubled since 1950, from 2,510 million to 5,280 million in 1990
- world economic production has increased six fold since 1950 - world GDP has increased from 1,671 US$ *per capita* in 1950 to 3,971 US$ in 1990 (1990 prices)
- primary energy consumption *per capita* doubled between 1950 and 1990, from 30 gigajoules to 61 gigajoules *per capita* - total primary energy consumption increased from 76,459 petajoules to 320,563 petajoules in the same period
- world fish catch has increased five fold since 1950
- 80% of natural resources are consumed by the OECD countries, which have only 16% of global population
- 17% of Earth's land area is soil degraded (23% in Europe) - this includes 10% of agricultural land world-wide
- human-made fixation of nitrate and sulphur is now as great as natural fixation

Sources: EEA[2] & UNEP[3]

Society's **ecological footprint**, an indicator developed to illustrate human impact on a finite planet, underlines the dilemma now facing the global community. A footprint represents

"the corresponding area of productive land and aquatic ecosystems required to produce the resources used, and to assimilate the wastes produced, by a defined population at a specified material standard of living, wherever on Earth that land may be located".[4]

Applying this concept shows that the earth's resources have to a large extent already been appropriated by the wealthier sectors of global society, particularly in urban settlements. The global ecological footprint clearly shows why sustainable development has become a global imperative:

"At present, both the human population and average consumption are increasing while the total area of productive land and stocks of natural capital are fixed or in decline ... The ecological footprint of the present world population/economy already exceeds the total productive area (or "ecological space") available on Earth."[5]

Ireland's Ecological Footprint

Ireland's Ecological Footprint is already 1.23 times the size of the land available

In preliminary calculations by the UCD Environmental Institute, based on a standard methodology, the average size of Ireland's ecological footprint is 2.38 hectares per person, or a total of 86,325 km[2] - some 1.23 times the size of the State (70,394 km[2]).

Features such as low population density and a high percentage of productive agricultural land have allowed Ireland to retain a relatively small footprint for a developed country. However, as this preliminary footprint measurement includes only four categories of domestic consumption (i.e. fossil fuels, built-up land, food and forestry), the results may be regarded as presenting a conservative illustration. Given that substantial socio-economic development needs remain, ecological footprinting provides a means of demonstrating the importance of sustainable development considerations in relation to lifestyle and consumption patterns.[6]

Principles

In approaching the definition of policies and actions to achieve the aim of this Strategy, the Government remains committed to the principles which have informed Irish environmental policy in recent years.[7] The transition to sustainable development, however, requires these principles to be given fuller practical expression.

The **precautionary principle** requires that emphasis should be placed on dealing with the causes, rather than the results, of environmental damage and that, where significant evidence of environmental risk exists, appropriate precautionary action should be taken even in the absence of conclusive scientific proof of causes. This is more than simply giving the environment the benefit of the doubt. It is a spur to responsible action and a stimulus to scientific and technological development. Reasonable action to avoid potentially serious risks to the environment and human health maintains choice, control and quality.

Integration (of environmental considerations into other policies) is a leading mechanism for sustainable development. At **Government level**, integration is important to ensure consistency across the range of policies contributing to sustainable development; it also encourages mutually supporting policy formation and delivery, and enables environmental concerns to be addressed in an effective and comprehensive manner. At **sectoral level**, integration is fundamental to the decoupling of economic growth and environmental degradation; it promotes economic and environmental efficiency through reduced materials and energy use, waste prevention and minimisation, re-use and recycling, and it assists the realisation of economic advantage founded on environmental quality.

National policy, in line with EU policy, has up to now emphasised the integration of environmental considerations in energy, agriculture, industry, transport and tourism policies. The concept is also relevant in other sectors, notably those which are based on natural resource use, such as fishing, forestry and mining, and it is increasingly important in a trade context.

Integration must also be pursued at **macro-economic and fiscal policy levels**, to reflect the value of natural as well as human-made capital, to account for natural resource use and depletion, to internalise environmental costs and to provide a more balanced and full measurement of national growth and prosperity.

Principle 1 of the *Rio Declaration on Environment and Development* states that *"human beings are at the centre of concerns for sustainable development"*.[8] Integration of environmental considerations into **social policy** envisages:
- fair access to a clean, healthy environment;
- maintenance of public health and elimination, as far as practicable, of environmental risks;
- equity in the use of environmental resources;
- full access to education and information concerning the environment; and
- sustainable planning, development (including urban development), and human settlement policies.

Effective environmental policies require the active participation of society, so that lifestyle changes compatible with sustainable living can become established.

The **polluter pays principle** regarding cost allocation and action by public authorities has influenced public policies at OECD and EU levels for over twenty years[9], and has been incorporated in all recent Irish environmental legislation. Its objective is to allocate correctly the costs of pollution, consumption of energy and environmental resources, and production and disposal of waste to the responsible polluters and consumers, rather than to society at large or future generations; in turn, this provides an incentive to reduce pollution and consumption. Cost internalisation through the use of market based economic and fiscal instruments, in line with the polluter pays principle, is now widely perceived as a flexible and efficient means of addressing sustainable development objectives. While some environmental charges and taxes are in place in Ireland which lean on polluters and users of resources, use of these instruments is not yet widespread; policy objectives in this area are outlined in Chapter 19.

The principle of **shared responsibility** for the environment requires a broadly based involvement of public bodies, private enterprise and the general public so as to achieve environmental policy objectives. Public participation in environmental protection is already encouraged in Ireland through, for example, the provision of information, awareness raising, statutory consultation and reporting mechanisms, support for non-governmental organisation (NGO) initiatives and the development of Local Agenda 21 measures. Shared responsibility aims at engendering commitment throughout society, which in turn fosters a sense of public ownership of the environment. Voluntary action by individuals, through lifestyle choices, as well as by economic and social operators, are essential to realise the aims of this Strategy.

Priorities for Action

Sustaining the environment while securing development requires:

- a balance between the conservation and utilisation of resources;
- concrete action on the basis of practical programmes and clear targets; and
- an ability to measure and monitor sustainable development performance.

Accordingly, the Government's priorities within the framework of this Strategy are to:

- maintain the quality, quantity and diversity of natural endowments;
- undertake a high level of environmental protection so that renewable resources are conserved and not depleted beyond their renewal rates; ensure that non-renewable resources are used prudently and efficiently with a strong emphasis on the use of substitute resources, where practicable, on the concentration of critical natural capital, and on the needs of the future;
- ensure that the creation of wastes, and inputs of substances and emissions, are minimised to take account of the carrying capacity of the environment;
- ensure that spatial planning policies support sustainable development;
- set out sustainability objectives for agriculture, forestry, the marine, energy, industry, transport, tourism and trade so as to encourage long-term growth and competitiveness within a quality environment;
- accelerate progress towards a more environmentally sustainable society based, *inter alia*, on sustainable settlement and housing policies, promotion of sustainable consumption and lifestyle, and greater individual and community participation in protecting the environment;
- move towards the development of economic instruments and pricing mechanisms to internalise environmental costs in economic activity, as well as towards green accounting methods;
- promote information, increased awareness and education as means of supporting participation and shared responsibility;
- pursue the development of indicators to measure progress towards sustainability; and
- establish arrangements for implementing the Strategy, with particular reference to the roles and responsibilities of central, regional and local government, and the need for broadly based participation of the social partners, the voluntary sector and the public.

Chapter 4
Environment and Economic Development

Current Development Trends

Although Ireland's environment has not generally suffered from intensive development pressures in the past, trends are now changing, with significant implications for environmental quality:

Population[1]

- The population increased by 21.6%, to 3.62 million, between 1971 and 1996.
- The decline in the number of births annually since 1980 has been an important demographic dynamic. However, the population is relatively young, with 26.7% in 1991 being less than 15 years old and 11.4% more than 65 years old.
- In the period to 2006, the CSO has predicted an increase in the labour force in the order of 0.7% to 1% per annum depending on outward migration assumptions.[2]
- In the longer-term, to 2026, the CSO also predicted a marked decline in the young population and a strong increase in the population aged 65 and over.

Settlement patterns[3]

- Average population density is low, at 51 persons/km², but varies from over 100 persons/km² in eastern and southern areas to less than 25 persons/km² in many western areas.
- There is an increasing trend towards urbanisation, and especially suburbanisation, characterised by low density, residential, business and commercial development at the outskirts of towns and cities.
- Over half of the population (57% approx.) live in urban settlements greater than 1,500 in population. While over a third of the national population live in the general Dublin area and its environs, the inner city accounts for only one fourteenth of the Dublin region population.
- Around 70% of the urban population lives at or near the coastal area.

Land use[4]

- Agricultural use accounts for 68% of land cover. Intensification of agriculture has brought change, including specialisation, mechanisation, increased animal numbers and need for housing for overwintering of animals. Reforms of the EU Common Agricultural Policy have seen the emergence of other forms of land use such as organic farming, forestry, wind energy and agri-tourism.
- Wetlands and bogs account for 14% of land cover. Raised bogs of conservation importance now amount to 99 sites covering 17,790 hectares, from an original area of 311,300 hectares. Some 112,300 hectares of blanket bog of conservation importance now remains from an area of 774,990 hectares.
- Forest cover, at 8% of the land area, is the lowest in the EU. The proportion of broadleaf species in Irish forests, at 16%, is also very low. Forest cover is increasing at a rate of around 0.33% a year, making it one of the significantly changing aspects of the terrestrial environment.
- While land loss due to urbanisation is not as significant in Ireland as in much of Europe, the demand for urban generated low density residential development on the outskirts of cities is a noticeable trend. New forms of commercial and business development, such as business parks and out of town retail centres, seek to locate at points of high accessibility on the periphery of cities, creating their own sphere of influence, but also potentially threatening the viability of town centres.

"Urbanisation has created new demands on the countryside as a visual amenity, a place for recreation, a location for second homes and a repository of cultural, historical and other values."

- Environmental Protection Agency[5]

Fig 4.1 Land Cover Statistics for Ireland
(excluding Northern Ireland)

	Percentage Area
Artificial Surfaces	1.2%
Agricultural Areas	68.1%
Forest and Semi-natural Areas	14.0%
Wetlands (including Bogs)	14.3%
Water	2.4%

Source: CORINE[6]

Economy[7]

• Irish economic performance is buoyant. Average GNP growth of 0.2% per annum in the early 1980s has increased to rates of 4.4% per annum on average in the years 1992-5, with growth of 7.3% in 1995 and an estimated 6.25% in 1996. GNP growth of 5.5% is forecast in 1997.

• In 1996, consumer prices remained subdued with an annual average increase in the Consumer Price Index (CPI) of 1.6%, output grew by an estimated 7.25% (measured by GDP) compared to an OECD average of 2.5%. Manufacturing output growth is estimated to have been about 9%, while high-technology sectors again expanded strongly, albeit at a more moderate pace than in 1995, with particular significant production increases being recorded in computers and pharmaceuticals.

• Unemployment still remains a major national problem. The results of the 1996 Labour Force Survey indicate that employment grew by 46,000 in the twelve months to mid-April. This growth is a feature of most economic sectors other than agriculture. The labour force continued to expand in 1996, however, reflecting demographic factors and an unusually large increase in female participation rates. Unemployment, as measured by the Labour Force Survey, fell by only 1,000 in the year to mid-April 1996 but has fallen by 40,000 since mid-April 1993. In 1996 as a whole, it is estimated that unemployment fell by 10,000.

Despite the strong economy the Live Register has remained stubbornly high: the average Live Register for 1996 was 279,000, up from 278,000 in 1995.

"... Ireland should replace the traditional adversarial approach that presents industrial development and environmental protection as opposites. The new approach should simultaneously maintain high environmental quality and promote a competitive enterprise sector."

- Forfás, Shaping our Future[8]

Growth and Sustainability

The relationship between economic development and environmental quality has sometimes been perceived as adversarial. Traditional economic activity, with increasing production and consumption, was seen to intensify the use and depletion of natural resources, impact adversely on the quality of environmental media, and generate growing volumes of wastes and emissions. On the other hand, strict environmental requirements have sometimes been regarded as impeding growth, for example, by delaying new projects, increasing capital investment needs, raising production costs or threatening the loss or relocation of industry.

It is now acknowledged[9], however, that the relationship between economic growth and pressure on the environment is not straightforward. Emissions of some pollutants increase in line with economic activity, but many pressures on the environment (for example, sulphur dioxide emissions, untreated waste water) appear to decrease as economies prosper. This is partly attributed to the increasing economic share taken by service activities, which are generally characterised by low pollution levels per unit of production. In Ireland, as in most developed countries, the services sector has been a key direct source of employment growth over the past decade.[10] As economies grow, technologies change, and more efficient methods of production may reduce natural resource use and pollution levels per unit of production. Willingness to pay for environmental quality appears also to increase with income. In effect, growth increases public preference for a clean environment, and contributes financial resources for effective action.

On the other hand, it is clear that economic growth has in practice up to now increased energy, transport and materials use, as well as generation of waste and emissions. Even where greater production efficiencies are achieved, these can be offset by volume increases (a particular feature in the transport sector) and by increased demand for luxury goods and services. Reliance on regulatory controls alone, which do not capture externalities, may also reduce incentives to increased efficiency and technological innovation.

All development impacts on the environment. Sustainable development cannot eliminate such effects altogether. It aspires, however, to change the balance of impacts from negative to positive, pursuing policy choices which promote economic efficiency with less intensive natural resource use and less environmental stress. The following chapters of this Strategy consider the issues arising for key economic sectors. In many instances, concerns about the trade-offs involved centre on employment and competitiveness issues. These are now addressed in their relationship to sustainable development.

Employment

Development meets social and economic needs. Despite the strong performance of the Irish economy unemployment remains unacceptably high; the average Live Register for 1996 was 279,000, up from 278,000 in 1995.[11] Job creation continues to be the highest priority of national economic policy. Sustainable development policies do not conflict with the objective of job creation, and can encourage diversity in employment opportunities. Long-term employment will be underpinned by sustainable development policies which guarantee a high standard of envi-

ronmental protection and an environmental quality approach throughout productive sectors.

An estimated 155,000 jobs, outside farming, are dependent to a significant degree on a quality environment.[12] Many potential areas of employment growth also depend on the preservation of a high quality environment. Over the past decade, employment across the EU appears to have increased at a much higher rate in the environment-related sectors (including recycling, water and waste water services, instrument engineering) than in the rest of the economy. In Ireland, increased employment in environmental sectors, particularly instrument engineering and water technology, has developed at some four times the rate of employment growth elsewhere.[13]

High environmental standards are an incentive, rather than a deterrent, to the location of high performance industry in Ireland. They are also guarantors of product quality and acceptability for export markets - critical to an open economy in an era of globalisation. Lower standards place both the environment and employment at risk, as any short-term gains are offset by, for example, cost and resource inefficiencies, lack of incentive to innovate, potentially greater health and safety risks, and future difficulties with market acceptability and adjustment costs.

Sustainable development requires policies that maximise efficiency and broaden the base of employment. The extent of employment which can be generated by sustainable development policies, however, depends on:
• the nature of the policies devised;
• the efficiency with which they are pursued;
• the ability of business and industry to capitalise on them; and
• the receptiveness of consumers and trading partners.
Under this Strategy, employment maintenance and generation will remain a priority.

Competitiveness and Innovation

It is a commonly-quoted perception, arising from a debate which has continued for over twenty years, that the costs of environmental requirements can have a negative impact on competitiveness. Yet there is much international evidence to support the counter-argument that environmental protection promotes long-term competitiveness and encourages innovation.[15] Environmental standards are only one of a range of determinants of competitive advantage, including:

- tax regimes;
- factor conditions (e.g. transportation and education systems, availability of infrastructure, and specialised factors such as the presence of a specific world class research institute);
- demand conditions (including market share, consumer preferences, behaviour of multinational companies);
- relationships with supporting industry (e.g. expansion, diversification and sophistication of the supply industry); and
- domestic rivalry.

The relative position of environmental requirements within this range is suggested by estimates made by the International Labour Organisation (ILO) which attribute only 1% of plant closures world-wide to environmental regulation.[16]

Research carried out in a number of OECD countries into the impact of environmental programmes on the economy has generally concluded that any negative macro-economic effects of environmental policies are quite small.[17] At the micro-level, issues of local and short-term competitiveness are often a matter of debate. Small firms, which are usually more susceptible to any competitive force, generally have greater fears in this regard than large industry. This was also borne out in the study *Cleaner Manufacturing Technologies in Ireland*[18], carried out in 1993 for the Department of the Environment. Overall, stricter environmental policies do not appear to have had much long-term negative impact on either micro- or macro-economic competitiveness in OECD countries, and the perceived negative impact of environmental policies on economic competitiveness may be overstated.

National industrial policy has for some time recognised that it is in Ireland's best interests to advance ahead of other countries in environmental protection, anticipating trends, and leading rather than following. The Culliton Report (1992)[19] singled out the food industry as a sector where a proactive approach to environmental protection, building on the market opportunities of the "green", wholesome image of Ireland and its food products, could be a major factor in international competitiveness and industrial development. More recently, both the Forfás Report, *Shaping Our Future*[20] and the *White Paper on Science, Technology and Innovation*[21] recognise that the environment has become a key factor in promoting knowledge-based high value-added projects in Ireland, with a demand for qualified employees.

This approach is now reinforced by the report of the Joint Oireachtas Committee on Sustainable Development, published in March 1997, which concluded, *inter alia*, that *"Ireland has a definite competitive advantage in terms of its Green Image that must be exploited to its full by not only the food sector but other economic sectors such as tourism, the general green consumer industry and the fledgling environment protection industry".*[22] The Committee focused on highlighting market niches and opportunities which can be exploited by Irish industry in the growing global environmental market, and identified business opportunities for Irish enterprises in the areas of tourism, food, consumer products and environmental protection goods and services.

The economic sectors themselves must meet the competitive forces of the market-place and the challenges of consumer demand. Ability to innovate - achieving cleaner production, improving process technology, providing eco-friendly products and services - is critical to competitive success. The 1995 report of the Science, Technology and Innovation Advisory Council[23] pointed out that, contrary to the general trend, employment in innovative companies and industries increased internationally over the past two decades.

The Government will support enterprise in achieving environmentally responsible growth and employment.

- High planning and environmental standards will remain a precondition for development. Government has recognised, in *Partnership 2000*[24], the need to consider further streamlining of the planning system to minimise delays and uncertainties, and is committed to the introduction of accelerated procedures for major projects involving significant employment and added value.

- Greater flexibility of approach, complementing regulatory measures with market mechanisms, will be developed to allow economic sectors to achieve environmental objectives and realise environmental advantage in the most cost-effective manner.

- The Government supports the general approach of the EU White Paper *Growth, Competitiveness, Employment*[25], in advocating a shift in the tax burden away from labour and towards polluters. Such a shift would provide a means of implementing the "polluter pays principle" and underpinning the internalisation of environmental costs. It will also redress the balance between different industrial inputs and support labour-intensive, non-polluting industries. Appropriate measures will be developed for the 1998 and subsequent budgets.

- Environmental industry is a growth area, which offers many opportunities for exploitation by Irish industry. These include pollution control technology and equipment, biotechnology development and applications, and environmental consultancy services. The opportunities for Irish industry will be explored in a coordinated way and supported by Forbairt and An Bord Tráchtála (which already has a promotion unit for this purpose).

- Substantial investment in environmental infrastructure will be maintained, with a three-yearly review, to support construction, management, maintenance and supply jobs, and support sustainable growth.

- Active labour-market policies for improved vocational guidance, education and training will be put in place. These will support the transition to cleaner production and technologies, and the wider uptake of environmental management, auditing and reporting.

PART 3 - STRATEGIC SECTORS

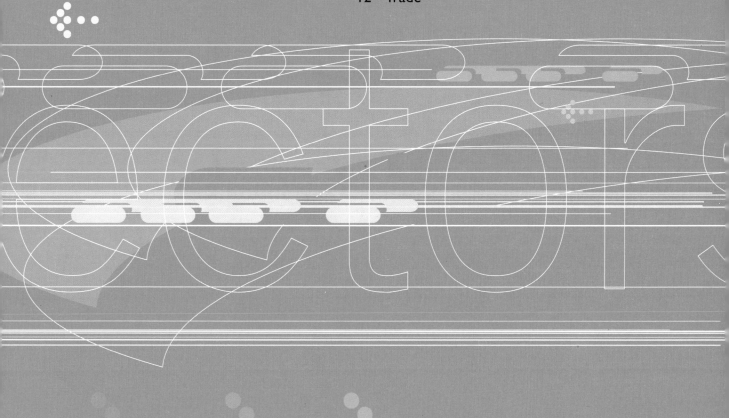

agriculture

5

SUSTAINABLE AGRICULTURE

- provides high quality food from a high quality environment

- maintains the character of the countryside and its landscapes, habitats and species

- secures an acceptable quality of life for the rural community

An action programme towards sustainable agriculture

Agriculture inextricably links the environment, the economy and social development. Although significant environmental impacts and some unsustainable trends may now be associated with the agriculture sector, much of today's landscape is the result of beneficial interaction between the farming community and nature over long periods of time. There is a widely shared appreciation that agricultural activity must be undertaken in an environmentally sustainable manner if it is to be economically viable in the long-term. Substantial action is already being taken to integrate environmental considerations more fully into agriculture. This Strategy defines an agenda to reinforce that action.

• The Government will extend environmental cross-compliance as a standard consideration in respect of agricultural support generally or in selected schemes.

• The *Code of Good Agricultural Practice to Protect Waters from Pollution by Nitrates*, launched in July 1996, and including recommended nitrogen application rates, will be promoted by local authorities, Teagasc and farmer representative associations. The implementation of the *Code* will be closely monitored. Efforts to prevent build-up of nitrates in waters will maintain and, where necessary, improve on the quality of drinking water.

• The use of revised recommended application rates for phosphorus fertilisers for grassland (launched by Teagasc in December 1996) will be encouraged and promoted so as to reduce soil P levels, where excessive to crop requirements at present, down to the recommended levels over a period of five years. In particular, this Strategy targets a reduction of 10% *per annum* in artificial P fertiliser usage over the next five years.

• Appropriate adjustments will be made by the Department of Agriculture, Food and Forestry to the specification for the *Rural Environment Protection Scheme* (REPS) to reduce phosphorus losses from agriculture which contribute to eutrophication of rivers and lakes.

• The Department of Agriculture, Food and Forestry will produce comprehensive guidance and advice on agricultural practices for the purpose of protecting all environmental media and the ecosystems they support, and promoting sustainable agriculture.

• Nutrient Management Planning (as now statutorily provided for in the *Waste Management Act, 1996*), will be promoted mandatorily by local authorities in areas where EPA water quality data identify agriculture as a significant contributor to eutrophication of rivers and lakes. Emphasis will be placed on such planning on an individual farms basis and in catchment and regional areas.

• Teagasc will continue to provide advice and educational services to farmers, including the promotion of awareness of the nutrient value of farm wastes and the achievement of a more sustainable balance between soil inputs and outputs. The services will be reviewed to allow greater targeting, in consultation with EPA, towards the catchments of eutrophic rivers and lakes.

• Intensive agriculture is a scheduled activity for the purposes of Integrated Pollution Control (IPC) licensing under the *Environmental Protection Agency Act, 1992*. IPC requirements for new activities were introduced in September 1996 and IPC requirements for existing activities will be phased in from 1998.

• To assist in maintaining an environmentally-sound farming sector, the Government is introducing, for a three-year period to 1999, improved capital allowances for targeted investment by farmers in pollution control measures.

• A system of environmental management of farming in proposed Natural Heritage Areas, including sustainable stocking densities, will be elaborated between the Department of Agriculture, Food and Forestry, the Department of Arts, Culture and the Gaeltacht, Teagasc and REPS planning agencies, as well as environmental and farm organisations.

Agreed conditions in this regard, correctly applied, will provide for sustainable farming systems in such areas, as well as placing restrictions on environmentally-damaging activities.

- The Department of Agriculture, Food and Forestry is seeking the approval of the European Commission to extend the application of REPS in overgrazed areas from 5 to 15 years. Measures will also be put in place to ensure that the environmental benefits achieved under REPS in designated commonage areas are not diminished by non-participants in the scheme.

- An uptake of 30% of farmers in REPS will be achieved by the year 1999.

- The National Biodiversity Plan, to be completed by end 1997, will identify the actions necessary to preserve biodiversity, including species and habitats, from human activities, including the pressures of agriculture.

- The Department of the Environment will review the regulatory thresholds for environmental impact assessment of drainage works in 1997.

- The Department of Agriculture, Food and Forestry will coordinate action to improve information on the use of pesticides, and to reduce the environmental risks associated with their storage, use and disposal.

- The Department of Agriculture, Food and Forestry will continue its support for organic farming, including financial support for measures to improve marketing and public awareness of the environmental benefits of organic products.

- A farm plastic films recovery scheme, a voluntary initiative involving industry and farming operations, is commencing operation in 1997, and will contribute to national recycling targets.

- The need for precaution in the use of genetically modified organisms (GMOs) in food production is recognised. The new Food Safety Authority will be established in 1997, and will have responsibility for novel food. Better labelling

provisions in Community legislation are being sought for products containing GMOs.

Fig 5.1 Key Trends in Irish Agriculture

Changing agricultural practices
- production of silage
  - increased from 0.3 million tonnes in 1960 to over 20 million tonnes in 1990
  - number of farms using baled silage increased from 2-3% in 1990 to 56% in 1994
- change from manures and dungsteads to slurries
  - 28 million tonnes of winter slurries must be stored and spread on land each year
- enlargement of fields to facilitate mechanisation

Intensification
- increase in livestock numbers
  - sheep flock grew by over 5 million animals from 3.3 million in 1980 to 8.5 million in 1990; the sheep flock peaked in 1992 at 8.9 million and was 7.9 million in 1996
  - national poultry flock which fluctuated between 9.3 million and 9.9 million in the 1980 to 1987 period grew to a high point of 13.7 million in 1994 and was 13.2 million in 1996
  - pig numbers have increased from 1.19 million in 1990 to 1.62 million in 1996

Extensification
- reduced tillage (decrease of nearly 25% in area under arable crops between 1980 and 1990)
- set-aside and Rural Environment Protection Scheme
- organic farming

Environmental impacts
- soil erosion from overgrazing, particularly by sheep
- eutrophication of inland waters by phosphorus from organic (animal wastes) and anthropogenic (chemical fertiliser) sources
- loss of habitats and species, leading to reduction in biodiversity

Waste Management
- organic farm wastes
  - increased amounts of animal slurries utilised by spreading on agricultural land
- non-organic wastes
  - increased use of plastic sheeting for baled silage
- silage effluent
  - approximately 1.4 million tonnes *per annum*, usually combined with slurry for disposal

Introduction/Overview

Agriculture is the primary land use in Ireland, accounting for 4.9 million hectares (including upland pasture and commonage areas) out of a total land area of 6.9 million hectares. It represents around 7% of GDP and 10.6% of employment; these proportions are significantly higher than the respective comparisons for the EU as a whole. If the food sector is included, overall employment amounts to some 14% of the national total. The economy relies heavily on agriculture and its associated industries. Around 18% of total exports come from this sector, together with in the region of 40% of net foreign exchange earnings.[1]

Major changes have taken place since Ireland joined the EEC in 1973. Under the influence of the Common Agricultural Policy (CAP), these changes have resulted in substantial increases in animal and farm productivity and in farm incomes. There is now a greater degree of specialisation, which in some cases has involved a greater concentration of intensive agricultural practices, notably in the pigs, poultry, mushroom and cereals sectors. These concentrations, together with
- a reduction in the outwintering of cattle, in favour of more animal housing,
- the replacement of hay bedding and dung by slatted floors and slurry,
- increased fertilisation of land, and
- a switch from hay to silage feed,

have impacted on the environment to a significant degree.

The environmental impacts of agriculture have been most evident in the increasing incidence of water pollution and the effects of overgrazing on soil and biodiversity. Potentially unsustainable trends are also identifiable, for example, in the area of waste management. Nonetheless, Irish agriculture, with its predominantly grass-based production systems, remains the most extensive and environmentally-friendly in Europe in its use of land resources. The majority of Irish live-stock producers qualify for EU extensification premia, which require a relatively low stocking rate of less than 1.4 livestock units per hectare, and the value of production per hectare, at £731.39, is half that of the European average.[2]

Substantial EU co-financed investment in environmental protection measures continues to be undertaken by the agriculture sector under the *Control of Farm Pollution Scheme*[3] (CFP) and the *Farm Improvement Programme*[4] (FIP). A total of some 1 million cattle and 800,000 sheep have been housed, with effluent storage of 6.1 million cubic metres and fodder storage of 2.6 million tonnes. Some 26,000 applicants were grant-aided to a total of £121 million between 1986 and 1995 under the FIP. A further £145 million was allocated in grant aid to some 25,800 applicants under the CFP Scheme between 1989-93 and under funds agreed for the period 1994-99.[5]

Agriculture is undergoing a process of major structural, social and economic change. This is primarily a consequence of external factors, modifications in the CAP and changes under the General Agreement on Tariffs and Trade (GATT). With the introduction of CAP reform, agriculture policy is now based on lower support levels, greater market orientation and more environmentally-friendly farming practices which are promoted under the *Rural Environment Protection Scheme*[6] (REPS), introduced under the CAP Reform Accompanying Measures.

"By end February 1997, approximately 23,200 farmers had been approved under REPS, and, as a result, some 772,000 hectares of agricultural land (c. 16% of the total) are being farmed in an environmentally-friendly manner. It is envisaged that there will be 43,000 REPS participants and spending of £350 million by 1999."

- Department of Agriculture, Food and Forestry[7]

CAP reform has resulted in a move towards direct payments to farmers with some bias in favour of extensive production. This will have some sustainability benefits, in terms of a slowing down in the intensification of farming and correcting imbalances between production and the carrying capacity of the soil. However, extensification may also lead to larger farms and field sizes, lower labour inputs and consequently less attention to hedgerow maintenance, soil conservation and other positive aspects of current agricultural practices.

Agricultural Interactions with the Environment

Farmers have traditionally been the guardians of the countryside and its heritage. They are aware of the importance of protecting the natural environment, both in its own right and as the resource base for their livelihood, and they have made substantial investments to these ends. The rich rural landscape of Ireland is to a very significant extent a creation of agriculture.

Modern agriculture places pressure on the environment. The EPA has indicated that the *"total organic load generated from agricultural activities in Ireland is equivalent to that generated by about 68 million people"*.[8] Agricultural production and processes give rise to numerous and varied impacts affecting air, water, soil and landscape. Many of these impacts are intensifying in Ireland and, if unchecked, will seriously erode and destroy environmental assets. Apart from the immediate impact on the local environment and its resources, the long-term damage and destruction involved could also have serious implications for the wider economy and society.

Environmental requirements and standards must inform the operation of the agricultural sector. REPS and the CFP Scheme have increased the extent to which agricultural support is being made conditional on compliance with good environmental management and practice. The general issue of eco-responsibility, or cross-compliance, under which environmental requirements are imposed on farmers as a condition of receiving support payments, is receiving increasing attention in the EU. The Government will extend environmental cross-compliance as a standard consideration in respect of agricultural support generally or in respect of further selected schemes.

Intensive livestock farming

Irish agriculture is primarily based on livestock rather than tillage farming, with pasture, hay and silage accounting for some 70% of land use and total crops, fruit and horticulture accounting for 8%. Trends since 1970 show that while the area under grass has remained more or less unchanged, the proportion of arable land has decreased and the area under forest has increased. The emphasis on livestock and related products is highlighted in the analysis of Gross Agricultural Output for 1995 (see Fig 5.2). Livestock related agriculture, including dairying, meat production, poultry and related commodities accounts for nearly 87% of the Gross Agricultural Output in that year.[9]

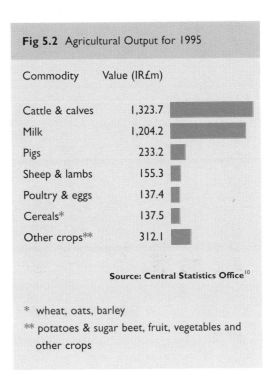

Fig 5.2 Agricultural Output for 1995

Commodity	Value (IR£m)	
Cattle & calves	1,323.7	
Milk	1,204.2	
Pigs	233.2	
Sheep & lambs	155.3	
Poultry & eggs	137.4	
Cereals*	137.5	
Other crops**	312.1	

Source: Central Statistics Office[10]

* wheat, oats, barley

** potatoes & sugar beet, fruit, vegetables and other crops

The intensification of livestock farming has led to a rapid and significant growth in numbers.

Except for a reduction in sheep numbers since 1992, the general trend continues to rise, as shown in Fig 5.3. Poultry numbers also increased dramatically; the national flock, which fluctuated between 9.3 million and 9.9 million in the 1980 to 1987 period, grew to a high point of 13.7 million in 1994 and was 13.2 million in 1996.

Fig 5.3 Livestock Numbers, 1991-1996

	1991 (000s)	1992 (000s)	1993 (000s)	1994 (000s)	1995 (000s)	1996 (000s)
Cattle*	6,912.0	6,975.7	7,026.6	7,064.5	7,122.1	7,422.8
Sheep	8,888.2	8,908.5	8,647.3	8,433.4	8,369.5	7,934.0
Pigs	1,303.7	1,385.8	1,521.6	1,530.4	1,550.4	1,620.8
Poultry	12,052.8	12,039.2	12,900.0	13,725.8	13,248.4	13,170.5

Source: Central Statistics Office[11]

* includes cows and heifers-in-calf in the dairy sector as follows:

1991 - 1,460.5; 1992 - 1,462.4; 1993 - 1,471.3;
1994 - 1,494.4; 1995 - 1,520.1; 1996 - 1,548.4.

This growth has involved major developments in farm management practices, such as fertiliser usage, mechanisation, use of winter housing and investment in pollution control. Widespread dissemination of information on best management practices, advice and the application of research by Teagasc, have also had the effect of increasing land productivity. However, growth has increased pressures on the environment particularly as regards waste management (mainly relating to cattle and pigs) and overgrazing (mainly involving sheep). In addition to effects on soil and water, intensive livestock production also gives rise to increased emissions of ammonia, which contribute to acid rain, and of methane and nitrous oxide (N_2O), which are greenhouse gases.

Methane and N_2O emissions combined are substantial contributors to Ireland's total greenhouse gas emissions; measured on the basis of greenhouse warming potential, they account for 46% of Ireland's emissions of primary greenhouse gases, compared to an EU average of 20%. Methane and N_2O emissions were 811 kt and 29.4 kt respectively in 1990, with about 80% in each case resulting from agriculture. Provisional figures for 1995 indicate no change in methane (812 kt) and a decrease in N_2O (26 kt). Agriculture remains the principal source in the case of both gases, but the proportion of N_2O from this source has fallen to 73%.[12] Both of these greenhouse gases are under consideration as part of the negotiations to strengthen the commitments under the UN *Framework Convention on Climate Change* (see Chapter 8). Gaseous emissions of ammonia from the agriculture sector amounted to 123 kt in 1994, of which almost 100% results from agriculture.[13] Ammonia emissions are under investigation in the development of policy within the EU to combat acidification and eutrophication. Control of emissions of these three gases will require new and continuing attention at national level in the implementation of this Strategy.

Organic waste management

The management of wastes arising from agriculture has particular implications for the maintenance of water quality. Grazing animals produce some 28 million tonnes of manure during the indoor winter period, which must be stored and land-spread. Pig and poultry manure output is over 2 million tonnes. In addition, about 1.4 million tonnes of silage effluent are also produced. Farm wastes have a high polluting potential relative to domestic sewage or industrial wastes, as indicated in Fig 5.4.

Fig 5.4 Polluting Potential of Various Wastes

Wastes	BOD content (mg/l)	Phosphorus content (mg/l)
Cattle manure slurry	17,000	630
Silage effluent	65,000	560
Domestic sewage	450	15
Brewing	600	20

Source: Environmental Research Unit[14]

The potential of agricultural wastes to cause water pollution should be qualified to take account of the relatively low pollution potential of manures produced by cattle and sheep at pasture. After allowing for these, however, the agricultural waste volume is calculated at six times the levels from domestic sewage and industrial wastes.[15]

Compared to traditional manures and dungsteads, the large quantities of animal manures produced on dairy and beef farms using slatted sheds (and accounting for 85% of total animal output) require different disposal practices to minimise the potential for pollution. Disposal by land-spreading has a significant potential for nutrient enrichment of waters in the agriculture context, particularly if disposal takes place outside the growing season or when weather or ground conditions are unsuitable. The problem is exacerbated in some parts of the country by heavy rainfall and areas of poorly draining soils, and also by the concentration of intensive farming, especially pigs and poultry, in certain geographic areas (e.g. almost 50% of the total poultry flock is located in Co. Monaghan).[16]

Careful management is required to minimise the losses of nutrients from land spread wastes to adjacent waters. The housing and feeding of higher numbers of livestock for extended periods in the farmyard greatly increase the threat of pollution from "dirty water" due to improper storage of waste and drainage of roofs and yards. The widespread use of silage as the main cattle fodder, replacing hay, introduces another potential pollutant of water courses, i.e. run-off from silage pits.

It is an objective of this Strategy to continue to improve the management of farm wastes. It must be accepted that there are finite limits to the capacity of soil to absorb organic wastes, and that appropriate arrangements are essential to stay within these limits.

- Positive steps are being taken through REPS, which requires all participants to draw up a waste management, liming and fertilisation plan, with the objective of minimising nutrient losses.

- A more intensive focus is now being placed on nutrient management planning (see below).

- Updated guidance on farm pollution control from the Department of Agriculture, Food and Forestry will focus, *inter alia*, on waste storage and treatment.

- Intensive pig and poultry rearing activities will progressively become subject to Integrated Pollution Control licensing over the remainder of this decade.

• While recognising that anaerobic digestion on its own does not solve all the problems of nutrient pollution, the agricultural sector will be encouraged by Government to explore the technical and economic feasibility of agri-waste digestion in association with other waste producing sectors.

Nutrients: Phosphorus and eutrophication

Monitoring of national water resources has established that eutrophication of rivers and lakes is the most significant threat to the maintenance of high water quality. (In this regard see also Chapter 13). Eutrophication involves nutrient enrichment of the water leading to accelerated plant and algae growth, lowering of water quality and interference with fisheries and other uses of the water. The primary cause of eutrophication in Ireland is phosphorus (P), although nitrates can be a contributor in certain circumstances.

A number of sources, including sewage and industrial wastes, contribute to phosphorus loadings. However, losses from agriculture, both organic farm wastes (from farmyards where waste management practices are inadequate and from leaching and run-off from land) and mineral fertilisers, are a significant factor. Case studies on Lough Conn and Lough Derg have attributed 50-60% of the P loading to agriculture, while studies in the Lee catchment attributed 80% of P loading to this source.[17]

"On a national basis, much more phosphorus than is required for optimal production is being used in intensive agriculture."

- Environmental Protection Agency[18]

Phosphorus is required for both plant and animal growth, but its application in the form of mineral fertilisers and as manures/slurries can have important consequences for water quality. National trends show a steady increase in soil P levels between 1950 and 1991, when the average P level increased from 0.8 mg/l to 9.3 mg/l. Since 1991, the average P appears to have dropped to about 8 mg/l and to have stabilised around that level.[19] Teagasc has reported

increasing evidence from research that there is potential to reduce P inputs to grassland without reducing yields. Phosphorus balance studies also indicate significant P inputs in excess of P removals, resulting in the build-up of excessive P levels in the soil in some areas. P inputs in 1988, for example, were estimated to be more than double the outputs, and this excess had been continuing for years.[20] Current excess of P input has been estimated at about 46,000 tonnes a year.[21] A recent project[22] on eutrophication in the Inniscarra Reservoir on the River Lee, Co. Cork bears out the findings on P levels. Excess phosphorus in the soil increases the risk of losses to waters, with consequent implications for eutrophication.

Apart from the environmental costs of excessive soil enrichment, there is also an economic cost where money is being expended unnecessarily on mineral fertilisers. Approximately 60,000 tonnes from a total P input of some 140,000 tonnes a year is artificial. While in Europe the level of application of artificial P has steadily declined by about 2% *per annum* for the last ten years, it has remained fairly constant in Ireland over the same period. In order to seek a balance in the inputs and removal rates of P, efforts should be focused on reducing artificial P levels. Teagasc has estimated that savings in excess of £25 million nationally could be achieved annually if fertiliser applications were tailored more closely to crop requirements.[23]

Nutrients: Nitrates and water quality

The European experience shows that excessive nitrate levels in waters contribute to eutrophication and to the contamination of drinking water sources. While there is limited evidence to date of problems arising from the use of nitrogenous fertilisers in Ireland, the concentration of nitrates in waters in some areas has increased significantly compared with normal background levels. Consumption of nitrogenous fertilisers has been increasing fairly steadily, from 275,000 tonnes in 1980 to just over 400,000 tonnes in 1993[24], and

EPA has referred to evidence that the efficiency of the utilisation of nitrogen in fertiliser is decreasing as the quantity used increases.[25]

Elevated nitrate levels are found in some rivers, particularly in the South-East, and in certain groundwaters in areas where tillage farming is carried on.[26] Existing efforts to prevent the build-up of nitrates in waters will maintain and, where necessary, improve on the quality of drinking water with important public health benefits. Drinking water quality analyses for 1995 indicate that only 0.8% of samples exceeded the statutory quality standard of 50 mg/l NO_3.[27]

Between 20% and 25% of drinking water supplies nationally come from groundwater sources. In certain areas, the proportion of drinking water obtained from groundwater is much higher than the national average (e.g. 90% in North Cork, 86% in Co. Roscommon)[28], and groundwater is often the only source of supply in rural areas unserved by public or group water schemes. These resources are vulnerable to human activities, including the use of chemical fertilisers and the growing volume of agricultural and other wastes disposed of by land-spreading. As remediation of contaminated water supplies is often either technically impracticable or prohibitively expensive, a preventive approach is essential.

Nutrients: Management responses

Good management can prevent water pollution from agricultural sources. Action, supported by enhanced legislative provisions, is already under way. The emphasis of this Strategy will be to ensure that management action is well planned, concerted, effective and backed up where appropriate by stringent legislative controls. The environmental objective of management action is to reduce and prevent the pollution of surface waters and groundwaters by nutrients from agriculture. The range of actions being, and to be, pursued includes the following.

- In December 1996, revised recommended application rates for phosphorus fertilisers for grass-

land were launched by Teagasc[29]; these took account of levels already in the soil. Use of the new application rates will be encouraged and promoted in the agriculture sector, so as to reduce soil P levels, where excessive to crop requirements at present, down to the recommended levels over a period of five years. In particular, this Strategy will seek to achieve a greater balance in the P budget, and towards this end targets a reduction of 10% *per annum* in artificial P fertiliser usage over the next five years.

- Appropriate adjustments will be made by the Department of Agriculture, Food and Forestry to the specification for REPS to reduce phosphorus losses from agriculture which contribute to eutrophication of rivers and lakes.

- The *Code of Good Agricultural Practice to Protect Waters from Pollution by Nitrates*,[30] launched in July 1996, which includes recommended nitrogen application rates, will be promoted by local authorities, Teagasc and farmer representative associations. A Code of Good Practice for Phosphorus will also be developed by 1998.

- Nutrient Management Plans provide an opportunity both to minimise adverse environmental effects and to make the most efficient use of economic resources. More attention, accordingly, is now being given to nutrient management planning, both on an individual farm basis where there is an increasing awareness and interest among farmers, but also in catchment and regional areas. This is particularly important where the organic wastes produced by intensive livestock farming exceed the soil nutrient requirements of the area. Nutrient management plans are a feature of REPS. The Erne Catchment Nutrient Management Scheme, launched in 1996 and being funded by the EU Peace Fund, offers a Nutrient Management Planning service to intensive farmers on both sides of the Border for the Bunnoe and Dromore sub-catchments of the River Erne in Counties Cavan, Monaghan and Fermanagh.

This pilot scheme will serve as a model for future services of this kind.

- Nutrient Management Planning has been given a statutory basis by the *Waste Management Act, 1996*. The Act provides that a local authority may, on foot of water quality analyses carried out by the authority or the EPA, serve notice on landowners/farmers to furnish a nutrient management plan, based on soil analysis of the holding, setting nutrient application rates so as to prevent or limit water pollution, and requiring records to be kept on production, treatment and application of farm wastes and the use of mineral fertilisers. The Department of the Environment will request local authorities to use these powers in areas where EPA water quality data identify agriculture as a significant contributor to eutrophication of rivers and lakes.

- To assist in maintaining an environmentally sound farming sector, the Government is introducing, for a three-year period to 1999, improved capital allowances for targeted investment by farmers in pollution control measures.

- Teagasc will continue to provide advice and educational services to farmers, including the promotion of awareness on the nutrient value of farm wastes and the achievement of a more sustainable balance between soil inputs and outputs. The services will be reviewed to allow greater targeting, in consultation with EPA, of the catchments of eutrophic rivers and lakes.

Management action will be supported and informed by appropriate research by Teagasc and EPA. Current projects commissioned by the latter, under the *Operational Programme for Environmental Services, 1994-99*[31], include:

- an investigation, headed by the Zoology Department of UCG, of eutrophication processes in the littoral zones of western lakes, including Lough Corrib; and

- a study by Teagasc/TCD on agricultural soil phosphorus losses to water. The aim is to develop a model to predict soil P losses given soil type, soil P level and precipitation amounts so as to facilitate better targeting of pollution control resources.

Overgrazing

"Soil genesis is a long process - the formation of a layer of 30 cm of soil takes from 1,000 to 10,000 years. It is formed so slowly that soil can be considered as a non-renewable resource."
- Europe's Environment: The Dobris Assessment[12]

Overstocking and overgrazing by sheep are particular problems in western and upland areas. Headage payments contributed to a significant expansion in the numbers of sheep in the country. Between 1980 and 1990, the size of the Irish sheep flock grew by over 5 million animals, with total sheep numbers reaching a high point of 8.9 million in 1992 (see Fig 5.3). Large numbers of grazing animals remove vegetative cover and compact the soil, resulting in faster run-off of water and consequent soil erosion. The problem is most acute on lands held in common ownership in Counties Donegal, Kerry, Galway, Leitrim, Mayo, Sligo and Wicklow, where blanket peat soils in areas of high rainfall are particularly vulnerable. Despite their low carrying capacity, these are also the areas of highest sheep density. In June 1995, there were almost 1.1 million sheep in Co. Galway, with a further 0.65 million in Co. Mayo; sheep numbers in Co. Wicklow were over 0.5 million, just under 0.55 million in Co. Kerry and 0.73 million in Co. Donegal.[33]

Average stocking rates, originated by Teagasc, are also a factor in the equation. Irish rates are significantly higher in some respects than those operating in Britain - 1.7 sheep per hectare on blanket bog (year round grazing) compared to between 0.25 and 0.37 sheep per hectare (summer grazing only) in Britain.[34]

Other environmental problems arising from overstocking and overgrazing include the degradation of blanket bog and heather moor - important natural habitats - with consequent effects on plant and animal species, and the siltation of streams and lakes by soil and peat released by erosion. Siltation can damage fisheries, particularly at the spawning/fry stage, with consequences for both species protection and commercial uses. There are also economic consequences for the agriculture industry itself. Land degraded by overgrazing may no longer be able to support livestock, or other uses. The loss of this land for agricultural use, combined with its lack of potential for other use as a result of its degraded state, reduces the overall productive land resource. This has implications for the wider economy and, in particular, the destructive effect on landscape may adversely affect the tourism industry.

It is essential to the sustainability of agriculture and its natural resource base to ease pressures in sensitive areas by reducing sheep numbers. It is recognised, however, that the socio-economic implications of overgrazing make it difficult to arrive at a simple solution to the problem.

- A partial response has already been made under REPS, whereby a special allowance is paid to farmers to remove their sheep from sensitive uplands for six months of the year. The practice of commonage is an additional factor in the equation, which requires control and management to ensure equitable sharing and sustainable use.

- Since 1994, it has no longer been possible to move sheep quota rights from non-disadvantaged into disadvantaged areas. This restriction is now helping to reduce the concentration of sheep stocks on the mountains and uplands of disadvantaged areas which could be adversely affected by overgrazing.

- A system of environmental management of farming in proposed Natural Heritage Areas, including sustainable stocking densities, is being agreed between the Department of

Agriculture, Food and Forestry, the Department of Arts, Culture and the Gaeltacht, Teagasc and REPS planning agencies, as well as environmental and farm organisations. The Department of Agriculture, Food and Forestry is seeking the approval of the European Commission to extend the application of REPS in overgrazed areas from 5 to 15 years, and is putting in place measures to ensure that the environmental benefits achieved under REPS in designated commonage areas are not diminished by non-REPS participants.

Pesticide use

Pesticide use in Ireland, while low by European standards (see Fig 5.5), nonetheless presents potential problems, particularly if pesticides are misused. Improper storage, handling, use and disposal methods can result in pollution of waters and soil, and may affect biodiversity by threatening insect, bird and animal life, and damaging flora. Sheep-dip is a prime example of the risks involved, given its highly toxic nature and the usual siting of sheep dipping close to watercourses.

Trends in the use of pesticides are difficult to identify, because of the limited availability of data. In 1996, EPA published the results of a countrywide survey of pesticide residues in water supplies.[35] From over 3,300 analytical results on water samples, spread over 26 counties and serving 1.8 million consumers, only 5 were above the statutory drinking water quality standards. On re-testing, the supplies with positive results were shown to be clear.

The regulatory system introduced to give effect to Council Directive 91/414/EEC on pesticide use[36] is designed to ensure that no unacceptable influence on the environment occurs in terms of contamination of soil, water and air and effects on flora and fauna. Improvements in the regulatory regime for plant protection products involve more in-depth examination in regard to operator safety, the fate and behaviour of individual plant

Fig 5.5 Consumption of Pesticides in Selected Countries

Country	Total Tonnes [37] (active ingredients)	Agricultural Area [38] (000 ha.)	Pesticide Use in Ratio to Agricultural Area (tonne/ha.)	
Austria [b]	3,565	3,449	1.03	
Belgium [1]	9,885	1,380	7.16	
Denmark	4,103	2,740	1.50	
France [b]	84,709	30,220	2.80	
Germany	28,930	17,160	1.69	
Greece	8,583	5,740	1.50	
Ireland [c]	2,761	4,900	0.56	
Italy [a]	91,671	17,220	5.32	
Netherlands	11,551	1,980	5.83	
Spain	80,760	29,760	2.71	
Sweden [3]	1,464	3,359	0.44	
United Kingdom [b] [2]	27,748	15,880	1.75	
EU Average			2.69	

1993 figures, except (a) 1990, (b) 1992, (c) 1994
(1) includes Luxembourg,
(2) Great Britain only
(3) special sales tax has been applied to pesticides in Sweden since 1987

Source: OECD/Department of Agriculture, Food and Forestry[39]

protection products in soil, water and air, and the impact on non-target species (terrestrial vertebrates, aquatic species, arthropod species, soil macro- and micro-organisms).

To ensure continued sustainable practice in regard to pesticides, the Department of Agriculture, Food and Forestry will coordinate action to:

- improve statistics relating to the use of pesticides;

- replace older less environmentally-friendly pesticides with newer more environmentally-benign products;

- improve standards of storage, handling use and disposal; and

- achieve a quantitative reduction in the level of risk associated with use.

Non-organic farm wastes

It is estimated that some 12,000 tonnes of waste plastic sheeting arise in the agricultural and horticultural sectors each year.[40] This represents about 35% of the total non-domestic polyethylene film waste generated in Ireland. While the generation of this waste is quite evenly divided between various uses, including fertiliser bags, silage covers and bale wraps, the significant increase in the use of baled silage, from 2-3% of all farms in 1990 to 56% in 1994[41], suggests that further growth in the quantity of plastic waste may be expected. Proper disposal of these wastes is essential to protect the environment from the hazards of plastic, which include threats to wildlife, disruption of drainage systems and water flows, and visual intrusion on the landscape.

In 1996, the Farm Films Producers Group (Ireland) (IFFPG) was formed by manufacturers, importers and distributors, with the support of the IFA, to increase the collection and recycling of plastic films from agriculture. It is intended that IFFPG will apply to be designated an approved body for the purposes of the *Waste Management (Farm Plastics) Regulations, 1997*, under the *Waste Management Act, 1996*. The Regulations afford plastics producers the option of complying with requirements based on a mandatory deposit/refund system, or of participating in an approved recovery scheme. In 1997, IFFPG will start operating an approved Irish Farm Films Recovery Scheme for the recovery of plastic films from farms where it is economically feasible to do so. The scheme is a significant voluntary initiative by the industry and IFA towards meeting national waste recovery and recycling objectives.

Landscape, habitats and species

Agricultural land use and practices can contribute to the loss of habitats and species, leading to a reduction in biodiversity. In historical terms, the introduction of agriculture into what was previously almost entirely natural forest broadened the range of plant species. Due to the largely extensive nature of Irish agriculture, landscape quality has been, with some exceptions, well conserved, and a high percentage of natural and semi-natural habitats has been retained. However, there has been some loss of biodiversity with, for example, the drainage of wetlands and the removal of hedgerows.

A system of environmental management of farming in proposed Natural Heritage Areas, including sustainable stocking densities, will be elaborated between the Department of Agriculture, Food and Forestry, the Department of Arts, Culture and the Gaeltacht, Teagasc and REPS planning agencies, as well as environmental and farm organisations. Agreed conditions in this regard, correctly applied, will provide for sustainable farming systems in such areas, as well as placing restrictions on environmentally-damaging activities.

Priority habitats will be designated as Special Areas of Conservation (SACs) under the *European Communities (Natural Habitats)*

Regulations, 1997 (see also Chapter 13). The effect of these designations, which will be compulsory, will be to further address any unsustainable farming or developmental practices in these areas, and to give additional support to that already available under REPS to environmentally-friendly farming.

As indicated in Chapter 13 also, a national Biodiversity Plan will be completed in 1997. Ireland supplied a "Country Report"[42] in 1995 to the UN Food and Agriculture Organisation covering measures to protect and conserve agricultural plant genetic resources. A complementary EU initiative (under Council Regulation 1467/94[43]) is co-funding, over a five-year period, research on the conservation, characterisation, collection and utilisation of genetic resources in agriculture. The Department of Agriculture, Food and Forestry recognises the need to develop more fully national policy in these areas, and will do so within the framework of this Strategy.

The general exemption of the development of land for agricultural and forestry use, including land reclamation and animal housing, from planning regulation means that such developments could potentially have an adverse impact on the environment, and affect the long-term sustainability of other uses such as tourism and amenity. However, even exempted development is subject to a number of conditions designed to limit its impact on the landscape, while large developments of forestry, land reclamation and peat extraction are now subject to planning permission requirements and environmental impact assessment procedures.

Drainage, frequently undertaken for agricultural purposes but also for flood relief, has caused significant damage to aquatic habitats and wetlands, including turloughs, wetland systems for which Ireland has particular international responsibilities. In the future all proposals to undertake drainage, whether for agriculture related, urban flood relief, or other reasons, will include careful consideration of the potential effects on biodiversity and the environment generally. The Department of the Environment will review the regulatory thresholds for environmental impact assessment of drainage works in 1997.

Organic farming

The organic farming sector supports sustainable agricultural development through the production of environmentally-friendly goods and services. It is desirable that lands in conversion to organic farming should reach full organic status, and that a greater market share, implying an increased availability to consumers, should be achieved for organic produce. Subsidisation of high-intensity agriculture, however, provides a comparative market advantage over low-intensity or organic farming. Correct pricing and ongoing support are needed to level the playing field between high and low intensity products.

The *Operational Programme for Agriculture, Rural Development and Forestry, 1994-99*, provides investment aid (an indicative amount of £0.8 million) for the marketing, promotion and distribution of organic produce over the period 1994-1999. In addition, the organic farming supplementary measure to REPS offers financial incentives to farmers who farm organically in accordance with a five-year REPS plan.

The Department of Agriculture, Food and Forestry will continue its support for organic farming, including financial support for measures to improve marketing and public awareness of the environmental benefits of organic products.

Agricultural research

Research is ongoing, funded by the Department of Agriculture, Food and Forestry, in the area of sustainable agriculture. As part of the Teagasc Environment Protection Programme under the *Agriculture, Rural Development and Forestry OP,* research is focused on the following priority areas:

- the development of viable nutrient and waste management strategies designed to minimise the impact on the environment of agriculture and other developments in rural areas; and

- the development of strategies for the enhancement of rural landscapes and the ecological management of set-aside areas, including habitat re-establishment studies.

Sub-programmes covered by this research programme include:
- sustainable farming systems;
- the environmental impact of phosphorous;
- the environmental impact of nitrogen;
- waste management;
- land use management; and
- soil fertility.

The projects involved scientifically underpin the implementation of EU and national legislation concerning agriculture and the environment.

Food safety

"Ireland has many environmental advantages which are important in meeting the increasing consumer demands for good quality, nutritional and safely produced food."
- Forfás, *Shaping Our Future*[44]

Of all industrial sectors, the food sector is the most highly, if not uniquely, dependent on a good environmental image as the key to good quality food. The food and drink industry contributes significantly to the national economy, accounting in 1994 for 29% of GNP, 21% of total exports and almost 20% of the total industrial workforce.[45] Both the Culliton Report and the 1996 Forfás Report, *Shaping Our Future,* recognised the need for a high quality environment to secure the position of the agri-food industry and realise its development potential. More and more, national environmental quality is seen as underwriting the quality of food products directly derived from that environment. Growing concern among consumers, both in Ireland and in export markets, about food quality and safety, highlights the need to protect the environment and maintain high environmental standards.

The agri-food sector must achieve and maintain high environmental standards in its operation in order to respond to consumer concerns and realise its economic and employment potential. Integrated Pollution Control (IPC) licensing is being progressively applied in the sector, and the phasing in of IPC requirements for existing activities, which has already commenced, will be completed by the end of the decade. In addition, substantial voluntary action demonstrating the sector's own environmental responsibility, is open to the agri-food sector, in common with industry generally, by means of initiatives including the new approaches identified in Chapter 9.

Genetic modification

The use of genetically modified organisms (GMOs) in food production is an issue of significant current concern to consumers.

Biotechnology has emerged as one of the most promising technologies for sustainable development into the next century, with potential both to improve environmental protection and to transform the competitiveness and growth base of a range of economic activities. BioResearch Ireland was formed in 1987 to develop biotechnology expertise and facilities, and to commercialise the results of biotechnology R&D.

While modern biotechnology can have a positive effect on health, food safety and the environment, there has nonetheless been growing public concern about the long-term health and environmental impacts of genetic modification. Equally, with increasing use of genetic modification tech-

niques in food production, concern has grown about the extent of consumer information made available, notably through labelling of products containing or consisting of GMOs.

Ireland's environmental regulatory controls in the area of biotechnology are based on EU Directives; the Environmental Protection Agency implements the *Genetically Modified Organisms Regulations, 1994*, which give effect to Council Directives 90/219/EEC on the contained use of genetically modified micro-organisms[46] and 90/220/EEC on the deliberate release into the environment of genetically modified organisms.[47] In 1996, the Government decided that the Minister for Health would assume responsibility for the implementation of Council Regulation (EC) No. 258/97 concerning novel foods and novel food ingredients.[48] Regulatory control will be undertaken in this regard by the proposed Food Safety Authority of Ireland, which will be established in 1997.

EPA operates on a precautionary basis in the discharge of its regulatory functions under the Directives and the Regulations. Improved safety measures in respect of contained uses (i.e. within laboratories) were agreed by the Environment Council during the Irish Presidency. It is recognised that the provisions of Directive 90/220/EEC are deficient in respect of the labelling of products containing or consisting of GMOs, and Ireland is actively supporting the development of transparent labelling provisions to be brought forward by the Commission in 1997 as part of proposals to revise the Directive.

(6)

SUSTAINABLE FORESTRY

- enhances the natural environment, including natural systems such as the carbon cycle

- harmonises with landscape and incorporates ecological issues including protection of sensitive areas, biodiversity and water quality

- supports the quality of rural life by providing employment and amenities

- provides timber on a sustained yield basis

An action programme towards sustainable forestry

National forestry policy, as evidenced in the *Operational Programme for Agriculture, Rural Development and Forestry, 1994-99* and the *Strategic Plan for the Development of the Forestry Sector in Ireland*, already takes account of many sustainable development issues and considerations. This integration will be further developed under the forthcoming National Sustainable Forestry Plan. Specific actions arising out of existing policy, or new initiatives which will be developed in addition to it, are summarised below.

- The threshold at which planning permission and environmental impact assessment (EIA) is required for afforestation has been reduced with effect from 1 October, 1996, from 200 hectares to 70 hectares. In addition, planning permission and EIA will now be required for cumulative afforestation which results in a total area planted exceeding 70 hectares.

- The Minister for the Environment will take new powers in relation to forestry control in the next Local Government (Planning and Development) Bill to enable planning permission to be required for plantations which would not warrant EIA.

- Forestry legislation will be reviewed to reflect the principles of sustainable forestry development, as set out under the Helsinki process. As part of this process, Ireland will also develop a national sustainable forestry plan and national criteria and indicators by which progress can be measured, and the Department of Agriculture, Food and Forestry will develop a Code of Practice for sustainable forest management over the full forestry rotation period.

- The Department of Agriculture, Food and Forestry will implement a strategic plan for the forestry sector in Ireland, which will take account of sustainable development requirements.

- The Department of the Environment has issued draft consultation guidelines for planning authorities in relation to forestry and the need to protect views and scenic areas, landscape and water quality, and the natural and archaeological heritage, and to avoid rural isolation. These guidelines will be finalised in 1997. In accordance with the guidelines, planning authorities will be entitled to designate areas which they consider to be sensitive to forestry development, and the Forest Service will notify these authorities of all proposed forestry developments, regardless of size, within such designated areas.

- The Department of Agriculture, Food and Forestry will regularly review its existing environmental controls, including its existing guidelines in relation to the landscape, fisheries and archaeology, and will introduce new guidelines on wildlife and habitat diversity, harvesting and clearfelling, use of chemicals and herbicides, and amenity and recreation. Particular attention will be paid to the planting of broadleaf trees on the margins of large coniferous plantations.

Introduction/Overview

Approximately 8% of Ireland is currently under forest which compares to the EU average of over 30%. The low Irish figure, however, masks substantial increases in afforestation which have taken place in recent decades (see Figs 6.1 and 6.2). The degree of afforestation must be seen in the context of a baseline of approximately 1% of forest cover at the turn of this century. The current afforestation policy will increase this proportion to 10% by the end of the century and to 17% (almost 1.2 million hectares) by the year 2030.[1] An estate of this size is considered to be the minimum necessary to produce the annual volume of timber needed to support the required range and level of timber processing industries.

Fig 6.1 Issues in Irish Forestry

Increase in area afforested
- the total area under forest has increased in this century from 1% to 8%
- forest cover is increasing at a rate of about 0.33% per annum
- the current rate of afforestation is the highest in the EU
- the area afforested is still the lowest in the EU

The predominance of coniferous species in the past is now changing
- 84% of Irish forests comprise conifers, mostly Sitka spruce
- the emphasis in forestry guidelines and conditions for grants is now on greater diversity and preference for native and broadleaved trees
- broadleaved species accounted for almost 20% of planting in 1995, compared to 2-3% in the mid-1980s

Increase in private afforestation
- privately-owned forests account for just over 30% of all forests
- annual planting by private operators (including farmers) reached 73% of total planting in 1995
- in 1995, 85% of all private afforestation was undertaken by farmers

The primary objective of forestry in Ireland is the production of timber for a variety of end uses. The growing forestry industry and trade in wood products have significant economic value. An estimated 16,000 people are currently employed in the sector, of which 7,000 are directly employed in forestry. Annual timber production in 1996 was 2.32 million cubic metres, and supported some 100 sawmills and three panel board mills. The value of the contribution of the sawn wood and panel board processing sectors to the national economy was estimated in 1993 at £87 million. The value added to industrial input timber and wooden furniture

was estimated at £166 million. Irish forests supply around 60% of domestic requirements for structural and construction grade timber, while exports, comprising some 250,000 cubic metres, consist mainly of palletwood destined for the UK market.[2]

Fig 6.2 Forest cover in EU Member States

Country	Area Under Forest
	%
Austria	46
Belgium	22
Denmark	10
Finland	69
France	30
Germany	30
Greece	44
Ireland	**8**
Italy	29
Netherlands	9
Portugal	35
Spain	27
Sweden	62
United Kingdom	10
EU (15) Average	>30

Source: **Department of Agriculture, Food and Forestry**[3]

Forestry is a valuable element of regional development. It offers an alternative land use, thereby creating diversification in rural areas; it provides farmers with an alternative agricultural activity, a long-term asset and new income opportunities; it benefits the rural economy by the provision of additional and alternative local employment, both in primary afforestation and in the industrial sector. This helps to maintain the rural population, especially in areas where other land based activities do not generate adequate incomes. Current policy focuses on farm forestry, which is now the largest single component of the forestry programme; farmers account for over 80% of private afforestation (which represented 18,627 of the 25,627 hectares afforested in 1996). A total of 1,300 farmers undertook afforestation projects in 1995, and afforestation grants totalling £19 million and forestry premiums amounting to over £4 million were paid in that year.

The long cycle of forestry development (40 years for Sitka spruce) means that the forests of today are the result of decisions made and actions taken decades ago. A range of controls (discussed in this chapter) has been introduced in recent years and the Department of Agriculture, Food and Forestry is committed to their regular review and improvement.

Forestry Interactions with the Environment

Forestry provides a number of environmental benefits. Forests play an important part in the carbon cycle. The *National Climate Change/CO$_2$ Abatement Strategy*[4] (1993) recognised the role of forestry as a carbon sink, which can make a significant contribution to meeting the challenge of climate change.

Forests also act as an atmospheric filter, removing pollutants from the atmosphere. Developed forestry reduces soil erosion by wind and water and controls land slips. Forestry is both a valuable and renewable resource and a sustainable balance between timber production and harvesting has been standard practice in well-managed forests for decades. Forestry can also add to the amenity of urban and rural landscape where developed in a sensitive manner. It provides opportunities for recreation and tourism and form a part of our natural heritage; as well as providing pleasure and amenity to citizens and tourists alike, there is a spin-off benefit in employment in these sectors.

The benefits of forestry, however, have to be weighed against possible adverse environmental effects, in particular areas at the afforestation and forest operation stages, including:

- visual intrusion;
- the impact of monocultural coniferous plantations;
- impacts on water courses and water ecology;
- the loss of, or damage to, sites of archaeological or of scientific interest;
- reduction in the range of flora and fauna;
- isolation of rural dwellings; and
- damage to rural roads during planting and harvesting.

Planning and landscape implications arise not only in the location of the forestry but also in the provision of access roads, bridging/fording of streams, and other works necessary for its commercial operation. These considerations will increase in importance under the planned major afforestation programme, and must be taken into account in its implementation.

Land use

"(Increasing afforestation is) ... perhaps the most rapidly changing feature of land use in Ireland."

- Environmental Protection Agency[6]

Ireland has the lowest level of forestry cover in the EU. Government strategy in recent years, however, has been to increase significantly the land area under afforestation with planting targets of 25,000 hectares *per annum* set down under the present afforestation programme. The planting rate in Ireland - an average 19,000 hectares *per annum* throughout the 1990s - is now the highest *per capita* forest planting programme of any developed country. Forest cover as a percentage of total land area is increasing at a rate of about a third of one percent every year and is probably the most significant change in land use that has taken place in recent times in Ireland. This planting programme is being supported by the under the EU *Operational Programme for Agriculture, Rural Development and Forestry, 1994-1999.*

A sustainable forestry sector is of paramount importance from a land use perspective. A range of controls already exists with a view to achieving the necessary balance. These include the need for planning permission and environmental impact assessment in certain circumstances. The Department of Agriculture, Food and Forestry requires applications for forestry grants to comply with guidelines on the protection of habitats, fisheries, archaeological sites and landscapes of high amenity value[6] (which are being reviewed in 1997). Where environmental considerations are identified in these regards, relevant State agencies and local authorities are consulted. The Department of Arts, Culture and the Gaeltacht will review the management of archaeological monuments within forested areas, in particular with reference to the potential impact of afforestation on as yet unidentified archaeological monuments, the management of monuments within existing forests, and the enforcement of conditions placed on afforestation grants to protect known monuments.

The experience has been that problems can arise in relation to specific afforestation projects. Some problems arise from the conflict between development and non-development which is not unique to forestry. However, the fact that in most cases there was no statutory process which allowed structured input from the general public into the forestry consent process contributed to some problems. In order to address some of these issues, the Department of the Environment, in conjunction with the Department of Agriculture, Food and Forestry, has introduced a revised regime of control on forestry development.

An Environmental Impact Assessment (EIA) threshold of 70 hectares (ha) for both initial afforestation, and contiguous afforestation by a single developer over a three year period, has been introduced. This reduced EIA threshold (originally 200 ha) applies to planting commencing on 1 October, 1996, and will be reviewed after 3 years. In this context afforestation will be deemed contiguous if it is within 500 metres of another plantation being developed by the same person. The Department of Agriculture, Food and Forestry has introduced a system of notification of local authorities for all projects over 25 hectares in respect of which grant applications were received on or after 1 April, 1996. Local authorities have a month in which to make observations on the proposed projects. Where the local authority responds, its views will be taken into account by the Forest Service.

The draft *Guidelines for Planning Authorities on Forestry Development*[7], issued by the Department of the Environment in January 1997 for consultation purposes, set out the proposed procedure under which local authorities may designate areas which they consider to be sensitive to forestry development. The draft Guidelines are based on factors such as the need to protect views and scenic areas, landscape quality, protection of the natural and archaeological heritage and the avoidance of rural isolation. In these sensitive areas, it is proposed that local authorities will be notified of all proposals for afforestation regardless of threshold and the Forest Service will have regard to any observations made by the authorities. The Guidelines also suggest that planning authorities consider preparing local indicative forest strategies to form the basis for decisions on planning applications and consultations on forestry applications. In issuing the draft, the Department of the Environment is facilitating the widest possible consideration of all the issues involved. The Guidelines will be finalised in 1997.

The Department of Agriculture, Food and Forestry will regularly review its existing environmental controls, including its existing guidelines in relation to the landscape, fisheries and archaeology, and will introduce new guidelines on wildlife and habitat diversity, harvesting and clearfelling, use of chemicals and herbicides, and amenity and recreation. Particular attention will be paid to the planting of broadleaf trees on the margins of large coniferous plantations.

It is also intended to take new powers in relation to forestry control in the next Local Government (Planning and Development) Bill to enable planning permission to be required for plantations which would not warrant EIA. The appropriate levels for such controls will be judged in the light of the experience gained through the new local authority notification system. These changes will assist in ensuring that the afforestation programme continues to contribute to Ireland's sustainable development while at the same time minimising problems which may arise in specific cases.

Predominance of coniferous species

A trend in past afforestation has been the predominant planting of coniferous rather than native and broadleaved species, to the extent that 84% of forests comprise coniferous species. The 16% of the Irish forest estate which is made up of broadleaves is considerably less than in practically all other EU Member States, where the average proportion of broadleaved forestry is 40% of the total (see Fig 6.3). The emphasis on quick-growing softwoods reflected the exceptionally suitable conditions of the Irish climate for such species, supporting rapid growth and providing quick returns on investment.

Fig 6.3 Percentage of Broadleaves and Conifers in EU National Forests

Country	Broadleaves %	Conifers %
Austria	24	76
Belgium	51	49
Denmark	32	68
Finland	10	90
France	64	36
Germany	31	69
Greece	82	18
Ireland	**16**	**84**
Italy	75	25
Luxembourg	64	36
Netherlands	40	60
Portugal	56	44
Spain	58	42
Sweden	7	93
United Kingdom	33	67

Source: Department of Agriculture, Food and Forestry[8]

Forestry plantations change some wildlife habitats and biodiversity. Coniferous woods, however, can support a high density of wildlife and high species richness, but they are more vulnerable to disease and pest infestation, and may therefore require higher use of pesticides and fungicides. Although disease and infestation have not been major problems in Irish forests to date, greater diversification would reduce the risk. Diverse forestry also increases the amenity value for tourism and recreation.

Current forestry policy places greater emphasis on the planting of broadleaved species, including native species, with the target for annual broadleaf afforestation set at 20% of total annual afforestation. This has particular value in terms of landscape, heritage, amenity, and habitats. In economic terms, it also offers long-term opportunities for the production of hardwood timber, allowing a greater diversity of associated industries and products. However, this policy requires the use of better quality land, which can raise issues of potential conflict with other uses competing for the same land.

Impacts on soil and water

"Ultimately, the sustainability of plantation forestry in Ireland depends on the sustainability of the soil resource"
- E.P. Farrell[9]

While forests can be beneficial in preventing soil erosion, felling and harvesting operations in productive forests can introduce pressures which increase the threat of erosion. This has consequences not only for the forest itself, but also for nearby waterways and any fish stocks therein. Care must be taken that all forestry operations, including felling and harvesting, cause the minimum of disruption to soil stability and conserve its productivity for as long as possible.

Forestry plantations on peatland, which represent over 40% of Irish plantations, may pose particular problems arising from the nature of the soil. The oxidation of carbon from the peat caused by forestry development depletes the soil, threatening its sustainability. It also releases additional carbon into the carbon cycle, which may offset the carbon sequestration effect of the forestry.

Peatlands formed a significant component of forestry from the 1960s to the 1980s, but now comprise a very minor percentage of planting.

Coniferous plantations, particularly on poorly buffered soils, contribute to acidification, which leads to a depletion of nutrients and a reduction of soil productivity. Poor drainage design can cause problems of sediment and flash flooding, which in turn can increase aluminium stripping and leaching on poor soils. A survey[10] carried out by the ERU in the late 1980s found evidence of acidification in rivers feeding Loughs Doo and Naminna, Co. Clare, and the Lugduff River which flows into the Upper Lake at Glendalough, Co. Wicklow. Common features were poor buffering and coniferous afforested catchments, particularly in the Glendalough area where there are mature forests. The adjoining Lugduff river was more acidic than the Glenealo River, which drains the adjoining non-afforested catchment. Historical data are, however, sparse.

Arising from concerns in relation to water acidification, the EPA established a Working Group in January 1997, including representatives from central and local government and forestry, agriculture and fisheries interests, to review research findings to date on the impact which afforestation on different soil types may have on water quality, and to consider the effectiveness of existing guidelines in protecting sensitive surface waters against increased acidification and enrichment. Its work will lead to recommendations to the Department of Agriculture, Food and Forestry for inclusion in revised guidelines on afforestation.

Impacts on landscape and biodiversity

It is important that any potential adverse impacts of increasing afforestation on natural landscapes and habitats are addressed and minimised. The recent emphasis on broadleaved species and greater diversity within plantations, and the requirement for compliance with the guidelines on the protection of habitats, fisheries, archaeological sites and landscapes of high amenity value as a condition of grant-aid, help to ensure that this afforestation is carried out in a sensitive fashion which enhances and benefits the natural environment.

Certain areas, such as boglands of national or international conservation importance, and areas which are protected or qualify for protection under EU Directives 79/409/EEC on the Protection of Wild Birds[11] and 92/43/EEC on the Protection of Habitats[12], are explicitly excluded from the afforestation programme. The Department of Agriculture, Food and Forestry is committed to introducing new guidelines covering wildlife and habitat diversity in forests.

Ireland has a relatively small area of indigenous forest, much of which is protected by conservation measures. About 5,200 hectares of semi-natural forests are protected in national parks and nature reserves, while the proposed Natural Heritage Areas include other important woodland ecosystems.

Forestry management

Fig 6.4 Criteria for Sustainable Forest Management

- Maintenance and appropriate enhancement of forest resources and their contribution to global carbon cycles
- Maintenance of forest ecosystem health and vitality
- Maintenance and encouragement of productive functions of forests (wood and non-wood)
- Maintenance, conservation and appropriate enhancement of biological diversity in forest ecosystems
- Maintenance and appropriate enhancement of protective functions in forest management
- Maintenance of other socio-economic functions and conditions

Source: Department of Agriculture, Food and Forestry [13]

At the 1993 Ministerial Conference on the Protection of Forests, held in Helsinki, Ireland and 44 other countries signed a Resolution on General Guidelines for the Sustainable Management of Forests in Europe. The Resolution defines sustainable management as:

"the stewardship and use of forests and forest lands in a way and at a rate that maintains their biodiversity, productivity, regeneration capacity, vitality and their potential to fulfil, now and in the future, relevant ecological, economic and social functions, at local, national and global levels, and that does not cause damage to other ecosystems".[14]

In 1994, as part of the Helsinki follow-up process, a draft list of six criteria and twenty indicators for sustainable forest management, agreed by the participating countries, was issued. The intention is that the list will be refined as the process continues. In line with its commitments in this area, and in accordance with the Rio Forest Principles[15], a national sustainable forestry plan (following on from the strategic plan for the forestry sector) is being prepared by the Department of Agriculture, Food and Forestry for publication later this year. The Plan will include, *inter alia*, matters of national criteria and indicators, and address the issue of timber certification/eco-labelling. The related issue of tropical timber certification is addressed in Chapter 12.

Sustainable forestry practices require attention at all stages, from the initial preparation of ground for planting (where sustainability may require, for example, natural or less toxic alternatives to the use of herbicides and pesticides), to the construction and use of access routes, to planned felling and replanting operations. Guidelines on the use of chemicals and pesticides, and on harvesting and clearfelling, will be issued by the Department of Agriculture, Food and Forestry as part of its strategic plan for the forestry sector.

The loading and haulage of timber from forests has significant implications for non-national roads in some areas. This will require appropriate investment as forestry expands and matures (just over 50% of the productive forest estate is under 25 years of age at present). The impact of heavy vehicles related to initial land development, drainage and planting is also considerable.

Coillte is already statutorily required to take account of the environmental effects of its forestry developments and practices. The Department of Agriculture, Food and Forestry will continue to ensure through cross-compliance (in relation to grants, subsidies and other supports) that private forestry operators do likewise.

Forestry based industry

Productive forestry provides the raw materials and resources for economic development which is often focused on areas where alternative industries are unavailable. The location of forestry and downstream production operations in disadvantaged rural areas helps to maintain the local economy and society. The strict implementation of planning requirements (including environmental impact assessment) and, where applicable, of Integrated Pollution Control licensing under the *Environmental Protection Agency Act, 1992*, will be essential to ensure that such operations are established and carried out in accordance with the principles of sustainable development.

(7)

SUSTAINABLE USE OF MARINE RESOURCES

- protects and enhances the marine environment

- uses renewable resources in a sustainable fashion, while preserving biodiversity

- provides economic and social support for coastal and island communities, while conserving the natural resource on which they depend

An action programme towards sustainable use of marine resources

- Ireland will continue to support efforts, under the EU Common Fisheries Policy (CFP), to optimise the management and conservation of sea fisheries in the interests of sustainable and renewable use.

- In this context, Ireland will support the development within the CFP of further measures to reduce the catching of juvenile fish, through improvements in the selectivity of fishing gear and other technical conservation measures, and monitor and quantify the by-catch of cetacea in fishing gear, as required by the Habitats Directive.

- National measures will be maintained to conserve inshore fish-stocks of salmon, sea-trout and bass. A new salmon management strategy is being implemented on a phased basis.

- The Minister for the Marine has introduced proposed legislation to establish a new licensing and regulatory system for aquaculture. The new system will include an independent Appeals Board.

- The *Dumping at Sea Act, 1996*, will be implemented to prohibit waste dumping in the majority of situations and ensure rigorous control of residual disposals.

- Existing regulations for preventing pollution from port operations and ships in harbours will be reinforced by the express duty of port companies established by the *Harbour Act, 1996,* to have due regard to the consequences of their activities on the environment.

- Ireland will ratify the Convention for the Protection of the Marine Environment of the North-East Atlantic (OSPAR) in 1997.

- A Quality Status Report, required by the OSPAR Convention, is being prepared for the Irish and Celtic Sea and areas west of Ireland and Scotland in cooperation with the UK authorities.

- Cooperation with UK authorities on management and monitoring of the Beaufort's Dyke munitions dumpsite will be continued, and an inventory of other dumpsites will be developed in preparing the Quality Status Report under the OSPAR Convention.

- The Minister for the Environment will formulate a policy directive to planning authorities, An Bord Pleanála and the Environmental Protection Agency indicating that there should be a presumption against the location of new landfills adjacent to coasts or estuaries.

- The Framework Strategy for the development of the marine sector, to be published shortly by the Department of the Marine, will take full account of the requirements of sustainable development.

- The Department of the Marine, in consultation with the Department of Transport, Energy and Communications, is devising an updated and comprehensive strategy to ensure that offshore oil and gas exploration and development do not adversely affect the marine environment.

- The Government will continue to press, in the appropriate international fora, for the implementation of a strict new code governing the shipment of nuclear materials, and will seek to have the existing *Code on the Safe Carriage of Irradiated Nuclear Fuel, Plutonium and High-Level Radioactive Wastes in Flasks on Board Ships* made mandatory.

Introduction/Overview

The marine sector, which includes natural resource based industries such as sea fishing, aquaculture and related processing, tourism/leisure and offshore gas and oil exploitation, is important to an island economy like Ireland. Sustainable use of marine resources, which if properly managed can be considered renewable resources, offers significant economic and employment benefits and opportunities. There is concern worldwide, however, about the increasing unsustainable use of marine resources: such use can arise from over-fishing, pollution by ships and offshore installations, sewage and industrial effluents, radioactive substances, tourism and recreation, and other activities.

Fig 7.1 Key trends in the Irish Marine Sector

Growing aquaculture industry
- 25% of all fish production now comes from fish farming
- value of production from the sector doubled between 1989 and 1994

Declining fish stocks
- significant fish stocks are depleted or overexploited
- downward trend in stocks of demersal fish (cod, whiting, plaice, sole)
- salmon catches peaked in the early 1970s

Employment
- some 16,000 persons are employed in the fisheries sector, including 2,500 in aquaculture

Marine transport
- 76% of Irish trade (by volume) is carried by sea
- 35% of passenger traffic to other countries is by sea

Energy production
- marine exploitation of natural gas provides some 20% of the Irish energy requirement

Waste discharges
- 80% of our municipal waste water discharges into Irish seas
- an estimated 80% of marine litter originates from land

Growing awareness of these threats to the marine environment has led to a number of initiatives in international cooperation in recent years:
- the entry into force of the UN Convention on the Law of the Sea (1994);
- the Washington Global Programme of Action for the Protection of the Marine Environment from Land-based Activities (UNEP, 1995);
- the UN Agreement on Straddling and Highly Migratory Fish Stocks (1995); and
- the FAO Code of Conduct for Responsible Fisheries (1995).

The UN has also designated 1998 as the International Year of the Oceans.

A major review of policy in relation to the marine sector generally is now under way in Ireland; a synthesis of views expressed during extensive public consultation has already been published by the Marine Institute in 1996.[1] A Framework Strategy for the development of the sector will be published shortly. The Strategy will focus on policies to maximise the return from existing activities and develop new uses of the marine resource, and will take full account of the need to ensure that the development of the sector is in accordance with the principles of sustainability.

Marine Activities' Interaction with the Environment
Commercial sea-fishing

"It is essential for continued harvesting that the limits which nature imposes on the quantities of fish that can be taken from the sea be respected."

- UN Food and Agriculture Organisation[2]

Fisheries are an important renewable resource, provided that they are used sustainably. While the global fish catch increased five-fold between 1950 and 1990 it has not increased since then. Maintaining catch levels now requires ever greater effort and technology, as well as an expanded range of operations. In addition to unsustainable levels of catches, fish stocks and marine biodiversity are also depleted through by-catches of immature fish and by depletion of other species which serve as food for commercial stocks.

It is now internationally recognised that the long-term preservation and improvement of fish stocks, through careful management and responsible fishing, is vital for the future of the industry. For example, the UN Commission on Sustainable Development, at its fourth session in 1996, agreed that significant fish stocks at global level are depleted or overexploited, and noted that urgent corrective action is needed both to rebuild depleted stocks and to ensure the sustainable use of all fish stocks.

At EU level, the Common Fisheries Policy (CFP) already takes account of sustainability requirements in respect of fish stocks, and imposes quotas on certain traditionally fished key economic species. These quotas are based on Total Allowable Catches for major fish stocks, which are determined annually on the basis of scientific advice on the state of these stocks. The CFP also provides for longer-term conservation objectives to be set, where these are appropriate. These measures are supported by technical requirements in relation to permitted net configurations and mesh sizes, minimum landing sizes for fish to protect immature stocks, and a programme of balancing overall fleet structures and activities with fish stocks.

Ireland has been generally supportive of efforts at EU and international level to optimise the management and conservation of the sea fisheries resource in the interests of its sustainable utilisation, and will maintain a progressive stance on these issues. Conservation and management policies and regulations must be underpinned by strict monitoring and enforcement, if the long-term future of the fishing industry is to be ensured. In Irish waters, strong enforcement of regulations under the CFP will be continued, and prosecutions will be taken in cases of illegal fishing, including the use of illegal nets and fishing methods. National measures will also be maintained to conserve inshore fish stocks, such as salmon, sea-trout, bass, lobster, crabs and whelks, which are not controlled by the CFP.

A new salmon management strategy is being implemented on a phased basis. Conservation regulations have been introduced for 1997 as the first phase of the implementation of the new management regime, and the key elements of the second phase of the strategy are in preparation. The strategy is based on ensuring that sufficient salmon return to their native rivers to spawn, and that the surplus is shared equitably between legitimate interests in the fishery.

The Irish fishing fleet, at some 1,400 vessels, consists mainly of inshore and mid-water boats. Over half of the fleet consists of vessels of less than 12 metres in length, which are generally restricted to inshore fishing and are heavily weather dependent. The pelagic fleet, on the other hand, has been renewed in recent years and is now technically sophisticated and capable of availing of a wide range of fishing opportunities, hundreds of miles from the Irish coast. The development of the Irish fishing fleet takes place within the framework of EU fleet policy, which aims at ensuring that the overall fleet remains in balance with the available fishing opportunities. Within this framework, Ireland will continue to seek to strengthen the ability of its fishing fleet to avail of national fish quotas and to develop opportunities in new areas and non-quota species.

It is important that fish stocks are allowed to replenish themselves, and are not overfished, if the Irish fishing industry is to have a future. The marine research measure under the *Operational Programme for Fisheries, 1994-99* (the *Fisheries OP)*, supervised by the Marine Institute, will support focused research on sea fisheries issues and will, *inter alia*, help to bring about a greater understanding of fish stock dynamics and thus to achieve maximum sustainable yield from fishing effort.

Aquaculture

Aquaculture, including finfish and shellfish farming, is a growing sector of the Irish marine industry (see Fig 7.2). It now accounts for 25% of Ireland's fish production, and provides employment for over 2,500 people, mainly in remote coastal communities. The estimated value of the output from the sector in 1995 was £49 million.[3] This represents a doubling of the value of aquaculture production since 1989. The *Fisheries OP* targets aquaculture as a key growth area, and Government policy is committed to supporting the sustainable development of the industry as a source of jobs and economic activity, particularly for remote coastal communities.

Fig 7.2 Growth in Aquaculture Production

	1989		1992		1999 (projected)	
	Tonnes	IR£m	Tonnes	IR£m	Tonnes	IR£m
Farmed salmon	5,800	21.8	9,700	30.4	19,000	62.7
Farmed sea trout	300	0.8	430	1.1	5,000	17.9
Freshwater trout	650	1.3	970	1.8	1,250	3.1
Rope cultured mussels	2,800	1.0	5,100	2.3	10,000	3.9
Bottom cultured mussels	10,760	1.3	8,730	1.4	26,000	3.1
Native oysters	400	1.1	300	0.8	660	2.2
Pacific oysters	380	0.4	1,750	2.4	6,000	6.7
Clams & other shellfish	0	0.0	80	0.2	1,230	3.5
Total	21,090	27.7	27,060	40.4	69,140	103.1

Source: *Operational Programme for Fisheries, 1994-99*[1]

Aquaculture, as a natural resource based industry, requires a clean, high quality environment in which to develop. Maintenance of high water quality standards is therefore essential for the industry. However, aquaculture development itself raises a number of environmental and sustainability concerns, including:

- potential adverse effects on wild fisheries;
- fish health problems (disease and parasites);
- usage of medicines and chemicals;
- localised water pollution and nutrient enrichment; and
- diminution of rights of access to State foreshore, visual impacts on scenic landscapes and impacts on the archaeological heritage - these concerns also have implications for tourism and recreation.

Sustainable aquaculture must therefore reconcile economic and social benefits with environmental impacts. This underlines the importance of environmentally-sensitive site selection, effective management and training, and improved fish husbandry and production strategies including fallowing.

The industry itself accepts the need to maintain the highest possible environmental standards in its fish husbandry and management practices, and codes of practice have been introduced voluntarily to ensure this. In order to address local concerns and differences, the Department of the Marine, with the participation of shellfish growers and fish farmers and other interests, is advancing a system of single bay management throughout the coastal zone. In addition, implementation of the Sea Trout Task Force Report is being supervised by the Sea Trout Monitoring and Advisory Group, and the Department of the Marine's action programme to conserve and rehabilitate sea trout stocks has been augmented to give full effect to the practical framework of action recommended by the Task Force.

Licensing of aquaculture already takes account of environmental and related considerations and makes provision for formal Environmental Impact Assessment in specified cases. Funding of development under the *Fisheries OP* is also subject to full compliance with EU Directives on the conservation of wildlife (including wild fish populations) and habitats (including coastal wetlands). To provide better regulation and to take account of developments in planning and environmental thinking since the existing legislation was passed, the Fisheries (Amendment) Bill, currently progressing through the Oireachtas, will establish a new licensing system for fish farming. New Ministerial powers will be provided to amend or revoke licences where conditions are breached. An Aquaculture Licence Appeals Board will be established, to which applicants or third parties can take their case. The new legislation will strike the necessary balance between the essential development needs of the industry and the acknowledged concerns of other interests, while ensuring that development is planned and regulated in a sustainable way.

Seaweed

Although the seaweed sector is comparatively modest at present, with an economic value of approximately £3 million per annum, the potential for future development of this natural resource is increasingly recognised. Research supported through the Marine Research Measure of the *Fisheries OP* is oriented towards the sustainable development of the resource, and will provide a basis for building on existing activities in the sector.

The OSPAR Convention

The Convention for the Protection of the Marine Environment of the North-East Atlantic (the OSPAR Convention) provides a stricter and more comprehensive environmental protection regime for the North-East Atlantic, including all Irish coastal waters, than is currently available under the Oslo and Paris Conventions, and will replace these Conventions on its entry into force in 1997. The Convention requires Contracting Parties to take all possible steps to prevent and eliminate pollution of the marine environment, including necessary protection measures against the adverse effects of human activities. Obligations are specified in this regard in respect of each of the main potential sources of marine pollution, i.e. land-based activities, dumping or incineration of waste at sea, and pollution from offshore installations and pipelines. Ireland will ratify the OSPAR Convention in 1997.

Offshore Energy Installations

The marine environment can be rich in fossil fuels and is at present, through natural gas production, providing some 20% of total Irish energy requirement. It is important that the substantial investment involved in marine natural resource exploitation should be mobilised and operated in a manner which respects the environment.

The Department of the Marine, in consultation with the Department of Transport, Energy and Communications, is devising an updated and comprehensive strategy to ensure that offshore oil and gas exploration and development do not adversely affect the marine environment. This will also ensure that international obligations, such as those under the OSPAR Convention, are fully respected. The necessary powers to underpin this approach, insofar as both locational and operational considerations are concerned, are available under the *Energy (Miscellaneous Provisions) Act, 1995*, and are complemented and reinforced by other statutory provisions for protection of the marine environment, including the *Dumping at Sea Act, 1996*.

Marine Transport/Shipping

It has been estimated that some 80% of all goods produced in the world are transported by sea. Ireland's geographical location at the apex of major shipping routes increases the risk of impacts from maritime casualties, including oil spillages. The Irish Sea, as a semi-enclosed sea, is particularly vulnerable to these impacts and to the effects of the disposal of garbage from ships.

The *Sea Pollution Act, 1991*, the *Merchant Shipping (Salvage and Wreck) Act, 1993*, and the *Oil Pollution of the Sea (Civil Liability and Compensation) Act, 1988*, establish the legal framework for prevention of and response to pollution discharges (accidental or operational) from ships. This framework also supports Ireland's participation in the MARPOL Convention for the Prevention of Pollution from Ships.[5] It also provides a liability regime for the payment of compensation for damage to the marine environment and remedial action that may be required. The emphasis will, however, continue to be on prevention of pollution, through enforcement of operating and safety requirements.

The existing legal framework for protection of the marine environment has been reinforced by the *Dumping at Sea Act, 1996*. This Act has considerably wider application than the *Dumping at Sea Act, 1981*, which it supersedes; it will extend Irish control in relation to dumping from 12 miles to 200 miles and in some areas to 350 miles (depending on the extent of the Irish Continental Shelf). The 1996 Act strictly regulates dumping at sea and gives effect in Ireland to the dumping at sea provisions of the OSPAR Convention.

Plans are in train also for accession to the Oil Pollution Preparedness, Response and Cooperation Convention (which is to be expanded in the near future to include emergencies involving hazardous and noxious substances). The Convention is designed to facilitate international cooperation and mutual assistance in preparing for and responding to major pollution incidents.

Eight new port companies were established for major commercial ports under the *Harbours Act, 1996*, with effect from 3 March 1997; these companies will be required to have due regard to the consequences of their activities on the environment. Improvements in waste reception facilities in ports, which are being undertaken on a progressive basis by harbour authorities, will contribute to the practical implementation of this requirement. Investment in reducing pollution and improving environmental protection in fisheries harbours will continue under the *Fisheries OP*. Controls under the Foreshore Acts in relation to development proposed on the foreshore will address pollution issues/concerns posed by such development.

Shipment of Nuclear Materials

The shipment of irradiated nuclear materials has increasingly become a matter of concern, in par-

ticular in relation to traffic in such materials through the Irish Sea. This traffic will increase when the THORP facility in north-west England goes into full operation, and a proposed mixed oxide fuel fabrication plant is commissioned. Ireland has already initiated international action in this regard, leading to agreement at the 1995 Assembly of the International Maritime Organisation (IMO) on a Resolution on the shipment of nuclear materials and the strengthening of the *Code on the Safe Carriage of Irradiated Nuclear Fuel, Plutonium and High-Level Radioactive Wastes in Flasks on Board Ships (the INF Code)*.[6] Following a special consultative meeting convened by the Secretary-General of the IMO in March 1996, the IMO's Marine Safety and Marine Environment Protection Committees are now examining the question of extending the INF Code.

Ireland will continue to press for the implementation of a strict new code governing the shipment of nuclear materials. In particular Ireland is seeking to:

- have the INF Code made mandatory;
- have an evaluation of INF cargo flasks undertaken by the IMO. Such evaluation should take account of the specific hazards associated with marine transportation;
- have a notification structure put in place whereby coastal states would be informed of the passage of INF cargoes past their coast; and
- have a liability regime established to deal specifically with marine transportation of INF materials.

The European Commission brought forward a proposal to extend the EU Directive on the carriage of hazardous materials to include substances covered by the INF code. This matter was given priority during the Irish Presidency of the EU and political agreement was reached in December 1996.

Chemical Munitions Dumps

The existence, off Irish shores, of a number of munitions dumpsites is also an area of concern. Arising from concerns about its environmental and safety implications, a survey of the Beaufort's Dyke munitions dumpsite was completed, in cooperation between Irish and UK authorities, late in 1996. The survey provides a sound basis for the future management and monitoring of the site, and a high level of cooperation between Irish and UK authorities and scientists will be continued. An inventory of other dumpsites around the Irish coast will be compiled in the preparation of the Quality Status Report under the OSPAR Convention.

Land-based Activities

"Domestic waste water discharges are considered as one of the most significant threats to coastal environments worldwide."

- Global Action Programme[7]

Sustainable management of the marine environment involves reducing the many polluting inputs from land-based activities; for example, sewage, industrial effluents (containing heavy metals and/or persistent organic pollutants), radioactive substances and litter. Policies and measures to eliminate or reduce these inputs at source, or to control them by the application of appropriate discharge limits, are set out in Chapters 9, 10, 13 and 16.

In addition, the Minister for the Environment will formulate a policy directive to planning authorities, An Bord Pleanála and the EPA indicating that there should be a presumption against the location of new landfills adjacent to coasts or estuaries.

Bilateral Cooperation with the UK

"While international action has been taken to prevent the discharge of plastics and other persistent wastes from vessels, it has been estimated that approximately 80% of persistent wastes originate from land."

- Global Action Programme[8]

Good cooperation exists between Ireland and the UK on a range of issues relating to the marine environment, notably the important shared resource of the Irish Sea. The work of the Irish Sea Science Coordination Group laid important foundations in this regard, which will be built on

in the preparation of the Quality Status Report required under the OSPAR Convention. Ireland and the UK will be responsible for the preparation of this Report in respect of the Irish and Celtic Seas and areas to the west of Ireland and Scotland. The Report, which will comprehensively assess the health of those areas, will constitute an important input into formulation of future policy for the sustainable development of the marine resource.

Marine Biodiversity

In 1991, Irish waters, extending 200 miles from the coast, were declared a sanctuary within which all whales, dolphins and porpoises are protected, and subject to a total ban on hunting. This was the first European sanctuary for whales and dolphins to be created within the exclusive fishery limits of an entire country. These animals, together with seals, otters and marine turtles, are among the species specifically protected under the *Wildlife Act, 1976.* Ireland has also ratified the *International Convention for the Regulation of Whaling.*[9]

Conflicts can arise between marine wildlife (including birds, seals and otters) and commercial marine enterprises (including sea-fishing and aquaculture). These include both damage caused to fish stocks and fish farms by wildlife, and threats to wildlife from fishing practices and ships' wastes. Studies currently underway will help to quantify the impacts of seal populations on fish stocks. As required by the EU Habitats Directive, by-catch of cetacea in fishing gear will be monitored and quantified.

Steps taken to ban waste incineration and the dumping of hazardous noxious substances at sea, together with measures to prevent pollution from ships, will help to decrease the threat to wildlife from these sources. The expansion of fishing operations to include new species of fish must take account of the impact on biodiversity, including disturbance of seabed-dwelling species and the effects on the food chain, including that of sea birds and mammals.

energy

(8)

SUSTAINABLE ENERGY POLICY

- ensures security of energy supply in order to support economic and social development while protecting the environment

- maximises efficiency of generation and emphasises the use of renewable resources

- promotes energy conservation by users

- minimises emissions of greenhouse gases and other pollutants, both by clean generation and by sustainable consumption levels in all sectors

- maintains local air quality and limits and reduces the Irish contribution to regional and global environmental problems

An action programme towards sustainable energy

- Energy conservation and demand side management programmes will be encouraged and monitored. The Irish Energy Centre will continue to develop its energy conservation programme, including the promotion of energy efficiency in industry, provision of technical advice, information campaigns and support measures.

- Under the Department of Transport, Energy and Communication's *Renewable Energy Strategy*, installed electricity generating capacity from renewables will reach 10% of total installed capacity by the end of 1999; further growth under the Strategy will increase this to 14% by 2010.

- The Minister for Finance, in consultation with the Minister for Transport, Energy and Communications, will introduce new incentives to encourage investment in renewable energies.

- For purposes of the UN climate negotiations, Ireland has adopted an indicative national objective of limiting the growth in total emissions of carbon dioxide, methane and nitrous oxide up to the year 2010 to 15% above their 1990 levels.

- A study has been commissioned to evaluate the scope for intensifying (or introducing new) policies and measures to limit greenhouse gas emissions.

- Action will be continued to reduce emissions of sulphur dioxide and nitrogen oxides (NO_x) from power generation; these actions include fuel substitution, energy conservation and installation of low-NO_x burners in some power stations, supported as necessary by voluntary agreements with energy producers.

- Ireland will ratify the Second Sulphur Protocol (Oslo Protocol) in 1997.

- In relation to emissions of NO_x, Ireland will work towards achievement of the more stringent emission ceilings now being developed at UN ECE and EU level.

- Energy is a scheduled activity for the purposes of Integrated Pollution Control (IPC) licensing under the *Environmental Protection Agency Act, 1992*, and IPC licensing requirements will come into operation for the sector by the end of the decade.

- The threshold at which peat extraction becomes liable to Environmental Impact Assessment will be reduced.

- The Government will continue to oppose any expansion of the international nuclear industry, and to avail of all opportunities at bilateral, EU and wider international level to advance its concerns in this regard. Closure of the Sellafield operations remains an objective, and will be pursued through legal action should sufficient evidence of pollution or public health impact be obtained. Possibilities in this regard are being pursued in particular under the provisions of the Paris and OSPAR Conventions. Ireland has ratified the Nuclear Safety Convention, and is actively promoting a new Global Convention on Radioactive Waste Management, which is expected to be finalised in 1997.

Introduction/Overview

Energy consumption is unavoidable. It is both a sector in its own right and fundamental to all other sectors of the economy. Ireland suffers a number of marked disadvantages insofar as energy is concerned due to its small size and island location. Ireland's isolation from the European energy infrastructure accentuates the need for security of energy supplies, efficient energy infrastructure, and for development of indigenous resources to the maximum possible. The nuclear energy option is not a part of Irish energy policies because of concerns about safety. Current high economic growth and the expectation that this will continue will have energy demand consequences. Using energy more efficiently, cleaning up energy production, using energy sources which minimise damage to the environment are sustainable energy policy objectives. It should be recognised, however, that there may be high costs involved in managing the objectives of strong economic growth, competitive energy costs and environmental quality.

The concept of sustainability in the energy sector must be managed in a manner that secures the international competitiveness of Irish energy prices and ensures that economic dislocation is avoided. These objectives are vital in a peripheral economy like Ireland's, which is still on the economic development path.

Energy is a significant sector in the Irish economy. The annual final energy demand bill of approximately £2.5 billion is equivalent to about 10% of GNP.[1] Investment by the State in the energy sector totals some £5 billion. Thousands of jobs are provided in such diverse operations as peat extraction and milling, electricity generation and transmission, and the natural gas network, while the availability of energy to power industry and enterprise supports a far greater number of other jobs.

Fig 8.1 Key Sustainability Issues in Irish Energy

Increasing total consumption of energy
- total primary energy requirement increased by 24% between 1980 and 1993
- increased energy consumption arose in the transport, domestic, commercial and services sectors in particular
- *per capita* consumption of energy is also increasing

High degree of dependence on imported fuels
- it is estimated that imported energy will account for 93% of total supply by 2010

High degree of dependence on fossil fuels for electricity generation
- fossil fuels (oil, coal, peat, natural gas) make up well over 90% of total fuels used

Increasing emissions of CO_2 from burning of fossil fuels
- emissions of CO_2 increased from 30.7 million tonnes (MT) in 1990 to an estimated 33.9 MT in 1995

Low use of renewable energy resources
- renewable resources (primarily hydropower and biomass/wood) currently provide only 2% of electricity generation capacity

Energy use

The use of energy in Ireland is growing. Between 1980 and 1993, the total primary energy requirement (TPER), which is a measure of all energy consumed, grew by 24%.[2] The amount of energy consumed *per capita* is also increasing, in contrast with the European average which has remained steady since 1980. It is projected that Irish energy consumption *per capita* will continue to increase.[3]

Energy consumption in Ireland is lower than the International Energy Agency (IEA) European average when measured in Total Final Consumption (TFC) *per capita*. Per head of population, Ireland has a rating of 2.23, compared to the average of 2.37. However, in terms of energy intensity (i.e. relationship between energy consumption and economic output), Ireland (0.16 in 1993) is on a par with IEA Europe. Ireland's rating has been improving over recent years. In the period from 1980 to 1993, while the annual growth in GDP averaged almost 3.6%, the average annual growth in TPER was only 1.7%. However, in the five years from 1988 to 1993, TPER grew relatively more quickly (at approximately 70% the rate of GDP), probably because the stimulus of the huge price rises of 1973 and 1979 had worn off. Overall, this is a welcome development, indicating a move towards the decoupling of economic growth from increased energy usage. The IEA, in its 1994 review of Irish energy policy, noted that energy intensity in relation to GDP will continue to improve, decreasing to 0.11 by 2010.[4]

Growing energy consumption has been driven principally by marked increases in energy use in the transport and commercial sectors. The industrial sector, on the other hand, has decreased its energy consumption by 19% since 1980. This is due to a number of factors including energy efficiency and fuel switching, as well as changes in the structure of industrial activity over the period. The relative position of each sector in 1980 and 1993 is shown in Fig 8.2. As in other developed countries, electricity continues to take a greater share of final energy consumption as the economy becomes more sophisticated technically and more wealthy.

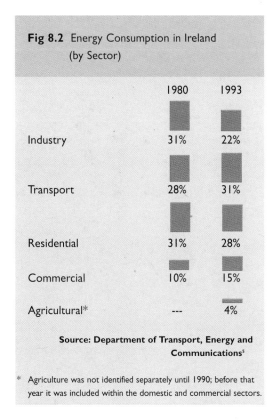

Fig 8.2 Energy Consumption in Ireland
(by Sector)

	1980	1993
Industry	31%	22%
Transport	28%	31%
Residential	31%	28%
Commercial	10%	15%
Agricultural*	---	4%

**Source: Department of Transport, Energy and
Communications**[5]

* Agriculture was not identified separately until 1990; before that
year it was included within the domestic and commercial sectors.

Energy supply

Indigenous natural resources - primarily gas and
peat, but also, to a lesser extent, renewable
resources such as hydro, wind and biomass -
supply some 32% of the energy Ireland requires.
Other resources such as coal and oil, and increasingly, as indigenous supplies run out, natural gas,
must be imported. As an island nation, security of
supply has been, and will continue to be, a major
issue for Irish energy policy and a constraint on
fuel mix choices and environmental options. To
ensure continued supply of gas when indigenous
supplies are depleted, Bord Gáis Éireann (BGÉ),
with EU assistance, constructed a natural gas
interconnector linking Ireland with the UK. The
cost of this project was £253 million. Further, for
security of supply reasons among others, a feasibility study into an interconnector linking the
Northern Ireland gas grid with the BGÉ grid is
being carried out, also with EU assistance.

Imported sources account for approximately
two-thirds of domestic energy requirements[6], at

a cost of some 2-3% of GNP. As indigenous
reserves of peat and natural gas are finite, alternative indigenous resources are being developed
and exploited in order to avoid complete dependence on imported energy supplies. It is vital
that Ireland vigorously promote its offshore oil
and gas exploration programme. Increasing
emphasis is also being placed on the development of renewable resources (e.g. wind, hydro,
wave/tidal, biomass, etc.), and expanding their
penetration of the market, although it will be
some decades before these can offer a substantial
alternative to current sources. The role of fossil
fuels will continue heavily to influence the world
and Ireland's energy mix for many decades.
Nuclear energy provides a non-carbon energy
option in many countries.

The breakdown of Irish energy supply from different sources shows a greater dependence on
fossil fuels, particularly peat, and the absence of
nuclear power, compared to the overall figures
for IEA Europe, as in Fig 8.3. This degree of
dependence on fossil fuels has implications in
relation to greenhouse gas emissions and acidification, which will be dealt with later.

Fig 8.3 Energy Supply in Ireland relative to
IEA Europe, 1993

	Ireland	IEA Europe
Oil	48%	43%
Hydro	1%	3%
Natural Gas	20%	18%
Nuclear	-	15%
Geothermal	-	0%
Coal	20%	18%
Other solid fuels	11%	3%

Source: International Energy Agency[7]

Ireland is dependent on imports for approximately 70% of its oil product needs, with the balance being supplied from INPC Whitegate. The Government recently reiterated its commitment to retaining a domestic refining capability on security of supply grounds. It is recognised that emerging standards on fuel quality will impose additional costs at refinery level in meeting new standards as they are adopted. Options in relation to financing the necessary investments are currently being examined.

Interactions with the Environment

Energy affects the environment at many stages during its production, distribution and use. While total energy consumption by all sectors is a major source of atmospheric pollution, energy production accounts for 37% of carbon dioxide (CO_2), 54% of sulphur dioxide (SO_2) and 39% of nitrogen oxide (NO_x) emissions.[8]

Air pollution

Air pollutant emissions from the use of fossil fuels consist primarily of CO_2, SO_2 and NO_x.

Carbon dioxide (CO_2)

CO_2, the main gas generated by human activity which contributes to climate change, arises in the main from the burning of fossil fuels. CO_2 emissions in Ireland increased from 30.7 million tonnes (MT) in 1990 to 31.9 MT in 1993, 33.3 MT in 1994 and 33.9 MT (provisional) in 1995.[9] While this rate of increase is less than might have been suggested by the economic growth over the period, a continuation of the trend would give cause for concern. The national *Climate Change/CO_2 Abatement Strategy* (1993) set the objective of limiting the growth in CO_2 emissions over the period 1990-2000 to 20% above their 1990 levels (a net increase of 11% when the estimated growth in carbon fixation by expanded afforestation is taken into account). It is now projected that CO_2 emissions in the year 2000 will be well within this target.

Substantial improvements in environmental performance can be expected to arise in step with the normal timing of investments to replace infrastructure and equipment as it wears out or becomes obsolete.

In Ireland, the electricity system has certain structural disadvantages compared to most EU partners regarding control of CO_2 emissions, notably lack of interconnection with other systems, high fossil fuel dependency, and already relatively high gas-based generation which limits the potential for fuel switching without significant strategic risks regarding energy supply security. In addition, nuclear power is not an option for the Government and the public. It is important that all sectors contribute to CO_2 abatement.

Climate change is universally recognised as one of the greatest challenges to the global environment. The Inter-Governmental Panel on Climate Change has concluded that *"The balance of evidence suggests that there is a discernible human influence on global climate".*[10] Average global temperatures have increased by between 0.3°C and 0.6°C in the past 100 years. In the absence of mitigating measures global average temperature is projected to increase by between 1°C and 3°C in the next 100 years. Increases in temperatures of this order are projected to significantly affect global food production, sea levels and weather patterns.

Fig 8.4 Emissions of Primary Pollutants (000 tonnes)

Year	Power plants	Residential/ Commercial combustion	Industrial combustion	Agriculture & Forestry	Transport	Other sources	Total
Sulphur dioxide (SO2)							
1980	101.5	34.7	78.6	...	5.4	2.2	222.4(a)
1985	39.34	39.73	57.14	...	4.38	0.6	141.19(b)
1990	103.03	29.475	38.0	1.215	5.355	0.825	177.9
1991	104.935	35.495	31.35	1.305	6.99	1.365	181.44
1992	96.59	33.785	32.705	1.33	7.645	0.95	173.005
1993	87.255	31.02	33.89	1.33	7.695	0.97	162.16
1994	95.515	30.94	39.63	1.515	8.22	0.76	176.58
1995	91.625	29.095	32.825	1.435	8.72	1.16	164.86(c)
Nitrogen oxides (NOx)							
1980	27.3	4.1	8.2	...	34.8	2.4	76.8(a)
1985	29.04	6.71	8.18	...	35.45	5.71	85.09(b)
1990	46.37	6.4	11.26	2.92	45.26	2.4	114.61
1991	46.19	7.41	9.315	5.665	49.04	2.24	119.86
1992	53.065	7.385	9.24	5.86	49.79	2.36	127.7
1993	46.945	7.195	9.34	5.86	45.48	1.47	116.29
1994	45.115	7.595	9.845	4.64	47.73	0.645	115.57
1995	41.39	7.555	9.55	4.425	50.83	0.985	114.735(c)
Volatile organic compounds (VOC)							
1980	0.1	12.4	0.2	...	34.8	31.8	79.3(a)
1985	0.08	16.54	0.57	...	24.3	22.24	63.73(b)
1990	0.25	7.95	0.34	83.2	62.58	25.65	179.97
1991	0.24	8.88	0.26	78.43	64.15	25.68	177.64
1992	0.265	7.69	0.19	79.56	65.38	26.0	179.085
1993	0.25	6.58	0.185	81.61	56.695	25.9	171.22
1994	0.255	5.62	0.15	82.87	58.705	26.8	174.4
1995	0.26	5.005	0.145	84.06	55.22	24.97	169.66(c)
Carbon dioxide (CO2)(million tonnes)							
1980	7.983	6.045	5.09	...	4.501	1.549	25.168
1985	8.255	6.534	4.114	...	4.479	1.651	25.033
1990	10.863	7.199	5.431	0.66	4.885	1.681	30.719
1991	11.362	8.762	3.73	0.684	5.124	1.981	31.643
1992	12.027	8.542	3.538	0.696	5.556	2.014	32.373
1993	12.047	8.239	3.481	0.696	5.543	1.931	31.937
1994	12.368	8.624	3.64	0.794	5.811	2.087	33.324
1995	13.051	8.514	3.442	0.751	6.209	1.964	33.931(c)
Methane (CH4)							
1990	0	3.58	0.2	660.13	1.2	146.21	811.32
1991	0	3.935	1.11	645.795	1.24	145.79	797.87
1992	0	3.47	0.74	650.145	1.24	146.28	801.875
1993	0	3.02	0.74	653.83	1.19	146.69	805.47
1994	0	2.645	0.13	656.45	1.25	146.71	807.185
1995	0	2.415	0.12	661.265	1.32	147.12	812.24(c)
Carbon monoxide (CO)							
1990	3.3	79.42	0.89	39.47	305.3	0.6	428.98(d)
1991	3.32	82.555	1.56	1.825	312.3	0.62	402.18
1992	3.46	75.465	1.55	1.885	303.38	0.83	386.57
1993	3.375	66.535	1.5	1.885	252.9	0.61	326.805
1994	3.43	60.21	1.635	1.49	262.26	0.615	329.64
1995	3.565	56.475	1.52	1.425	231.81	0.635	295.43(c)
Nitrous oxide (N2O)							
1990	1.38	0.745	0.435	24.01	0.18	2.62	29.37
1991	1.51	0.875	0.33	19.515	0.44	2.62	25.29
1992	1.62	0.83	0.33	19.58	0.45	2.62	25.43
1993	1.55	0.79	0.33	19.92	0.44	2.62	25.65
1994	1.635	0.83	0.38	20.05	0.46	2.62	25.975
1995	1.68	0.82	0.36	20.075	0.49	2.62	26.045(c)
Ammonia (NH3)							
1990	0	0	0	121.585	0.25	0	121.835
1991	0	0	0	120.215	0.25	0	120.465
1992	0	0	0	121.36	0.25	0	121.61
1993	0	0	0	122.435	0.27	0	122.705
1994	0	0	0	123.145	0.29	0	123.435
1995	0	0	0	123.665	0.3	0	123.965(c)

Source: Environmental Protection Agency[11]

(a) Bailey, (1988), natural emissions excluded
(b) McGettigan, (1989), natural emissions excluded
(c) Provisional estimates only for 1995
(d) Includes agricultural waste burning which is excluded in the other years
Figures in this table are based on most recent EPA estimates of emissions of primary pollutants in Ireland. Insofar as they may differ from previous published figures, this is attributable to the use of an improved methodology for the years 1990-1995 and of updated background data. Figures for 1980 and 1985 have not been revised to date using the updated methodology.

Sulphur dioxide (SO₂) and nitrogen oxides (NOₓ)

Emissions of SO_2 and NO_x in Ireland are set out in Fig 8.4. Emissions of SO_2 decreased by 25% between 1980 and 1995; emissions of NO_x, on the other hand, increased by 49% between 1980 and 1995.[12]

International agreement has already been reached on the first of a series of Protocols based on a critical loads approach and thus intended to achieve sustainability in the realms of acidification, eutrophication and photochemical pollution. Under the *Second Sulphur Protocol to the Convention on Long Range Transboundary Air Pollution*, which Ireland has signed, national emissions of SO_2 should be reduced to 157,000 tonnes from the year 2000 onwards (i.e. a reduction of 30% on 1980 levels).[13] Ireland will ratify this Protocol in 1997. Under the 1988 *Sofia Protocol* to the same Convention, NO_x emissions must be held at a level of 105,400 tonnes from 1994 onwards. A revised protocol based on the critical loads approach is under negotiation and will require further NO_x reductions after the year 2000. Ireland will work towards the achievement of the emission standards now being developed at UN ECE and EU levels, with due regard to the technical and economic feasibility in the Irish context and the need to cater for a growing economy.

The electricity sector is highly capital intensive. There is likely to be upward pressure on Irish electricity prices in the years ahead because of the need to undertake planned capital investment in electricity infrastructure, particularly upgrading the rural electricity networks and new generating capacity.

Peat extraction

Peatlands are unique ecosystems, and Ireland has the best remaining raised bogs in Europe. In 1987, the Government set a target of conserving 10,000 hectares of raised bog (primarily found in the Midlands) and 40,000 hectares of blanket bog, in recognition of the importance of this nat-

ural landscape and habitat. Many peatland areas have been selected for conservation as Natural Heritage Areas (NHAs). Peat extraction by definition irrevocably changes the landscape and habitat characteristics; it also risks water pollution by peat silt washed off the cutaway bog, which can harm aquatic life; and it can impact on the archaeological heritage.

Peat has been used as a fuel in Ireland for centuries. Bord na Móna owns and works 88,000 hectares of peatland, mainly in the Midlands. These are estimated to have a remaining working life of some thirty years, based on present rates of extraction. Bord na Móna is not acquiring or developing any new areas of virgin bog. Extraction of peat by private sector operators, however, has expanded significantly, from 300,000 tonnes in 1982 to a current level of around 1.3 million tonnes. This is putting increasing pressure on blanket bogs, and the recent introduction of mechanised extraction in upland areas has increased the rate and capacity of extraction. However, the Private Bog Development Grants Scheme has now been terminated.

New bog development

Peat extraction, if not subject to the requirements of Environmental Impact Assessment (EIA), is an exempted development under the Planning and Development Acts. It is recognised that the current threshold of 50 hectares at which peat extraction development must undergo EIA is too high; the Department of the Environment will shortly reduce this threshold to a more sustainable level. Since 1994, all new peat extractions greater than 50 hectares in area are also subject to IPC licensing under the *Environmental Protection Agency Act, 1992*.

The rehabilitation of cutaway bog can be carried out in an environmentally-appropriate fashion if alternative, sustainable uses are catered for; these can include locations for wind energy installations and the creation of wetlands, which can provide high quality wildlife habitats. However, it is important that the suitability of these alternative uses for particular areas of cut-away bog is carefully assessed so as to avoid creating further environmental problems or affecting the archaeological heritage.

A measure has been included in the *Operational Programme for Economic Infrastructure, 1994-99* (the *Economic Infrastructure OP*), which involves studies into the regeneration of certain cutaway peatlands. Cutaway developments will also be established involving the creation of 1,000 acres of new wetlands and around 500 acres of wildlife habitats. The total cost of the measure, which will be managed by Bord na Móna, will be approximately £2.2 million of which 50% will be grant aided by the EU. The completion of this project should add immeasurably to our knowledge regarding the principles underpinning the planning and development of amenity and wildlife areas and will form the basis for future development of Bord na Móna's cutaway peatlands.

Decoupling Economic Growth and Energy Consumption

As a developing economy, Ireland must maintain potential for, and realise, economic growth. Given international commitments to reduce the environmental impact of energy use, the challenge is to decouple economic growth from increased energy usage. Greater emphasis on demand side management and energy efficiency can reconcile the need for economic growth with the necessity to maximise energy intensity. Reduced and more efficient use of energy and the greater use of renewable energy sources can significantly reduce environmental degradation and contribute to mitigating global problems such as climate change. Combined with increased emphasis on renewable sources, fuel switching and environmental control techniques, energy efficiency enables more sustainable energy development. Enhanced energy efficiency is also of benefit in terms of reduced investment in generating plant, reduced dependence on imports, reduced strains on balance of payments, delayed depletion of scarce energy

reserves, and stimulation of indigenous technical competence and industrial capacity.

The degree of penetration of these policies is contingent, however, on the level of investment in efficiency, take up of technology, consumer behaviour and awareness.

Emissions from the energy sector depend on the structure and efficiencies of energy production, supply and end use. Emission reductions can be achieved by efficiency improvements in production and end use, fuel switching to cleaner/lower emission fuels and by emission regulations and standards to reduce polluting emissions from energy use. Policies and measures in these areas are outlined below.

Climate Change Strategy

Negotiations are currently taking place under the auspices of the United Nations *Framework Convention on Climate Change* to strengthen the convention commitments in terms of establishing legally binding quantified emission limitation and reduction objectives for greenhouse gases (including CO_2) in the post-2000 period, and agreeing policies and measures to meet these targets. These negotiations are expected to be completed by the end of 1997.

The EU position on these negotiations is to seek a 15% reduction in developed country 2010 emissions of CO_2, methane (CH_4) and nitrous oxide (N_2O) taken together below 1990 levels. Ireland has indicated that it will contribute to the achievement of the overall EU reduction objective resulting from the protocol negotiations by means of an indicative national objective of limiting the growth in the period up to 2010 in its total emissions of CO_2, CH_4 and N_2O (measured on a Global Warming basis) to 15% above their 1990 levels.

A major study has been commissioned jointly by the Department of the Environment and the Department of Transport, Energy and Communications to contribute towards the review and updating of the national CO_2 abatement strategy (1993). This study will identify and evaluate the scope for intensifying existing policies and measures and undertaking additional measures to limit and/or reduce greenhouse gas emissions. It will also make recommendations for the ongoing development of Ireland's greenhouse gas emissions abatement strategy.

The national CO_2 abatement strategy will be updated, in the light of the outcome of the negotiations currently taking place at EU and UN levels, to cover not only CO_2 but other greenhouse gas emissions. It will be based, *inter alia*, on the outcome of the study referred to above. As a cross sectoral strategy, it will draw on the policies and measures outlined below.

Energy Efficiency and Conservation

"... sustainability requires a clear focus on conserving and efficiently using energy."

- The World Commission on Environment and Development[14]

Energy conservation is a specific objective of Irish energy policy; it will play a major role in influencing the growth in demand while allowing for economic development. Depending on the level of investment and take-up, there is potential for significant savings in overall Irish energy consumption. The environmental benefits of such savings would make a significant contribution to meeting international commitments, including the targets set out in the national *Climate Change/CO₂ Abatement Strategy*. But there are also economic benefits; a more efficient use of energy resources has significant implications for cost-saving in the economy as a whole, as well as in individual industries and businesses, and in household budgets.

Measures have already been taken to pursue this objective. A national energy conservation programme, in place since 1994, included institutional changes, such as the creation of the Irish Energy Centre and the appointment of an Energy Advisory Board to advise the Minister for Transport, Energy and Communications on policy related to energy efficiency, renewable energy and associated research. An energy effi-

ciency sub-programme was included in the *Economic Infrastructure OP*, involving the expenditure of £34 million during the period of the programme. The Irish Energy Centre has a central role in this programme and is pursuing a number of avenues, including the promotion of energy efficiency in industry, technical advice, information campaigns and various other programmes.

Efforts towards energy conservation and efficiency must be aimed at different sectors. The industrial sector has already decreased its energy consumption significantly, without adversely affecting its economic performance; it may be possible to make some further contributions to energy saving by emphasising energy conservation criteria in the design and production stages, in greater promotion of energy-efficient goods and in the development of integrated CHP units. In the commercial, services and domestic sectors, where consumption is increasing, concerted efforts are required to reverse this trend without impairing the economic potential or quality of life. The activities of the Irish Energy Centre will help to educate consumers not only to save on energy use but also to focus on energy-efficient goods and processes. The further expansion of energy-efficiency labelling of domestic appliances will support this work. An increase in the market share held by energy-efficient appliances will indicate growing public awareness and acceptance of the need for energy efficiency.

Increased emphasis on energy efficiency in buildings is also important. The Building Regulations, discussed in Chapter 15, provide for thermal insulation standards for domestic and non-domestic buildings, in the interests of fuel and energy conservation. Action in the transport sector, where energy consumption is growing, is also vital; this issue is addressed in Chapter 10.

The overall objective is to limit growth in consumption through maximum efficiency/increased energy efficiency of the Irish economy.

To this end, energy conservation programmes will be encouraged and monitored. In particular, the downward trend in energy consumption per unit of GDP, which has already been noted as a welcome development, must be reinforced. Indicators of progress towards this objective will include measures of Total Final Consumption (TFC) per unit of GDP or TFC *per capita*; the overall level of demand for energy will also be relevant.

In addition to efficiency in end use energy consumption, it is also necessary to address the energy production sector. In particular, it is necessary to maximise the efficiency of conversion of primary energy to electricity through use of the most efficient technologies and lower emission fuels.

Fuel switching involves a shift from emission-intensive fuels to cleaner/lower emission fuels. For example, switching from coal to natural gas reduces CO_2 emissions while reducing emissions of particulates and SO_2.

Fig 8.3 set out the relative energy fuel mix. Consideration will be given as appropriate to the use of fuels with lower levels of emissions and to the achievement of higher penetration levels for such fuels, including natural gas. Fuel quality standards to control a range of pollutants will be established in the implementation of the proposed Fuel Quality Directive under the EU Auto Oil programme.[15] Fuel quality standards in relation to emissions from stationary sources are expected to be developed at EU level at a later stage.

Renewable Energy Sources

The energy system is currently dominated, and will be for some decades, by fossil fuels. Moving from this towards carbon-free energy sources such as wind, hydro, wave/tidal, solar, etc., or towards sources that are carbon neutral such as biomass, has been hampered by factors such as high costs, availability of finance and technology, problems related to market access and other barriers. Nevertheless, progress is being made.

Renewable Energy - A Strategy for the Future outlines the advantages of renewable energy sources for strategic, environmental and sustainability purposes. Given that indigenous supplies of natural gas are expected to deplete by the year 2003, and also that peat use for electricity production is expected to peak around the year 2000, it is important, in order to retain some security of supply, to develop alternative native supplies of energy. In the longer term, renewable energies are the only fuel source whose continued use can be sustained. On balance, each megawatt (MW) of energy produced from renewable energy instead of from conventional generation reduces CO_2 emissions by an average of 1,000 tonnes *per annum*[16]; it also reduces oil import requirements for power generation by £100,000 *per annum*.

To date, renewable sources have provided only about 2% of the Irish energy requirement, mainly from hydropower and biomass (primarily wood); the first wind farm is in operation since late-1992. However, there have been recent significant moves towards increased emphasis on and investment in renewable sources of energy. The Department of Transport, Energy and Communication's first Alternative Energy Requirement (AER1) was completed in 1995. This competition was designed to secure up to 75 MW of electricity generation capacity from alternative energy systems. The positive response to the scheme resulted in 34 contract offers to independent producers of electricity, amounting to a total electricity generation capacity of 111 MW[17] (see Fig 8.5).

Fig 8.5 Power Purchase Agreements under the Alternative Energy Competition

No. of Projects	Category	Projected Target
10	Wind Farms	73 MW
8	Combined Heat and Power	22 MW
6	Landfill Gas and Waste	12 MW
10	Small-scale Hydro	4 MW

In an effort to support the development of energy from biomass and waste, a second Alternative Energy Requirement competition (AER2) was launched in December 1995. This sought tenders for the building and operation of an electricity generation facility of between 10 MW and 30 MW, and offered a grant of up to £7 million payable to the successful bidder. The winning tender has recently been announced, and will involve a 30 MW waste to energy facility capable of treating some 490,000 tonnes of non-hazardous municipal solid waste *per annum*.

In April 1996, and following a major review of renewable energy policies and programmes, the Department of Transport, Energy and Communications launched *Renewable Energy - A Strategy for the Future* which sets out the long-term development of renewable energy. The strategy identifies a current practicable resource of up to 800 MW of renewable energy sources, and sets out measures to exploit this resource. Short and medium-term targets for electricity generation from renewable energy sources are established and set out in Fig 8.6. These will be secured through the third Alternative Energy Requirement (AER3) competition. The overall objective of the *Renewable Energy Strategy* is to increase the proportion of electricity produced from renewable energy sources. Subject to all the strategy targets being met, the renewable energy electricity generation capacity will be 10% of the total installed capacity by the end of 1999 and approximately 14% of total installed capacity by the year 2010.

Capital grant aid is available from the *Economic Infrastructure OP*, for projects which can deliver on these targets up to 1999. In addition, ERDF funding of up to £1 million will be made available subject to EU approval, for a pilot wave energy electricity generating plant to be built by the end of 1999.

Fig 8.6 Short and Medium-term Targets for Electricity Generation from Renewable Energy Sources

Wind
- an additional 90 MW of installed capacity by the end of 1999
- a further 30 MW each year for the period 2000-2010

Hydro
- an additional 3 MW of installed electricity generation capacity to be secured by the end of 1999
- a further 1 MW each year for the period 2000-2010

Biomass/Waste to Energy
- 7 MW of installed capacity by the end of 1999
- further developments to be decided in the light of the outcome of AER2

Source: Department of Transport, Energy and Communications[18]

The achievement of the AER3 targets will result in investment in renewable energy of £100 million by the end of the century. When coupled with AER1 and AER2, this represents a total investment in the order of £320 million in renewable energy between 1995 and 1999. Further fiscal incentives are being pursued by the Department of Transport, Energy and Communications which is represented on an inter-departmental committee established by the Minister for Finance to examine the potential of using the tax system to further environmental objectives.

Emission Regulations and Standards

Large point sources such as electricity generating plant are already subject to controls on emissions of SO_2 and NO_x. New generating plant and large users of fossil fuels are subject to IPC licensing. IPC licensing requirements will be extended to existing electricity generating plant by the end of the decade. In accordance with the EU Directive on Integrated Pollution Prevention and Control[19] (1996), energy efficiency will become a more explicit consideration in the IPC licensing system.

Energy Pricing/Taxation/Cost Internalisation

Low energy prices can act as a disincentive to reduce demand or adopt energy efficiency measures. From an environmental viewpoint, pricing should reflect the external costs of energy production and use - such as the costs of remediating energy-related pollution. The Government is examining this matter in the context of both energy pricing and environmental taxation, having regard to the need to integrate environmental and sustainability considerations into energy policies, the requirements of the "Polluter Pays" Principle, and the economic and social implications of increased prices. Costs which are at present reflected in environmental threats and degradation should be internalised.

While pricing can play a role in influencing energy demand, competitively priced electricity has been one of the fundamental planks of Irish energy policy, because of implications for industrial competitiveness and export performance should energy prices increase relative to other countries. However, developed economies have shown that high energy prices do not undermine competitiveness. Current energy prices in Ireland are low; electricity prices had not been increased for nearly ten years until 1996, and notwithstanding the increases approved for the period 1996-1998, electricity prices in Ireland still compare favourably with those in other European countries. Low energy prices do not encourage reduced demand or increased efficiency. However, there is likely to be upward pressure on electricity prices in the years ahead because of the need to undertake planned capital investment in electricity infrastructure.

In addition to pricing, other tools must also be used to achieve the objective of demand reduction and greater efficiency, including incentives, regulations, technical advice and awareness. There will be an increasing role for market-based instruments, designed to sensitise both producers and consumers towards responsible use of natural resources, and avoidance of pollution and waste.

Nuclear safety

Ireland's objectives on nuclear matters place a heavy emphasis on safety, environment and public health protection, and radiological protection.

The White Paper on Foreign Policy (1996) commits the Government to ensuring that *"environmental, health and safety issues associated with the nuclear industry (are) effectively addressed"*[20] in all relevant fora. To this end, the Government is actively pursuing a series of actions to address and resolve these issues, and has availed of all opportunities to raise its concerns on nuclear matters at bilateral, EU and wider international level, including within the International Atomic Energy Agency (IAEA) and the OECD. Ireland supports the key role of the IAEA as the global forum for the promotion of internationally acceptable safety standards in the nuclear industry.

The Government acknowledges the serious and continuing threat posed to the health and safety of the Irish public and Ireland's environment by:
- the operation of Sellafield;
- ageing nuclear reactors in Europe and in Britain; and
- the increased traffic on the Irish Sea involving irradiated materials (see Chapter 7).

A Ministerial Group on Sellafield and the Irish Sea was established under the Chairmanship of the Minister for the Environment in April 1995 to coordinate action on foot of measures contained in the *Policy Agreement for a Government of Renewal*. As a result, nuclear matters are receiving an unprecedented level of attention. Closure of the Sellafield operations remains an objective and will be pursued through legal action should sufficient evidence of pollution or public health impact be obtained. The Government's comprehensive policy incorporates a series of practical measures which will afford lasting benefits to the Irish public and environment, *viz.*:

- the successful opposition to the NIREX proposal for the construction of a rock characterisation facility at Sellafield as a precursor to the development of an underground structure for permanent storage of UK and foreign radioactive waste;

- ongoing examination of the possibilities for legal action against the Sellafield/THORP facilities, having regard in particular to the provisions of the Paris and OSPAR Conventions (see Chapter 7);

- high-level diplomatic approaches to the Governments of countries having or contemplating radioactive waste reprocessing agreements with the THORP facility at Sellafield, highlighting the Irish Government's concerns and opposition to the plant;

- opposition to a new mixed oxide fuel manufacturing facility at Sellafield;

- requests to the Oslo/Paris Commissions and the Nuclear Energy Agency of the OECD to undertake a thorough technical review and assessment of both the reprocessing and non-reprocessing options for spent nuclear fuel management, as well as their impact on radioactive discharges into the marine environment. Work is underway on these matters;

- presentation of a proposal to the Paris Commission seeking measures to tackle discharges of the radioactive isotope technetium-99 from Sellafield which are leading to increased concentrations of the substance in seawater, seaweed and lobster, particularly close to the discharge point off the Cumbria coast;

- advancing proposals within the International Maritime Organisation (see Chapter 7) which will substantially strengthen the safeguards and other controls applied to the transport of irradiated nuclear fuels at sea;

- an initiative within the context of the Inter-Governmental Conference to amend the EURATOM Treaty so as to place greater emphasis on public health and environmental protection considerations;

- the ratification of the Nuclear Safety Convention in July 1996 and Government efforts to have all Member States of the EU and the IAEA do so as soon as possible;

- the active promotion by Ireland of a new Global Convention on Radioactive Waste Management, which is expected to be finalised in 1997;

- the offer of State financial assistance and other support to the County Louth residents (STAD) taking court action against British Nuclear Fuels Limited. The assistance will apply to specific items of scientific investigation, research and other work relevant to the case; and

- by way of further support to the STAD action, extensive information on documentation held by the Departments of Transport, Energy and Communications, Environment, Health and Marine and the Radiological Protection Institute of Ireland has been made available. The Government has also offered medical and statistical expertise to assist the Louth residents with the interpretation of health-related data.

industry

⑨

In a highly competitive world, Ireland's high quality environment offers a priceless advantage to natural resource-based products and manufactured goods and services generally.

SUSTAINABLE INDUSTRIAL DEVELOPMENT

should recognise and respond to this unique opportunity by pursuing

- responsible growth, maintaining natural capital,

- eco-efficient, clean production, lowering input costs and adding value to output,

- eco-friendliness, addressing consumer concerns and preferences.

An action programme towards sustainable industry

Because Ireland has retained a largely unspoilt environment, there is a strong consensus on the need to maintain high environmental standards for industry. There is also a growing acknowledgment from industry that adherence to these high standards is in its own best interests and that industry should also act voluntarily to promote environmental excellence. Reflecting this twin-track approach of strict environmental regulation combined with pro-active voluntary measures, the following are some of the specific actions to these ends which will be taken under this Strategy:

- While legislation and regulation will continue to be important instruments for managing industrial impacts on the environment, a broader mix of instruments will be applied where environmental benefits are achievable as efficiently or more cost-effectively. This will include increasing the use of market-based instruments over time and using voluntary agreements with industry where appropriate.

- Integrated Pollution Control licensing is being extended on a phased basis by 1998, to most industries covered by the *Environmental Protection Agency Act, 1992*.

- The *Environmental Protection Agency Act, 1992*, will be amended to give effect to the provisions of Council Directive 96/61/EC on Integrated Pollution Prevention and Control (IPPC).

- The *Waste Management Act, 1996*, will be rapidly implemented. This will increase the focus on waste prevention and minimisation and on recovering, rather than disposing of, the by-products and wastes arising from industrial processes, and of products themselves and their packaging.

- Producer responsibility initiatives (such as the REPAK scheme already mobilised) will be encouraged to increase re-use and recycling of wastes, with regulatory support to ensure fair competitive conditions for participatory industries.

- A Pollution Emissions Register will be published by the EPA in 1997. Regulations will be introduced subsequently to establish by 1998 a more complete Toxics Release Inventory.

- The EPA will complete a national hazardous waste management plan by 1998.

- Ireland will support international efforts to develop legally binding instruments for the reduction and/or elimination of emissions of persistent organic pollutants to the environment.

- The Department of Enterprise and Employment will review the coordination of cleaner production mechanisms to ensure maximum efficiency and value in the uptake and replication of initiatives, and as a basis for future targeting of supports to the SME sector.

- The extension of the EU Eco-Management and Audit Scheme (EMAS) to all major industrial sites will be actively promoted.

- Grant assistance for industrial development will remain conditional on compliance with environmental regulatory requirements.

- Government will develop suitable economic instruments to improve the internalisation of external costs. This will include:
  - resource pricing, including a charging system for water and waste water services to industry;
  - possible green taxation measures, with particular emphasis on the removal of environmentally-unfriendly subsidies; and
  - exploration of market-based instruments, such as emissions trading, offering flexibility to industry to achieve environmental improvements.

- The EPA, in cooperation with the Central Statistics Office (CSO) and the Department of Transport, Energy and Communications, will develop a materials and energy balance for industry to determine the full extent of industry's environmental/natural resource impacts and advise on targets for greater eco-efficiency.

- Forbairt and An Bord Tráchtála, with the support and assistance of the Marine Institute as appropriate, will explore the opportunities for Irish industry in the growth area of environmental industry, including pollution control technology and equipment and environmental consultancy services.

- The Government has undertaken and will pursue a rapid mobilisation of new initiatives in the Science and Technology area, in line with the 1996 *White Paper on Science, Technology and Innovation*.

- Greater policy coordination at Departmental level in the areas of industry, environment and sustainability will be ensured through the development of the Green Network of Government Departments (see Chapter 19).

Introduction/Overview

The quality of raw materials is an increasingly important factor for industrial development and production. Irish products must compete on European and world markets on the basis of quality and price, and with the assistance of brand marketing underlining a distinctive image. Ireland is marketed as an attractive location, both in economic and environmental terms, for high performance multi-national industry. If Ireland's natural advantages are to continue to support socio-economic development, continued effort is necessary to ensure that this environmental image has real substance.

Fig 9.1 Sustainability Issues in relation to Industry

Land use and impact on landscape

Consumption of raw materials
- initial extraction (e.g. mining)
- growth in road freight transportation (also for finished goods)
- processing
- use of hazardous substances

Energy consumption
- improved energy efficiency
- use of fossil fuels

Emissions to air
- NO_x, VOC, CO_2, SO_2, odours, metals

Emissions to water
- waste water, chemicals, heavy metals

Production of waste
- industry is the largest producer of solid wastes, at 17.5% of total national waste
- industrial hazardous waste is estimated at nearly $1/4$ million tonnes *per annum*
- on-site incineration is the main method of disposing of hazardous waste

Industry in Ireland grew significantly from the 1960s, and now accounts for 27% of total employment and 38% of GDP. It is strongly export-oriented; manufactured goods - including quality-branded foods and drinks, fashion, high technology electronics, engineering and pharmaceutical products - make up over 70% of Irish exports, while some 68% of manufacturing jobs are dependent on exports.[1]

The range of manufacturing industry is wide. Relatively recent industrial development means that few of the traditional heavy industries, such as steel making, oil refining and oil-based petrochemicals, established here. Labour-intensive textiles, clothing and footwear sectors have been in decline in recent years. However, this decline has been balanced to some extent by significant growth in other sectors such as metals, engineering, minerals, electronics and chemicals. The food industry continues to develop, building largely on indigenous agricultural output, and industrial development policies have promoted a substantial growth in the electronic and computer industries. Modern industries, although in general more environmentally-friendly than those of the past, can still bring pressures to bear on the environment.

Multi-national companies now represent a considerable proportion of the Irish industrial base; over 1,000 overseas companies are located in Ireland, employing some 100,000 people, which represents well over 40% of total manufacturing employment. Many of these companies are in the fine chemical and electronics sectors, and are required, and accustomed, to operate to high environmental standards.

Small and medium-sized indigenous enterprises have a different profile. These enterprises represent a significant portion of the Irish economy; the Task Force on Small Business[2] estimated in 1994 that 98% of some 160,000 non-farm businesses fell within their definition of "small" (under 50 employees, turnover of under £3 million), and that small business accounted for around half of all private sector employment. This sector, while less well-equipped to meet environmental requirements, is nonetheless crucial to achieving sustainability in industry.

Analysis of the performance of Irish industry over the period from 1989 to 1992, carried out in connection with the *Operational Programme for Industrial Development, 1994-99*, showed that in terms of employment, output and productivity, Irish industry performed considerably better than the average for either the EU or the OECD. In the manufacturing sector, for example, overall output grew by 6% *per annum*, productivity by

4.9% *per annum*, and employment by 1% *per annum* over this period. This encouraging performance has continued, with average increases in output in manufacturing industry of 12.8% in 1994 and 20.1% in 1995, and an estimated increase of 9% in 1996.[3]

Increases in productivity, which are normally associated with increased efficiency in the use of inputs into the manufacturing process, are an important consideration in the context of sustainable development. While overall productivity in the manufacturing sector generally has increased significantly, the relative shift in output from traditional sectors such as clothing, textiles, footwear and furniture to the capital intensive sectors of chemicals, pharmaceuticals, electronics and electrical engineering, has been a significant factor in this increase. The sectors most likely to drive future increases in manufacturing output are electronics, pharmaceuticals, healthcare, food and drink and print and publishing.

Sustainable Development and Economic Growth

The principle of sustainable development underpins Ireland's industrial policy, the key objective of which is to promote a strong, internationally competitive enterprise sector, comprising both indigenous and non-national companies, which will make the maximum contribution to self-sustaining employment growth. The *National Development Plan, 1994-99*[4], sought to develop Ireland's natural resources as a foundation for increased industrial development, with particular emphasis on the development of the food-processing and timber industries. The Plan noted that sustainable industrial development entails:

- using cleaner technologies and production techniques to minimise emissions to air and water;

- preventing or reducing waste production and, where possible, increasing re-use or recycling activities; and

- pursuing a policy of conservation of energy and other raw materials.

Sustainable industrial development must allow industry to pursue its primary functions of generating wealth and employment while minimising impacts on the environment. It must also take account of future as well as present needs to increase employment and living standards. There is no easy balance: an ambitious environmental policy carries unavoidable costs. In common with policy trends elsewhere, this Strategy recognises that a mix of policy instruments:

- offers the best means of addressing public concerns about environmental protection; and
- creates the best framework for business and industry to achieve environmentally-sustainable growth in a cost-effective way.

Accordingly, Government will pursue a broad range of policy instruments, which will include increasing the use of market-based instruments over time and using voluntary agreements with industry where appropriate. In addition, greater policy coordination at Departmental level in the areas of industry, environment and sustainability will be ensured through the development of the Green Network of Government Departments (see Chapter 19).

For industry, the overall objective of this Strategy is to ensure that development:

- is environmentally sound, maximising advantage and maintaining quality;
- optimises the use of natural resources;
- minimises the production of waste and emissions;
- uses chemicals and other substances with potentially adverse environmental impacts sparingly and safely; and
- has a strongly defined clean production and clean technology ethos.

Industry's Interactions with the Environment

It is essential for industry to recognise and address its potential for extensive impacts on the natural environment.

"Pollution is a form of waste, and a symptom of inefficiency in industrial production."

- The World Commission for Environment and Development[5]

Industrial emissions

The relative absence of heavy industry in Ireland has resulted in a low level of pollutant emissions to air compared to most European countries. Growing road freight transport movements, arising from economic activity, contribute to increasing air emissions from the transport sector, while direct emissions from other sectors, including industry, have remained relatively stable or decreased.

Fig 9.2 Emissions of Primary Pollutants from Industrial Combustion (tonnes)

	SO_2	NO_x	VOC	CO	Smoke
1980	78,600	8,200	200	---	---
1985	57,140	8,180	570	---	---
1990	38,000	11,260	340	890	1,250
1991	31,350	9,315	260	1,560	960
1992	32,705	9,240	190	1,550	1,060
1993	33,890	9,340	185	1,500	1,000

Source: Environmental Protection Agency[6]

Industrial combustion accounts for around 22% of national emissions of sulphur dioxide (SO_2)[7] and for approximately 22% of national emissions of sulphur oxides (SO_x)[8]; the trend is positive, with the amount of SO_2 produced by industry having reduced by half between 1980 and 1994. Emissions of nitrogen oxides (NO_x) from industrial combustion represent 8.5% of the national total[9], and the quantity of emissions has remained relatively stable over the past 15 years. There is still scope for a reduction in these emissions from industry, however, for example through the use of low-NO_x burners in boilers.

Existing information indicates that industry emits limited quantities of Volatile Organic Compounds (VOC) (mainly from the use of solvents) and carbon monoxide (CO). However, the EPA[10] has noted that there are deficiencies in information, to the extent that emissions of VOCs from a range of industrial processes have not yet been reliably quantified.

As traditional pollutant emissions (SO_2, NO_x, VOC) have been controlled for many years under international conventions, national regulations and other measures, attention is increasingly focused on other substances. Together with the other Contracting Parties to the UN Convention on the Long-Range Transport of Air Pollution, Ireland is assisting in the elaboration of protocols to deal with persistent organic pollutants (POPs) and heavy metals.

As obligations to restrict national emissions to atmosphere of pollutants such as SO_2, NO_x, ammonia, heavy metals, POPs, CO_2, and VOCs become demanding, it will be necessary to allocate targets/ceilings to the contributing sectors of the economy. In this context, the Government will consider the appropriateness of market-based instruments such as emissions trading, insofar as these might provide a more cost-effective means for industry and other sectors of achieving such targets/ceilings.

Pollutant emissions from industry may also be discharged into water. In urban areas, waste water from industry commonly discharges into sewerage systems. The *Local Government (Water Pollution) Act, 1977*, requires discharges to waters and sewers to be licensed, and at the end of 1995, nearly 2,000 water licences were in force. Since the commencement of integrated pollution control licensing by the EPA in 1994, water pollution licences for certain industries are progressively being replaced by integrated licences covering all emissions and environmental impacts.

While the EPA identifies industrial activity as the single greatest cause of seriously polluted water[11], the extent of such pollution has been significantly reduced in recent years, and now accounts for only 0.6% (77 km) of over 13,200 km of river and stream channel surveyed. There is a need for more information on discharges to the aquatic environment of toxic, persistent contaminants. A research project in regard to the latter is to be undertaken under the *Operational Programme for Environmental Services, 1994-99* (the *Environmental Services OP*).

Fig 9.3 Proportion of Reported Fish Kills attributed to Industrial Sources

Period	Total kills	Industrial	Percentage of Total
1971-1974	98	37	38%
1983-1986	296	35	12%
1987-1990	334	46	14%
1991-1994	175	26	15%

Source: Environmental Protection Agency[12]

Other key pollutants of concern include organochlorines, polychlorinated biphenyls (PCBs), dioxins, furans and heavy metals. Levels of these pollutants in Ireland are generally low in comparison to other countries[13]; however, there are still gaps in the available information which must be filled. A report on dioxins in Ireland, published by the EPA in May 1996[14], concluded that their environmental impact is not significant in Ireland, with levels significantly lower than in many other European countries.

Industrial emissions are, in general, well regulated. In respect of industry with significant polluting potential, integrated pollution control (IPC) licensing is recognised by Government and the Social Partners in *Partnership 2000* as a major improvement on multi-media licensing which it replaces. IPC licensing will be commenced for existing activities in most industrial categories by end-1998. The Government will keep the system under review having regard to cost and competitiveness issues, including the capacity of the SME sector, in particular, to deal in the short term with new regulatory demands. The system will also be adjusted, as appropriate, by 1999 to implement Council Directive 96/61/EC on Integrated Pollution Prevention and Control.

Consumption of natural resources

Consumption of finite natural resources (both indigenous and imported) is a major issue for sustainable development. As noted in Chapter 8, the industry sector has decreased its energy consumption by 19% since 1980, due to a number of factors including fuel switching and changes in the structure of industrial activity over the period. While a number of energy-efficiency measures were also adopted by industry to achieve this reduction, there is still scope for further improvement. Assistance is being provided to industry in this regard through the Energy Efficiency Investment Scheme and the technical advice services of the Irish Energy Centre.

Maximum efficiency in the use of both energy and water in industrial processes is an important part of energy/resource conservation. Economic instruments and, in particular, correct pricing must increasingly be used to internalise all external environmental costs so that the real costs associated with the use of natural resources are correctly attributed.

A formalised system for charging industry the capital and operating costs of water and waste water services provided to it will be introduced by the end of this decade. Assessment of the options in this regard began in 1994 with the commissioning, by the Department of the Environment, of a study by the ESRI on charging industry the capital costs of waste water services.[15] The Department also commissioned a further study from the ESRI on the more general use of economic instruments to support environmental policy; this will be published in 1997.

Dangerous substances

Safety in relation to dangerous substances is closely related to potential impact on the environment and human health. The Health and Safety Authority (HSA) enforces a range of controls on dangerous substances used in industry, including:

- regulations concerning the protection of employees from the use in the workplace of lead, asbestos and chemical and biological agents;

- regulations protecting employees, the general public and the environment against major accident hazards, where dangerous substances are used or stored; and

- regulations governing the classification, packaging and labelling of a wide range of hazardous substances.

A review of the *Dangerous Substances Act, 1972*, is to be carried out by the HSA by 1998; this will also take account of:

- the implementation of the requirements of the ADR (European Agreement concerning the International Carriage of Dangerous Goods by Road);
- the implications of Ireland's 1996 ratification of the UN Convention on Chemical Weapons[16]; and
- the adoption of a new Directive on the Control of Major Accident Hazards Involving Dangerous Substances to replace EU Directive 85/501/EEC (the Seveso Directive).[17]

Solid wastes

The industrial sector is the largest producer of solid wastes in Ireland. Industry produces an estimated 7.4 million tonnes of non-hazardous waste a year, or nearly 17.5% of total national waste production (estimated at some 42 million tonnes).[18] The definition of industrial waste used by the EPA includes all non-hazardous, solid or semi-solid wastes originating from industrial or public utility premises and includes wastes arising from mines and quarries, construction and demolition sites, as well as wastes arising from food processing.

The definition of hazardous wastes, included in the *Waste Management Act, 1996*, reflects the properties of waste which render it hazardous, as set out in Directive 91/689/EEC.[19] Industry is the largest producer of hazardous wastes, estimated at over 243,000 tonnes *per annum*; however, more than 40% of this is reused, recovered and recycled. Incineration is the principal method used for the on-site disposal of hazardous industrial wastes.

The minimisation of industrial wastes is a major objective of national policy; measures such as cleaner production processes, life-cycle analysis and other eco-efficient approaches in the industrial sector will contribute to realising this objective. However, even with an extensive and sophisticated clean technology programme, there will always be some hazardous wastes requiring disposal. The issues involved in dealing with this waste will be addressed by the EPA in the preparation of the national hazardous waste management plan. Financial assistance of approximately £5 million for the provision of appropriate hazardous waste management facilities will also be available under the *Environmental Services OP*.

Chemicals

The estimated number of human-made chemicals on the world market almost doubled during the last three decades, and is projected to reach over 100,000 by the end of the century. Environmental risks arise from the significant increase in flows of chemicals from human activities, including industry, and in particular from the use of toxic chemicals and other hazardous substances. The accumulation of these in the environment, including in food chains, can profoundly disrupt biological processes. Used responsibly, chemicals make an essential contribution to modern social and economic goals and, with best practice, they can be used with a high degree of safety in a cost-effective manner.

Risk assessment is critical to the environmentally-sound management of chemicals; it aims at identifying, characterising and quantifying the potential adverse effects on human health or ecosystems of defined exposures to a chemical substance or mixture, or to a chemically hazardous process or situation. The OECD is carrying out a programme of work on risk reduction for chemicals and other substances, including lead and mercury; in February 1996, OECD Environment Ministers adopted a Declaration on risk reduction in relation to lead.[20]

In line with the Government commitment to provide for a Toxics Release Inventory (TRI)[21], the *Waste Management Act, 1996*, contains strengthened provisions for the making available of information on releases of specified substances into the environment, based on the concept of mass-balance accounting. Regulations to give formal effect to the TRI provision in the Act will be made by 1998. Under IPC licence conditions, the EPA already requires mass balances of specified toxic chemicals, showing overall usage and routes of disposal and loss, to be submitted for inclusion in a Pollution Emissions Register (PER). The first PER report will be published by the EPA in 1997.

Contaminated land

Land contamination by industrial activity is a limited problem in Ireland, compared to more heavily industrialised countries. At present, cases of land contamination are addressed on a case by case basis by developers and local authorities. The need for a national policy on soil and land quality will be addressed in the context of ongoing developments at EU level in relation to environmental liability. Current environmental requirements, including IPC licensing and monitoring operations, will help to prevent future contamination of land. The *Waste Management Act, 1996,* provides for both local authorities and the EPA to include in their respective waste management plans the identification and assessment of remediation needs in relation to waste disposal sites.

Voluntary Action by Industry: A New Approach

While public regulation and control have an important place in the environmental management of industry, substantial complementary action can be, and is being, taken voluntarily by industry to minimise its environmental impact and increase its efficiency. It is in industry's own interests to anticipate new developments and lead markets: the best performers have already adopted comprehensive and challenging environmental policies and the management systems to implement and communicate them. "Leaner" production, promoting better resource use, is economically as well as environmentally efficient. Industry can also benefit from "first mover" advantage, building new opportunities

in eco-industry and anticipating consumer environmental concerns, so as to lead rather than respond to competitive trends.

It is simplistic to assume that economic growth must necessarily be limited by the finite nature of non-renewable resources, such as fossil fuel energy and minerals. Advanced economies have proven their ability to stimulate the development of technological substitutes as scarcities emerge. But there is mounting concern internationally about other factors which, unless reversed, may limit growth in future, including:
- the increase in emissions and wastes, with potential adverse effects, which may not yet be fully recognised, for human health and the environment;
- the degradation of natural resources, including agricultural land, water and soil; and
- reductions in biodiversity and the accelerating rate of species loss.

As is clear from the EPA report, *State of the Environment in Ireland*, there are problematic trends for Ireland in these areas also. It is not sufficient to achieve efficiencies which are at the same time offset by volume growth, as is at present the case with energy and transport. Sustainable development depends as much on less intensive use of renewable resources as on optimised use of non-renewable resources and the development of substitutes.

Within the framework of this Strategy, demand as well as supply-side measures will be utilised to secure sustainable industrial development. Key issues for industry include:

- improving production processes, including efficiency of resource consumption;

- applying innovations in clean production technologies;

- utilising life-cycle analysis/assessment to identify environmental impacts through the stages of manufacturing, distribution, sale and use, and modifying product design to minimise such impacts;

- internalising the costs of environmental externalities;

- responding to consumer interests and needs, provided these are sustainable;

- taking advantage of the opportunities offered by eco-industry;

- integrating environmental considerations into management practice, through environmental management and auditing;

- taking responsibility for minimising waste and emissions; and

- assuming shared responsibility for the environment, and applying best practice, through voluntary action.

Sustainable consumption and production

Sustainable consumption has been defined as:

> *"the use of goods and services that respond to basic needs and bring a better quality of life, while minimising the use of natural resources, toxic materials and the emissions of waste and pollutants over the life-cycle, so as not to jeopardise the needs of future generations".*[22]

This concept is becoming increasingly important at international level, with work programmes developed in both the United Nations (CSD and UNEP) and the OECD. The European Union, through its review of the Fifth Environment Action Programme[23], has also stressed the need to address sustainable production and consumption issues. In addition to work by Governments and international institutions, other initiatives include the programme of the World Business Council for Sustainable Development, aimed at promoting environmental quality while satisfying societal and consumer needs, and the

"Sustainable Europe" project being carried out under the auspices of Friends of the Earth Europe.[24]

While all sectors must play their part in sustainable production and consumption, the role of industry is particularly important in implementing sustainable production principles. These include:

- enhancing product efficiency and durability;

- offering after-sales services to assist the environmentally-friendly use of products and to prolong useful life;

- eco-labelling and consumer information; and

- developing and marketing innovative services, e.g. rental rather than purchase, services rather than goods.

The principle of extended producer responsibility, incorporated in the *Waste Management Act, 1996,* places a responsibility on the producers of goods to have regard to the need for the prevention and minimisation of waste from activities producing goods and from the goods themselves, and as regards the recovery of wastes arising from the use of such goods. From a waste minimisation perspective, it places a focus on the life-cycle and durability of products, using ecologically-sound materials and lending themselves to environmentally-friendly use, reuse, and eventual recycling, either wholly or in their individual components; in addition, it requires that such products be manufactured by processes which avoid or minimise emissions of liquid and solid waste, and minimise the consumption of energy. Producer responsibility is now an integral part of environmental protection policy. The REPAK scheme, launched in 1996 by the Industry Task Force on Recycling[25], represents an important producer responsibility initiative in respect of packaging waste.

Eco-efficiency

Eco-efficiency is an important element of sustainable production, incorporating many of its principles. The World Business Council for Sustainable Development (WBCSD) has declared that

> "Eco-efficiency is reached by the delivery of competitively priced goods and services that satisfy human needs and bring quality of life while progressively reducing ecological impacts and resource intensity, through the life cycle, to a level at least in line with the Earth's estimated carrying capacity".[26]

Case studies by the WBCSD show that industry can derive substantial economic benefits from eco-efficiency. A life-cycle approach improves the way goods are produced, packaged, transported, sold, reused, recycled and, ultimately, disposed of. Use-sharing, renting, leasing and borrowing are also valuable options which can reduce material flows, both in terms of the consumption of natural resources and the production of waste materials.

Cleaner production

Cleaner production has been defined as *"the continuous application of an integrated preventive environmental strategy to processes and products to reduce risks to humans and the environment".*[27] In relation to production processes, it includes:

- the conservation of raw materials and energy;

- the elimination of toxic raw materials, e.g. through their substitution by less toxic materials; and

- the reduction in both quantity and toxicity of all emissions and wastes before they leave a plant.

In relation to products, cleaner production focuses on reducing impacts along the entire life-cycle of the product, from the initial extraction of raw material to the ultimate disposal of the product. A manufacturing life-cycle which incorporates return, reuse and recycling in a closed-loop system is becoming increasingly important as part of this process.

Use of cleaner technology and cleaner production to reduce and minimise waste production is an important facet of the environmental management programmes required by the EPA under the terms of IPC licences. However, small and medium-sized industries do not have a similar motivation and difficulties arise in the application of new clean technologies, due, for example, to lack of access to pilot facilities, international databases and expert assistance on applications. There is an increasing range of mechanisms for support and development in this area, for example, through the *LIFE* initiative[28], RETEX and the Cleaner Production measure of the *Environmental Services OP*, and through the services of Forbairt, the Clean Technology Centre (Cork RTC) and the Cleaner Production Promotion Unit (UCC). The Department of Enterprise and Employment will review the coordination of such mechanisms, so as to ensure maximum efficiency and value in the uptake and replication of initiatives and as a basis for future targeting of supports to the SME sector.

Environmental management systems

Progressive voluntary policies by business and industry can reduce the need for rigorous regulation, by, for example:

- allowing industry the scope to demonstrate its own environmental credentials in operating to high standards;

- reducing the environmental risks; and

- enabling industry to demonstrate that it can achieve best practice without such regulation.

Many forms of action are open to industry, including:

- participation in environmental management, eco-audit and other voluntary schemes;

- subscription to international codes of conduct, including the Chemical Industry's Responsible Care Programme, and the International Chambers of Commerce Business Charter on Sustainable Development; and

- the development of dedicated codes of practice to cover, for example, green procurement and purchasing, environmental criteria for equipment and vehicles, waste prevention and energy saving.

Environmental management and audit

Environmental auditing is an important tool for industry; only with full knowledge of its effects on the environment can the sector achieve the efficiencies that are central to sustainable production and demonstrate to clients, consumers and Government that it is effectively delivering improvements in environmental performance.

General environmental management by industry can be improved through the adoption of environmental management and audit systems such as the EU Eco-Management and Audit Scheme (EMAS).[29] The benefits of international certification systems, such as the ISO 9002 Quality Systems Management Certificate, are already recognised in relation to business competitiveness and image; similarly, certification under EMAS or ISO 14001 (adopted in September 1996 by the International Standards Organisation and CEN, the European Standards Organisation) can benefit industry in terms of:

- identifying, quantifying, and assessing the impact on the environment;
- identifying the management and organisational systems required to deal with environmental issues;
- ensuring good environmental performance and - as a minimum - ensuring compliance with in-house company policies and national legislation;
- providing a basis for formulating a corporate policy on environmental issues;

- identifying areas where improvements or cost-savings can be made;
- improving the corporate image of the company;
- attracting the support of the public for some elements of self-regulation by industry as a means of environmental conservation and protection; and
- identifying problem areas before they become acute.[30]

The Environmental Standards Consultative Committee of the National Standards Authority of Ireland (NSAI) will provide for participation by Irish experts in the development of European and international standards, in particular the ISO 14000 family of environmental standards. The NSAI will hold regular workshops, conferences and seminars to inform industry of developments in this regard.

It is Government policy actively to promote the extension of EMAS certification to all major industrial sites. The Minister for the Environment has designated the National Accreditation Board (NAB) as the Registration Body for Irish participants in EMAS, and the NAB will have a key role in pursuing this policy objective.

A new environmental training programme to help companies wishing to develop or update their expertise on environmental issues will be promoted by the Irish Business and Employers Confederation (IBEC) in 1997. The project, funded under the EU *LIFE* initiative, was developed in collaboration with the Environmental Protection Agency, An Taisce, and the Clean Technology Centre.

"Irish companies will need to incorporate environmental issues into all aspects of their business if they are to stay competitive. Training of staff in environmental management will be crucial".

- Dr. Mary Kelly, IBEC[31]

Environmental reporting

Environmental management systems facilitate industry in reporting to its stakeholders - including the local community and the wider public, shareholders, customers, suppliers and staff - about its environmental performance, including the use of energy and natural resources and the extent of emissions. A growing number of companies worldwide are taking up this challenge, to respond to increasing public and consumer awareness and to address market concerns related to environmental performance and the environmental quality of goods. Companies which cannot assure the public and consumers that they take account of and control their environmental impacts may find that they risk losing market share or market opportunities as a result.

Eco-labelling

The aim of the EU Eco-labelling scheme[32] is to stimulate the production of goods with the least impact on the environment and to identify these to consumers by an EU-wide label or logo. Consumer products other than food, drink and pharmaceuticals may be eligible for an eco-label if they meet strict ecological criteria. Participation in this voluntary scheme allows industry to demonstrate its commitment to eco-logically-friendly production by informing potential customers that its products meet stringent requirements and high standards based on life-cycle analysis. As consumers become more educated regarding the importance of environmentally-friendly goods and services, companies whose products bear the recognised eco-label will have a competitive advantage in the marketplace. The NSAI has been designated as the Competent Body for Irish companies participating in the EU Eco-labelling scheme.

Voluntary agreements

Voluntary agreements between government and industry (including manufacturing and services) are means of expressing shared responsibility for the environment. They allow industry to exer-cise leadership in recognising and acting on the principle of producer responsibility.

Examples of existing voluntary action in Ireland include the REPAK initiative (already referred to) which, in providing a basis for the recovery and recycling of packaging waste, is designed to help meet Ireland's obligations under the EU Directive on Packaging and Packaging Waste.[33] Also since 1996, the Society of the Irish Motor Industry is developing a voluntary scheme to recover and recycle spent automotive batteries. The Department of the Environment is seeking further expansion of this scheme to cover recycling of other vehicle materials.

Government will continue to pursue and participate in voluntary agreements provided they can secure real pollution prevention and reduction objectives. While such agreements can improve industry's public image, they will not be allowed to substitute for regulation unless they can demonstrate achievement and real environmental dividends.

Financial Sector

The potential of the financial sector to assist sustainable development has received relatively little attention in Ireland to date, despite the significant influence of financial institutions on industrial investment, and the relevance of environmental performance costs (including liabilities) to share performance and profits. The role of the financial sector has attracted greater interest at international level. Awareness in banking, insurance and other financial institutions of the costs and liabilities associated with poor environmental performance has become a new factor in the financing of business and industry. Increasing emphasis on environmental liability, particularly in relation to waste streams, is a concern not only for industry but for its financial backers and the financial community in general.

Eco-Industry

The global environmental technology industry has been expanding rapidly in recent years. OECD estimates predict that global spending on environmental products and services will be US$320 billion by the end of the decade.[34] The growing environmental protection industry currently supports more than 1 million jobs throughout the EU, and is estimated to expand at a rate of 5% per annum. The market for environmental goods and services is growing at a high compound rate in advance of economic growth generally, globally and in both developed and developing countries. Some 400 Irish firms are already engaged in this market to some extent; over 120 of these, employing some 5,000 people, are wholly engaged in providing environmental goods and services. The prospects for output and employment growth in this sector in Ireland are good, and will be developed.

Public policy, expressed, for example, through the *Operational Programme for Industrial Development*, and through the mandate of the Joint Oireachtas Committee on Sustainable Development, seeks to encourage Irish participation in world markets for environmental goods and services. An Bord Tráchtála has identified primary areas of potential for Irish eco-industry, and has established an Environmental Unit which is targeting opportunities for Irish companies in areas including the manufacture of equipment for dealing with industrial air pollution, water pollution, noise control and contaminated land. Environmental monitoring, consultancy, odour control and pollution prevention are also key areas of potential. The Unit is compiling a database of Irish environmental equipment and service companies, to provide potential customers with a comprehensive register of Irish supply capability. It has also produced an Environmental Technologies Directory[35], which details the wide range of Irish environmental expertise. Both of these initiatives promote Ireland's capability to provide environmental technologies and services to international customers. While a number of Irish companies are already successfully involved in the industry, there is considerable scope for more business to be won.

The Department of Enterprise and Employment and its agencies will support and encourage the development and export of Irish eco-industry, with a view to reaching a defined level of eco-industrial activity by the year 2005. This will involve identification and development of goods/services and export markets and provision of R&D support. Joint working arrangements have already been established between Forfás, Forbairt and An Bord Tráchtála to prepare Joint Development Strategies and consistent operational arrangements between the agencies in relation to sectors with good growth potential. The Marine Institute is preparing an RTD plan for the marine technology sector which will identify opportunities in the area of marine environmental monitoring and protection systems.

> *"Sustainable Development policies will, in the case of Ireland, lead to sustainable competitive advantage in industries such as food production, and tourism where a green image can enhance job creation".*
>
> - Joint Oireachtas Committee on Sustainable Development[36]

Joint Oireachtas Committee

As mentioned in Chapter 4, the report of the Joint Oireachtas Committee on Sustainable Development, published in March 1997, highlights market opportunities for Irish industry in relation to global demands for environmental goods, technologies and services. Many of the Committee's recommendations outline practical means to assist Irish industry to exploit world market opportunities. The report is a good basis upon which development authorities can devise more specific measures in the areas identified. The Committee's recommendations also focus usefully on areas in which better integration between environmental and economic policy and implementation, improved coordination between State Departments and Agencies, and greater consultation and partnership in setting and achieving objectives, can support and contribute to industry's efforts. For example, the Committee recommends, in relation to eco-industry:

- better cooperation, coordination and appropriate links between agencies, such as Forbairt and An Bord Tráchtála, which are involved in industrial and trade development and promotion;

- the development of a cross-agency strategic plan with clear-cut targets for job creation and sales in the Environment Protection Industry and the Green Consumer Market; and

- greater integration and coordination between Departments involved in environmental regulation and economic development policies.

Many of the Committee's recommendations are in line with the general thrust of this Strategy. Further consideration will be given to the Committee's report in operationalising the Strategy.

A Task Force on Enterprise and the Environment, established by the Minister for Enterprise and Employment in April 1996, has also examined market opportunities for Irish firms arising from both greater environmental consciousness among consumers and environmental conservation measures. The Task Force, reporting in 1997, has also considered the obligations and challenges facing Irish business resulting from environmental policies already in place and those likely to evolve in the future, and the actions which should be taken by both business and Government to respond to these challenges and to seize the economic opportunities they present. Its report provides additional direction and guidance for enterprise in addressing the challenges and opportunities of environmental integration.

Environmental Research

"State R&D programmes in support of enterprises ... must pay specific attention to the use of best practice, clean technologies in all their developmental projects, and should also maintain awareness of cleaner processes developed abroad which are potentially applicable in Ireland."

- Science Technology and Innovation Advisory Council[37]

The Science, Technology and Innovation Advisory Council (STIAC), which reported to the Minister for Commerce, Science and Technology in January 1995, recognised the economic importance of natural resource-based sectors and the need for strong, coordinated R&D policies to underpin their sustainable development. The Government's Task Force[38] on the implementation of STIAC recommendations noted the work of the EPA towards the development of national environmental R&D priorities, and the developing work of the Joint Oireachtas Committee on Sustainable Development. Given the existing role of the EPA in relation to the co-ordination of environmental research, the Department of the Environment intends that the Agency should lead the definition of R&D priorities relating to the environmentally-sustainable use of natural resources, in consultation with the relevant sectors and agencies, including the Marine Institute which has statutory responsibilities in the establishment of priorities for marine environmental research.

The 1996 *White Paper on Science, Technology and Innovation* called for science and technology (S&T) initiatives to realise the full economic benefits and potential of Ireland's natural resources. The Government has endorsed this recommendation and has created new structures to coordinate and prioritise S&T expenditure. These include:

- maintaining the Cabinet Committee on Science, Technology and Innovation;

- establishing an Interdepartmental Committee, comprising S&T-spending Departments and chaired by the Minister for Commerce, Science and Technology, to assess actual and proposed spending in the S&T area; and

- establishing an STI Advisory Council (as a sub-committee of Forfás) to provide Government with expert independent advice on S&T matters, and encourage greater awareness and debate on S&T.

Measures which will be taken in association with these new structures include:

- developing an integrated procedure for the prioritisation of S&T spending, as part of the annual Estimates and Budgetary cycle;

- reviewing and evaluating existing measures in such sectors as agriculture, food, marine and forestry to ensure greater coordination between Departments and agencies involved in this field; and

- coordinating, through Forbairt, a major effort, to develop, in both sustainable product and technological terms, firms in natural resource-based sectors.

In finalising its environmental research programme and priorities on the basis of response to the discussion document published in 1995[39], the EPA will be asked to maintain and build on its existing emphasis on environmentally-sustainable resource management, with due regard to the existing and potential role of natural resources in the national economy.

Extractive Industries

"Mining and quarrying can seriously alter the composition of a landscape, disrupting landuse and drainage patterns and removing habitats for wildlife."

- European Environment Agency[40]

Exploration

The techniques used in mineral exploration include soil and water sampling, airomagnetic surveys, geochemical surveys, rock sampling and drilling of boreholes or trenching activities.

While these are generally non-invasive, with little or no effect upon the environment, the fact that exploration is designed specifically to provide the information necessary to proceed to extraction or mining means that the long-term implications must be taken into account. Ground disturbance or excavation during the exploration phase is a rarity in general exploration, and is strictly controlled by the Department of Transport, Energy and Communications.

Mining

Mineral extraction is an activity which can never be reversed. It involves the depletion of a non-renewable resource and causes permanent changes to the earth. The issue from a sustainability viewpoint is whether or not the human-made wealth created from minerals, for existing and future generations, justifies the consumption of these finite resources and the environmental disruption involved. The greater the effort made to minimise the adverse effect on the environment, while preparing for, and both during and after, the mineral extraction, the more sustainable minerals development projects may be.

The environmental impacts of mining may include:
- ground and surface water pollution;
- air emissions;
- noise and vibration;
- visual impact (including landscape damage or alteration due to pits and waste rock);
- land subsidence;
- traffic;
- effects on elements of archaeological heritage;
- loss of habitat;
- loss of water supplies; and
- generation and disposal of large volumes of waste.

Most, if not all, of these impacts can be minimised by careful planning and monitoring, and enforcement of well-defined regulations. In addition, pollution prevention approaches can substantially reduce or nullify the volume and concentration of contaminants released into the environment. The integration of a strong environmental management approach into mining policy is critical to achieve this objective.

The *Guidelines for Good Environmental Practice in Mineral Exploration*[41], issued by the Department of Transport, Energy and Communications in September 1995, seek to integrate the best environmental approach into all phases of the exploration process - from the initial planning stage to operational issues related to prospecting, such as drilling, excavation, surveying techniques, and surface and groundwater protection. The Guidelines also emphasise the need to protect land and habitats from damage and to restore them fully where damage has occurred.

Environmentally sustainable mineral extraction involves a proactive corporate commitment from developers to extracting minerals in an environmentally-sustainable manner. The Green 2000 Advisory Group recognised that, with a clear corporate commitment to environmental protection, mining could be undertaken in an environmentally-sensitive manner. Developers should be committed to involving local communities in the project from the early planning stage right through to aftercare. It must be recognised that there are some circumstances and places where mining may not be permitted or only allowed to operate under restrictive conditions; these would include Natural Heritage Areas and areas of cultural and historical significance. It is also fundamentally important that full rehabilitation of the land and proper aftercare arrangements should follow decommissioning of all mines. The site should be restored to as close to its original appearance as is feasible. The National Minerals Policy Review Group, in its 1995 report[42], paid specific attention to the poor environmental image which mining has had in Ireland, and made a series of recommendations towards addressing the negative environmental effects of mining development.

IPC licensing of new activities in relation to minerals commenced in May 1994, and will be extended to established activities by 1999. New mining activity is therefore now subject to detailed planning and environmental controls. Under new provisions in the *Waste Management Act, 1996*, the EPA is also empowered to require that financial arrangements, including bonding, be made to ensure that financial liabilities associated with licensed activities are discharged. This will ensure proper provision for mining restoration and aftercare arrangements. In addition, special targeted tax relief was introduced in 1996 to address the problem of rehabilitation of mines after operations cease.

The Department of the Environment intends to keep under review the development control system, and other legislation impacting on mines, to ensure high environmental standards.

Quarrying

Quarrying for stone, gravel, sand, crushed rock, etc., is also based on an ultimately finite resource. Its products are used mainly in the construction industry, both as crushed rock and for the production of cement; ground limestone is also used in agriculture.

While the raw materials for the quarrying industry are not in short supply, the environmental impacts, which are similar to those of mining as outlined above, require greater consideration. In many cases, demand for aggregates for use by the construction industry could be adequately met by the recycling and reuse of construction/demolition waste, which has been estimated to amount to some 2.5 million tonnes annually.

SUSTAINABLE TRANSPORT

- helps to preserve the natural environment by minimising emissions of pollutants, reducing and managing transport waste and by careful land use planning to address the impact of transport infrastructure

- reduces environmental impacts and contributes to economic prosperity and development by maximising transport efficiency

- enhances social well-being by providing access and mobility to urban and rural populations and by reducing health risks and noise nuisance

An action programme towards sustainable transport

National transport policy, reflected in the *Operational Programme for Transport, 1994-99*, (the *Transport OP*) already takes considerable account of sustainability considerations. However, better integration is needed to address the growing environmental impacts of the transport sector. This Strategy sets out an agenda to "green" Irish transport, centering on:

- making transport more efficient;
- reducing the environmental impact and the intensity of transport; and
- support for moves at EU and international levels towards examination and implementation of the internalisation of external costs in transport.

Specific actions and initiatives will be taken in support of these objectives to establish a basis for more sustainable transport.

- Minimisation of potential growth in transport demand will be incorporated as a leading consideration in land use planning.

- Government policy and investment for road transport will support necessary economic growth. To this end, the roads programme will continue to target bottlenecks which represent inefficiencies in the infrastructural system.

- Increased efforts will be made to manage the existing road network more efficiently.

- Government policy will continue to support and improve public transport systems and infrastructure with a view to increasing their market share. Efficient, cost-effective and customer focused development of the rail network will be supported for its economic, social, environmental and regional development benefits.

- The agencies concerned, led by the Department of the Environment and the Department of Transport, Energy and Communications, will work together to provide more sustainable and environmentally-acceptable alternatives to private car transport, including better facilities for non-motorised transport and, where feasible, improved public mass transport modes.

- Implementation of the Dublin Transportation Initiative will be intensified.

- Noise controls will be developed under the roads (or other) legislation to limit permissible noise from road transport.

- Opportunities for non-motorised transport will be improved. This will include increased provision of cycle lanes and safer facilities for pedestrians.

- The Department of the Environment and appropriate agencies, such as the Dublin Transportation Office, will actively encourage greater public awareness of the unsustainable aspects of increasing use of vehicle transport.

- The Government will commission research to estimate more accurately the environmental externalities of road transport, and will make the results available both for public information and to the National Roads Authority (NRA) and local authorities. The NRA will be asked to amend various planning parameters to take greater account of these externalities and the cost benefits and viability of proposed major roads schemes will be assessed accordingly.

- The Government will support policy development at EU level and participate in measures towards internalising the external costs associated with transport.

- Ireland will strongly support the completion of EU proposals to reduce carbon dioxide (CO_2) emissions from motor vehicles and/or provide greater incentives for the use of fuel efficient vehicles. Pending full establishment of measures to reduce CO_2 emissions from motor vehicles, Irish vehicle tax provisions will be aligned more closely with this objective.

- Where allowable under EU law, consideration will be given to the application of tax incentives to encourage the placing of more efficient and less polluting vehicles on the market ahead of relevant EU deadlines.

- The scrappage scheme introduced in the 1995 Budget, which encourages the replacement of older cars with new, more efficient models, is being maintained for 1997 as a financial incentive to improve the age profile and efficiency standard of the vehicle fleet. Its effects will be monitored to ensure that it continues to meet this objective without creating other environmental problems, particularly in relation to disposal of vehicle waste. The Minister for the Environment is pursuing with the motor industry the development of more systematic voluntary arrangements for recycling vehicle materials.

- Ireland will support the EU Auto Oil programme as an appropriate means of addressing many of the environmental issues arising from transport emissions.

- Ireland will support the continued development at EU level of strict emission control standards for motor vehicles. In particular, Ireland will support a significant tightening of benzene and other limits in the context of the Auto Oil programme.

- The use of leaded petrol will be phased out by the year 2000.

- Vehicle testing will be extended to apply to private cars over four years old with effect from 1 January, 1998. Particular emphasis will be placed on adequate emission controls to reduce pollutants.

- Air transport is an increasing source of polluting emissions (particularly CO_2 and nitrogen oxides). Ireland is supporting the initiation of action by the EU to address this problem in a wider international context, and with due regard to effects on national competitiveness.

Introduction/Overview

Transport plays a central role in the Irish economy. National transport policy aims at:
- improving the internal and access transport network;
- meeting social and economic needs for the mobility of people and goods;
- offsetting the effects of Ireland's geographical peripherality; and
- facilitating successful participation in the EU internal market.

As an island nation, sea and air routes are vitally important to the Irish economy, providing access to and from Irish and world markets for both goods and passengers. Transport by sea is the dominant mode where freight trade is concerned, with over three-quarters of trade by volume passing through Irish ports. Air transport, on the other hand, accounts for 65% of all passenger traffic in and out of Ireland.[1]

Internal transport in Ireland is predominantly road based; 96% of passenger traffic and 89% of freight traffic is carried on the roads system. Virtually all of the remainder is carried by rail, which plays a useful part in the transport of bulk and other freight.[2]

In large urban areas, traffic congestion has become a serious problem, leading to increased air pollution, noise and a perceived diminution of the quality of urban living. Congestion also causes delays for commercial traffic, leading to economic and competitive disadvantages. The overall volume of traffic makes the roads less safe for pedestrians, particularly children, and for cyclists. Yet it is in the urban areas that there is the greatest potential to provide alternatives to the use of private motor vehicles, such as safer facilities for cyclists and pedestrians, and mass public transport modes (buses, trams, suburban rail services).

Fig 10.1 Sustainability Issues in Irish Transport

Increasing volumes of road traffic
- over 1.2 million vehicles were licensed at the end of 1995
- the number of private cars licensed increased by nearly 5.5% during 1995 to over 990,000
- vehicle kilometres travelled *per capita* increased by 47% between 1986 and 1995
- traffic congestion in urban areas is increasingly a problem

Emissions to air
- transport contributes over 17% of national CO_2 emissions; three-quarters of this comes from road traffic. Levels of these emissions are increasing, and are not amenable to control by end-of-pipe measures
- transport is now the largest source of emissions of NO_x, with vehicles contributing over 41% of national emissions
- levels of lead have been reduced as a result of the increased use of unleaded petrol

Land use
- demand for transport infrastructure (roads, rail, harbours, airports) encroaches on landscape, habitats, biodiversity and other uses

Energy consumption
- the transport sector accounts for the largest share of energy consumption - 31% of the total

In rural Ireland, the level of population dispersal poses particular problems for sustainable transport. Almost 40% of Irish households live in rural areas (defined as being outside settlements of fifty dwellings or more). A dispersed rural population increases dependence on road transport in general, and on private motor vehicles in particular. This high degree of dependency places some limitation on the scope for movement to more environmentally-friendly alternatives, such as mass public transport. Nonetheless, where economically and environmentally practicable, environmentally-friendly alternatives (e.g. rail) should be maintained and supported.

Sustainable transport involves minimising adverse environmental and social effects of transport, while maintaining opportunities for mobility. Measures to achieve this fall into two main categories, technological and operational. Technological improvements to vehicles and fuels can help to minimise emissions which harm public health and the environment. Operational measures such as traffic management and increased provision of public transport can reduce dependence on private vehicles, as can better facilities for non-motorised transport (e.g. provision for cyclists and pedestrians). Sustainable transport also calls for strategies which reduce total transport demand and transport demand growth, especially in private car movements, and which promote greater efficiency in transport arrangements generally.

All of these issues are currently being addressed in a variety of international fora. At EU level, the White Paper on the future development of the Common Transport Policy[3] (1992), the *Common Transport Policy Action Programme, 1995-2000*[4] (1995) and subsequent Green Papers, *Towards Fair and Efficient Pricing in Transport*[5] (1995), and the *Citizens Network*[6] (1996), all address the theme of sustainable mobility. The EU is now aiming at transport policies which will optimise the economic functioning of the sector while respecting and preserving the environment, now and in the future. In doing so, it recognises that transport is a key (and probably the most difficult) sector to be addressed from the point of view of sustainability.

The challenge for sustainable transport is to encourage patterns of economic growth which can be achieved with maximum transport efficiency and the least possible environmental impact, so that economic growth does not generate unlimited growth in demand for transport, with adverse environmental effects.

Transport Interactions with the Environment

Transport has extensive impacts on the environment. The use of land for transport infrastructure, whether road or rail networks, port or airport facilities, encroaches on landscape, natural habitats and biodiversity, and agricultural use. Motor vehicle traffic emits pollutants which affect air quality and human health, and gives rise to excessive noise, which affects the quality of life. Polluted surface water run-off from road surfaces may affect water resources. Traffic congestion, particularly in the urban environment, similarly affects human health, while the resultant delays are economically disadvantageous. Large volumes of traffic, especially when moving at speed, are hazardous to the safety of people (and also of wildlife). The human and social cost of road accidents, including the cost of hospital treatment, is high. Transport is also a substantial creator of waste products.

Growth in transport

Increased transport demand is both a function and a consequence of economic growth. Certain economic factors strongly encourage the growth in transport demand. These include:
- the dispersal of industrial activities away from traditional urban locations;
- changing production and stock-control methods requiring more frequent shipment of smaller quantities of goods;
- the growth of the service sector involving multi-site businesses, and of the tourism sector; and
- increased business/professional mobility.

Consumer and social factors, related for example to the demand for year-round availability of seasonal foods and of material goods and products, as well as individual lifestyle and mobility, also influence transport growth.

Since the 1960s, transport growth in Ireland has been concentrated on the roads. Economic growth, rising disposable incomes, and an increased emphasis on personal mobility have all contributed to increasing traffic on Irish roads. Over the period 1977 to 1995, this increase averaged an estimated 3.7% per year.[7] The average figure includes both the earlier 1980s, when a combination of economic recession and changes in motor taxation caused a slowing down of growth, and the period between 1988 and 1992, when growth averaged 5% *per annum*. Continued buoyant growth (7% in 1994 and 7.2% in 1995) may mean that the currently used projection of around 3% *per annum* growth in road traffic for the foreseeable future on a "business as usual" scenario is understated; the Dublin Transportation Office indicate that traffic flows earlier predicted for the year 2001 have already been reached.[8] Accelerating growth would exacerbate transport pressure on the environment, and make more urgent the need to take precautionary environmental measures.

Growth in traffic volume is also reflected in vehicle kilometres of road travel. Measured *per capita*, this increased from some 5,990 km in 1986 to over 8,800 km in 1995, an increase of 47%.

The total number of licensed vehicles on 31 December, 1995, was over 1.262 million, an increase of 60,000 since 1993. This figure includes over 990,000 private cars, an increase of more than 51,000 over the 1994 figure. The extent of this growth over the past 20 years, particularly in relation to private cars and goods vehicles, is shown in Fig 10.2. Ireland's level of car ownership remains low compared to other EU Member States. However, Irish car ownership in 1995 was some 27 cars per 100 people, reflecting increases of over 5.3% during 1994 and

Fig 10.2 Mechanically Propelled Vehicles (by Taxation Class), 1975-1995

Year	Private Cars	Goods Vehicles	Agricultural Tractors etc.	Motor Cycles	Others	Total
1975	510,651	52,367	65,166	36,711	16,256	681,151
1980	734,371	65,052	69,118	28,488	14,002	911,031
1985	709,546	93,369	68,552	26,025	17,266	914,758
1990	796,408	143,166	72,814	22,744	19,127	1,054,259
1995	990,384	141,785	77,925	23,452	28,957	1,262,503

Source: Department of the Environment[9]

nearly 5.5% in 1995. While still below car ownership of nearly 43 cars per 100 people for the EU as a whole, the Irish figure has increased from 22 cars per 100 people in 1989.[10] The combination of increasing disposable income and the age profile of the population suggest that there will be a continued and significant growth in the number of private motor vehicles.

Freight traffic

Freight traffic is concentrated on the roads, and the growth (see Fig 10.3) in heavy goods vehicles, i.e. those over 8 tonnes, is notable. However, there is no real alternative to road transport for the vast bulk of goods movements; for example, almost half of all road freight carried in 1992 involved journeys of less than 15 miles.

The age of goods vehicles is also a factor, particularly, in relation to the introduction of new technologies and the maintenance of high standards. Figures for the year ended 31 December, 1995, show that 66% of all goods vehicles were four years old and over, while 45% were six years old and over.[11] Positive developments in relation to new technologies and standards include those arising from Euro class I engines (mandatory since 1994) and Euro class II engines (mandatory since 1996).

Mandatory roadworthiness testing is in force for commercial vehicles. In 1995, 38.1% of goods vehicles (which represented 77% of vehicles tested) passed without having to remedy defects. A further 44.6% had to rectify defects in order to obtain a pass.[12] These defects, however, were primarily safety-related rather than environment-related. Ireland favours a greater link between vehicle testing and environmental performance, particularly in relation to emissions to air. This matter is being pursued at EU level.

As regards efficiency of road haulage, significant progress has been made in recent years through the liberalisation of road haulage markets in the European Union, involving the removal of restrictive and protectionist practices. Cabotage is due to be fully liberalised on 1 July, 1998.

Energy consumption

As a consequence of transport growth, final consumption of energy by transport increased by 34% between 1980 and 1993.[13] Transport now accounts for a greater share of energy consumption than any other sector. Specifically, the sector accounted for 31% of total energy consumption in 1993 compared to 22% for industry, 28% for the residential sector, 15% for the commercial sector and 4% for agriculture (see Fig 8.2).

Fig 10.3 Heavy Goods Vehicles Registered, 1960-1993

Year	Number
1960	195
1970	1,078
1975	3,093
1980	6,651
1985	7,073
1990	9,449
1995	12,116

Source: Department of the Environment[14]

Roads infrastructure

With a high proportion of internal transport dependent on the roads network, significant investment has been made and continues to be made in improving road infrastructure. This is particularly important from an economic point of view, to overcome competitive disadvantages caused by delays, congestion, etc. Addressing transport deficiencies and costs is of critical importance to meeting the objectives of Government policy regarding the growth and equitable distribution of income, facilitated by increased opportunity and mobility for economic development.

It is equally important to the economy and society as a whole that this process does not disregard external costs, which are considerable. OECD and EU estimates suggest that the external costs of land transport (e.g. congestion, noise, air pollution and accidents) can be up to 5% of GDP - a significant cost to the overall economy. The EU Green Paper *Towards Fair and Efficient Pricing in Transport* sets out options to be explored at EU level on how to achieve a proper internalisation of these costs so as to make transport more efficient, fair and transparent.

Current roads policy in Ireland aims at an overall balance. It focuses on key economic corridors, supports an adequate dispersal of economic development and seeks to bypass congested towns and villages. It concentrates on:
- upgrading and realigning existing roads, rather than building unnecessary new roads;
- bypasses to relieve congestion; and
- minimising the construction of new roads and motorways.

This policy reduces the impact of new road developments, and focuses resources on maximising the safety and efficiency of the existing network.

The Government will maintain this approach, with increased emphasis on the sustainability of construction, materials and use factors. The objective is to reduce and eliminate inefficiencies in road transport from every source; for example, the roads programme will continue to target bottlenecks which represent inefficiencies in the infrastructural system. Greater attention will also be paid to reducing the adverse impacts of roads infrastructure (and road traffic) on wildlife and biodiversity (e.g. by providing appropriate tunnels or other crossing points for animals), and on the archaeological heritage.

Rail transport

There has also been some growth in rail transport, as shown in Fig 10.4, although in absolute terms this is modest in comparison with road traffic.

Fig 10.4 Passenger/Freight Transport by Rail, 1970-1995

	1970	1980	1990	1995
Passenger Km (000s)	582	1,032	1,226	1,291
Tonne Km (000s)	529	624	589	603

Source: Department of Transport, Energy & Communications/CSO[15]

Current annual rail passenger numbers are in the region of 27 million. Much of this growth can be attributed to the suburban rail services, primarily in the Greater Dublin area, which provide an important alternative to the private car for commuters. Passenger use of suburban rail services has more than doubled over the past twenty years. A significant contribution to this increase has been made by the DART line in Dublin which has been particularly successful in attracting commuters in its catchment since its launch in 1984. Other commuter services, including those between Dublin and Kildare, Maynooth, Dundalk and Arklow have further enhanced the public transport option in the Greater Dublin area. However, there is still scope for further improvement, such as the extension of the DART to Greystones, Co. Wicklow, announced in 1995. The development of a light rail system in Dublin by 1999 is also intended to provide an attractive alternative to motor car use, and, when completed, help to relieve congestion in the city centre.

Investment under the *Transport OP* recognises the environmental importance of rail as a viable alternative to road transport. Funding for improvements in rolling stock, signalling and track network will have positive environmental effects, further encouraging commuters to switch from road to rail. Government policy will continue to support and improve public transport systems and infrastructure with a view to increasing their market share. Efficient, cost-effective and customer focused development of the rail network will be supported for its economic, social, environmental and regional development benefits.

Planning/Land use

Transport policy and planning and land use policy are fundamentally linked. The emphasis in national policy on the improvement of the existing road network, rather than the building of new roads, reduces the impact of new works.

However, physical planning and development patterns (including the expansion of outer suburban areas) addressed in Chapters 14 and 15, the national spread of economic activity, and the dispersed settlement patterns in much of the country, have a significant effect on the demand for transport infrastructure.

The pattern and density of urban development has a major influence on travel patterns. Many European cities are now pursuing the option of increasing urban densities around points of high accessibility, particularly points of high accessibility to public transport. This approach seeks to achieve the right activity or mix of activities in the right place by, for example, guiding businesses with large work forces or large numbers of visitors to locations with high accessibility to public transport and at the same time reserving locations adjacent to motorway junctions for businesses with a high dependence on road freight.

Encouraging high movement activities to locate in areas of maximum accessibility to public transport can help to reduce growth in transport demand. This requires a high degree of coordination at regional level and is a strategic issue to be considered in longer term planning. As a general principle, minimisation of potential growth in transport demand will be incorporated as a leading consideration in land use planning.

Air Pollution from Transport

"Road traffic has become potentially the greatest source of air pollution generally."

- **Environmental Protection Agency**[16]

Transport is a major contributor to air pollution. Its emissions are a serious concern, both nationally and internationally, because of their impact on the environment and on human health. The diversity and dispersion of transport make its emissions more difficult to address than those from stationary sources.

The major air pollutants arising from the use of motor vehicles fall into two main categories:

- those which have global effects, in particular carbon dioxide (CO_2); and
- the so-called conventional emissions whose effects are primarily local and regional, including nitrogen oxides (NO_x), carbon monoxide (CO), Volatile Organic Compounds (VOC), sulphur, lead and particulate matter (PM).

Individually, these emissions have unwanted effects:

- CO_2 is a major greenhouse gas implicated in global warming;
- sulphur and NO_x contribute to acidification and eutrophication; and
- CO, lead and PM threaten human health.

The combined impact of these pollutants can also be considerable. For example, NO_x and VOC combine to form low-level ozone, which damages both human and crop health. Such interactions make it more difficult to address the problem of emissions, as strategies directed at individual pollutants may not be fully effective. An EU framework Directive on ambient air quality has now been adopted.[17] This will be followed by subsidiary Directives which will specify air quality standards for a number of pollutants including NO_x, CO and tropospheric ozone. Ireland will support, and will seek to comply with, the new standards which are expected to be in line with WHO Guidelines and will extend the range of pollutants covered.

With no indigenous car manufacturing industry, Ireland does not control most of the technical means of reducing emissions from motor vehicles. Agreed action at international level is needed to change the types of cars and engines produced for sale. However, measures can be taken to reduce emissions to minimum achievable levels, for example, by fixing aggregate limits for different vehicle-related emissions.

Ireland will support the continued development at EU level of strict emission control standards. Specific domestic action can be taken in the area of vehicle testing, and in measures which encourage the introduction of new models to replace older, more polluting vehicles. The Government will consider, where allowable, the application of tax incentives to eligible best-technology vehicles which are placed on the market ahead of the relevant EU deadlines.

Carbon dioxide (CO_2) - a global problem

The effects of CO_2 in relation to global warming and climate change are addressed in Chapter 8. Ireland's National *Climate Change/CO_2 Abatement Strategy* (1993) recognised the extent of the transport sector's contribution to the problem of global warming. Some 17% of Ireland's energy-related CO_2 emissions arise from transport, with road transport responsible for over three-quarters of this.[18] CO_2 emissions from transport are projected to increase by more than a third between 1990 and the year 2000; in addition, the proportion of total CO_2 emissions which arise from this sector is expected to increase up to and beyond this date.[19]

Fig 10.5 CO_2 Emissions from Transport, 1990 (% of total CO_2 emissions)

	kT	%
Austria	16	28
Belgium	23	21
Denmark	14	26
Finland	13	25
France	126	34
Germany	173	18
Greece	18	25
Ireland	**6**	**20**
Italy	100	25
Luxembourg	3	24
Netherlands	31	20
Portugal	11	28
Spain	67	32
Sweden	21	43
United Kingdom	137	24
EU Total	**758**	**24**

Source: European Commission[20]

CO_2 emissions from transport are not amenable to control by technologies, such as three-way catalytic converters and fuel standards, which are effective in relation to other emissions. Demand restraint and greater fuel efficiency of vehicles are the accepted strategies required to limit transport related CO_2 emissions. Ireland will strongly encourage EU proposals to reduce CO_2 emissions from motor vehicles and incentivise fuel efficient vehicles.

Demand restraint is a more difficult proposition. Many countries have found that the demands of modern society for a high level of mobility means that even strong public/consumer awareness of the environmental and health problems caused by transport does not lead to a reduction in personal use of motorised transport. Nonetheless, the Department of the Environment will actively encourage greater public awareness of the unsustainable aspects of increasing use of transport, and will work with the Department of Transport, Energy and Communications to provide more sustainable and environmentally-acceptable alternatives. These will include better facilities for non-motorised transport and, where feasible, improved public mass transport modes.

The growing use of information technology services, including teleworking, teleshopping and other computerised facilities, will also help to reduce the need for transport in certain circumstances. The Government will encourage and support the use of these services so as to limit travelling requirements of business/industry.

Non CO_2 emissions

Non CO_2 emissions are more amenable to control. Vehicle emissions controls, primarily set at EU level, go some way towards reducing and mitigating the effects of these pollutants. Standards are already in force for emissions of carbon monoxide, nitrogen oxides and hydrocarbons. At present, these standards apply only to individual new road vehicles. All new petrol-engined vehicles, diesel-engined passenger cars and most light commercial vehicles, as well as heavy duty passenger and commercial vehicles with diesel engines, are covered by current standards.

Further proposals are being considered at EU level, including a proposal for a motor vehicles emissions Directive, which will strengthen existing controls on vehicle emissions. In addition to supporting the EU-led movement towards stricter vehicle emissions standards, there may ultimately be a need to adopt aggregate limit targets for different emissions from vehicles (such as those which operate in the energy sector) so as to set some limiting environmental parameters for air pollution from transport.

Nitrogen oxides

Nitrogen oxides (NO_x) are a major problem in relation to air quality. Transport is now the largest source of these emissions, with vehicles accounting for over 41% of national emissions of NO_x.[21] The other major source is power generation, but in that sector the upward trend in NO_x emissions is being addressed by the retro-fitting of NO_x controls at one of the larger power stations; similar controls are planned for a second station. NO_x emissions from transport, on the other hand, continue to increase. This is because the growth in transport counterbalances technological improvements in vehicle standards (e.g. catalytic converters) which would otherwise have the effect of reducing emissions. The EPA[22] estimates that vehicle emissions will continue to increase over the next five years before corrective measures, such as the compulsory fitting of catalytic converters to new cars, can bring about significant improvements.

Given that catalytic converters only became compulsory in new vehicles in 1993, the age profile of cars in use on Irish roads is important. At the end of 1995, 54% of private cars registered in Ireland were six years old and over, with 71% four years old and over.[23] Even when a significant proportion of the vehicle fleet is fitted with catalytic converters, it will still be necessary to ensure that vehicles are properly maintained so as to minimise emissions of NO$_x$ and other pollutants.

Fig 10.6 NO$_x$ Emissions from Road Transport in the EU, 1990 (% of total NO$_x$ emissions)

	kT	%
Belgium	189	55
Denmark	120	45
France	1,089	69
Germany	1,184	39
Greece	139	27
Ireland	**47**	**41**
Italy	1,006	49
Luxembourg	10	42
Netherlands	169	47
Portugal	117	53
Spain	499	40
United Kingdom	1,083	38
EU Total	**5,752**	**45**

Source: European Commission, DG XI[24]

Ireland will support a significant tightening of benzene and other limits in the context of the EU Auto Oil programme.

Fig 10.7 VOC Emissions from Road Transport in the EU, 1990 (% of total VOC emissions)

	kT	%
Belgium	129	35
Denmark	82	50
France	978	41
Germany	743	25
Greece	131	40
Ireland	**42**	**23**
Italy	866	36
Luxembourg	7	38
Netherlands	185	41
Portugal	60	29
Spain	469	42
United Kingdom	1,056	40
EU Total	**4,747**	**36**

Source: European Commission, DG XI[26]

Volatile Organic Compounds (VOC)

These include the aromatics, such as benzene, which are added to high-octane unleaded petrol. As well as being implicated in photochemical ozone pollution, benzene is a known carcinogen. The benzene content of petrol is already limited by Regulations, which transpose EU Directives, and is strictly enforced. As a further measure to discourage the use of high-octane unleaded petrol containing benzene, which is only required for high-performance cars, the 1996 Budget[25] included a proposal towards eliminating the excise differential on high-octane unleaded petrol, thus making it the same price as leaded petrol. This is intended to encourage motorists to use the cheaper, lower octane unleaded petrol, which can be used safely and without affecting performance in the majority of vehicles.

Lead

Lead emissions from petrol combustion, a known health risk, can be a particular problem in urban areas where high concentrations may arise due to significant traffic flows, slow-moving traffic and congestion. Major reductions in lead emissions have been achieved since the mid-1980s through a combination of a progressive reduction in the lead content of leaded petrol and the significant expansion of the use of unleaded petrol (see Fig 10.8), which now accounts for some two-thirds of the petrol market. However, as over 71% of motor vehicles registered in Ireland run on petrol[27], there is still considerable scope to reduce emissions further by expanding the use of unleaded petrol.

Fig 10.8 Percentage Sales of Unleaded Petrol in Ireland since 1989

Year	%
1989	7.0
1990	19.4
1991	25.9
1992	32.3
1993	39.6
1994	49.0
1995	56.5
1996	64.7

Source: Department of the Environment[28]

Particulate matter

While national standards are enforced in relation to emissions of black smoke, the data gathered do not distinguish the proportion of fine particulate matter in the smoke. PM_{10} (particulate matter measuring less than 10 microns in diameter emitted from engines) has been the cause of particular concern following studies in the USA which showed a correlation between concentrations of airborne particulate matter and human mortality.

Diesel-engined vehicles are generally more fuel efficient than those powered by petrol engines, and thus emit less CO_2 over a given journey, despite producing more CO_2 per gallon of fuel. However, diesel is not otherwise an environmentally-friendly alternative to petrol. It has a higher sulphur content than petrol, giving rise to increased emissions of sulphur dioxide (SO_2), and its emissions of fine particulate matter are implicated in health problems. The proportion of diesel-engined vehicles registered in Ireland was over 28% of all registered vehicles in 1995, and has been increasing in recent years, particularly in the private car sector.[29]

The problem of emissions from diesel, especially of particulate matter, is also being addressed in the EU Auto Oil programme. Ireland supports the measures proposed to reduce SO_2 and PM_{10} emissions, and will transpose them speedily into Irish law. A research project to investigate levels of PM_{10} in Dublin, being carried out under the *Environmental Services OP* will help to determine whether additional national measures are required in relation to fine particulate matter.

Vehicle Testing

In-service vehicle testing is recognised as a cost effective approach to reducing road traffic emissions. Compulsory roadworthiness testing is already in operation for heavy commercial vehicles over one year old (annual test) and light goods vehicles over four years old (biennial test). By 1 January 1998, private cars over four years old will also be subject to biennial testing.[30] The inclusion of a robust air pollution control element in this testing will ensure that vehicles are maintained in a satisfactory condition to minimise emissions. This should also encourage the removal of older, more polluting vehicles from the fleet and their replacement by newer, technically cleaner and more efficient models.

At EU level, the Auto Oil project[31] is bringing forward proposals on fuel quality, vehicle technology and emissions controls. These should be accompanied by a range of non-technical options (e.g. road pricing, traffic management, scrappage schemes), to achieve air quality standards in major conurbations. Ireland will support such integrated efforts to improve air quality and reduce the adverse impacts of transport.

Alternative Fuels

The EU White Paper on Energy[32] (1995) recognises that fuel diversification in relation to transport to reduce total reliance on fossil fuels is essential for both environmental reasons and security of supply. The Government will expand its support of research and development into alternative fuels, such as biodiesel (already being developed by Teagasc), for use in motor cars, as well as alternative power methods such as electric vehicles. The extension of electric-powered rail and light rail public transport systems in the Dublin area is also being supported as part of this objective.

Urban Transport

Environmental problems arising from transport cause particular difficulties when concentrated in urban areas. High traffic levels in large cities give rise to significant congestion. Apart from causing delays impacting on economic and social welfare, congestion creates noise and air pollution. These problems are best addressed by strategies which promote traffic management, demand management and public transport options.

Traffic management systems, such as those proposed by the Dublin Transportation Initiative (DTI)[33], are an option for both major urban centres and smaller towns. They include options such as enhanced traffic management and enforcement systems, traffic calming measures in city centre and residential areas, parking restrictions and facilities, coordinated traffic signals, and improved facilities for cyclists and pedestrians. DTI proposals in this regard are being implemented under the *Transport OP*, while similar measures are being undertaken in a number of other cities and towns throughout the country. The Government will intensify implementation of DTI (which will, *inter alia*, increase the proportion of peak period journeys by public transport in the City Centre area from 44% to 57%, and provide decongestion benefits of up to £1 billion over a thirty year period).

In addition to traffic management, transport solutions in urban areas require more intensive demand management and the provision of alternatives to private cars. These can include:

- better planning and land use policy and implementation;
- increased provision for cyclists and pedestrians, in particular for short journeys; and
- improved availability of more efficient public transport.

Public Transport

"Transportation strategies should reduce the need for motor vehicles by favouring high-occupancy public transport, and providing safe bicycle and foot paths."

- Agenda for Change[34]

Greater efficiencies, and environmental benefits, can be obtained by means of mass public transport. Studies at EU level have shown that collective transport is far more energy efficient than use of private cars, which very often have only single occupancy. Public transport also has a major social impact. People who cannot afford to run a car are dependent on public transport for any journey over walking distance. Where such people live in areas with poor or no access to public transport, they are particularly disadvantaged.

Improvements are being made in the major urban areas, particularly in Dublin, to reduce congestion by providing more and better public transport facilities (rail, bus, and in future, light rail). There is scope for much greater improvement, not only in the physical infrastructure, but in greater incentives to the public to switch modes, better coordination between different modes (e.g. ticketing practices, timetable co-ordination, route planning, etc.).

Transport Waste

Sustainable waste management requires that transport wastes (including old vehicles, tyres and batteries), should be recycled, reused and also requires suitable arrangements for final disposal. Ireland is participating in discussions at EU level on a proposal for a Directive on "end-of-life" vehicles, and will seek agreement on suitable arrangements to minimise the environmental damage which can be caused by these wastes. Industry, too, has a part to play in measures to this end, and the voluntary agreement entered into by the motor industry in relation to the collection and safe disposal of spent automotive batteries is a welcome initiative in this connection.

In renewing the vehicle scrappage scheme for 1997, the Government stated that it considers that the motor industry should reciprocate by initiating more systematic efforts for the recycling of vehicle materials. The Minister for the Environment is undertaking discussions with the motor industry to arrange a voluntary agreement to this end.

Transport Noise

"[the growth of traffic volume during recent years] ... more than offsets any possible results of tightening noise limits from road vehicles through engine/exhaust noise controls."

- European Environment Agency[35]

Transport is a major source of environmental noise, which is an important factor in determining the quality of life. In urban and suburban areas in particular, road traffic is the most frequent cause of disturbance to residents. As a non-fixed source, however, it is not always identified among the causes of complaints concerning noise pollution. Railway noise, although more limited in terms of the areas affected, can also be an environmental problem. Aircraft noise is dealt with below.

Where road vehicles are concerned, EU noise emissions limits have been significantly reduced over the past two decades. In response, car manufacturers have reduced mechanical noise to the point where a significant proportion of traffic noise is now due to tyres and road surfaces. Further measures to reduce noise from these sources will be explored. In particular, noise controls under roads (or other) legislation will be developed to limit permissible noise from road transport. However, unless growth in road transport can be limited by measures already outlined, traffic noise will continue to pose problems.

Insofar as railway noise is concerned, Iarnród Éireann will continue its programme of noise reduction through new technology and other measures.

Air Transport

Air transport is an increasing source of polluting emissions (particularly carbon dioxide and nitrogen oxides). Ireland is supporting the initiation of action by the EU to have this problem addressed in the wider international context, and with due regard to effects on national competitiveness.

Aircraft noise poses particular problems in the immediate environment of airports. Ireland is already implementing standards for noise certification and limitation which have been agreed in international fora such as the International Civil Aviation Organisation, the EU and the European Civil Aviation Conference. In addition, development planning in the vicinity of airports is monitored and controlled to minimise the impact of aircraft noise. Despite increases in traffic through the major Irish airports, the EPA reported in 1996[36] that noise reductions have been achieved by a combination of improvements in aircraft technology and greater attention to operational matters including noise abatement procedures and selection of take-off and landing routes/orientations to minimise the impact of noise.

Pricing and Cost Internalisation

Cost internalisation involves taking the external costs of transport (e.g. noise, pollution, congestion, health risks, etc.) into consideration when pricing the elements of transport. Such internalisation of costs gives a better signal to consumers of the real costs (financial and otherwise) of their transport practices, and can help to motivate changes in attitudes and, more particularly, behaviour, which can benefit the environment.

The environmental externalities of road transport have up to now been underestimated. The Department of the Environment will commission work to identify more accurately the cost of these externalities. The results will be made available both for public information and to the NRA and local authorities. The NRA will be asked to amend various planning parameters to take greater account of these externalities and the cost benefits and viability of proposed major roads schemes will be assessed accordingly. In line with the approach of the EU Green Paper, *Towards Fair and Efficient Pricing in Transport*, the Government will support policy development at EU level and participate in measures towards internalising the external costs associated with transport. This will assist in correcting the current distortion whereby car ownership is more highly taxed than car use, by focusing on internalising the costs of car use. Such measures could include road pricing (which may include road tolls, parking charges or electronic road pricing technologies), circulation taxes, fuel taxes, etc.

Road user charging has the potential to provide significant environmental benefits. These can help to control growth in traffic and obviate the need for heavy additional investment in expanding capacity. The Dublin Transportation Office and the NRA have initiated a study of road pricing in the context of the M50 motorway. Assessment of road user charging options, in particular road tolling, will have to take account of the diversion of traffic which might result, including the types of traffic likely to be diverted, the probable impact on adjacent residential areas and the expected additional road construction/maintenance costs arising from the diversion.

SUSTAINABLE TOURISM

- provides a high-quality product based on, and in harmony with, a high-quality natural environment

- minimises adverse impacts on local communities, as well as on built heritage, landscapes, habitats and species

- supports social and economic prosperity while protecting and enhancing the cultural and natural environments

An action programme towards sustainable tourism

Sustainable tourism involves a positive approach to harmonising the interactions between tourism, the physical environment and the host communities. National tourism policy, as set out, for example, in Bord Fáilte's development plan for the period 1994-99, *Developing Sustainable Tourism*, already provides good foundations for sustainability in this sector. Specific actions will be taken under this Strategy, additional to or in association with current policies. These will be designed to ensure a full integration of sustainable development principles in the sector and will involve the following actions.

- Tourism development will be taken into account, as appropriate, by the Department of the Environment in the preparation of land use policy guidelines for planning authorities, developers and the public.

- Planning authorities will make provision in their development plans for sustainable tourism, and ensure through the planning process that over-development does not take place.

- Bord Fáilte will consider the implementation of a managed network of scenic landscapes by 1999.

- The Department of Tourism and Trade/Bord Fáilte will issue appropriate guidelines on good environmental management to the tourist accommodation sector.

- The Department of Arts, Culture and the Gaeltacht will implement good environmental management, including energy conservation, in historic properties and other tourist attractions under its care.

- The Department of Arts, Culture and the Gaeltacht will consider implementing collective transport, such as operates in Glenveagh, in other National Parks.

- A national Coastal Zone Management strategy study will be completed in 1997 and lead to a national policy for the sustainable use of the coastal zone.

- The provisions of the Foreshore Acts in relation to preventing and penalising damage to beaches, sand dunes and seashore ecosystems will continue to be fully implemented.

- The Department of Arts, Culture and the Gaeltacht will ensure that all river cruisers licensed for hire are fitted with appropriate waste water storage and pumping facilities. Local authorities and the Department will ensure that the complementary shore pumping facilities are properly used and maintained.

- The Department of Arts, Culture and the Gaeltacht will develop appropriate management strategies to protect riverine archaeological monuments, which may be vulnerable to damage from cruising activities.

- Consideration will be given to the need for controls or restrictions on certain unsustainable leisure activities; the Department of the Environment, in consultation with the Department of Arts, Culture and the Gaeltacht, the Department of Tourism and Trade and the Department of the Marine, where appropriate, will provide suitable guidance for local authorities.

- Bord Fáilte, the Department of Tourism and Trade and the Marine Institute, where appropriate, will commission research on the "critical loads" of tourist destinations, including sensitive coastal or wilderness areas, to provide a firm basis for the establishment of sustainable tourist numbers.

- CERT, in conjunction with the education sector, will continue to provide suitable training emphasising the sustainable use of resources and highlighting natural products.

- Bord Fáilte, the Department of Tourism and Trade and the Department of Arts, Culture and the Gaeltacht will develop, and widely publicise, codes of conduct and practice to foster a greater awareness of the potential impact of tourist behaviour on sensitive areas and sites.

Introduction/Overview

"Among the major strengths which characterise Irish tourism is our clean physical environment."

- Operational Programme for Tourism, 1994-99[1]

Fig 11.1 Key issues in Irish Tourism

Management of increasing tourist numbers

- overseas tourists - at almost 3.7 million - exceeded the resident population of Ireland for the first time in 1994
- numbers of overseas tourists increased from 2.4 million in 1988 to 4.6 million in 1996; emphasis is now placed on growth in revenue rather than numbers

Concentration of tourists in certain areas

- the main centres for tourist accommodation (compared to resident population) are located on the west coast
- Connemara, the Burren, the Ring of Kerry, the Dingle Peninsula and the Wicklow Mountains have been identified as sensitive areas which are already subject to significant pressures from tourism

Seasonal profile

- 30% of all overseas tourists arrive in July and August
- domestic tourism is more than twice as peaked as overseas tourism

Increasing stress on landscape and infrastructure

- sensitive areas are subject to damage and erosion from tourism-related activities - e.g. threat to sand dunes from golf courses and horse trekking
- water, sewerage and solid waste infrastructure in some areas is inadequate or overloaded by pressure of tourist numbers
- roads in some areas are subject to damage and congestion arising from the growth in tourism traffic, especially coach tours

---

Tourism is one of Ireland's major indigenous industries, and one of the fastest-growing. It makes a significant contribution to the national economy, particularly through its foreign exchange earnings which have a high multiplier effect in terms of the national income. Total tourism revenue exceeded £2.3 billion in 1995 (continuing the steady growth experienced since 1993), and the sector now contributes around 7% of GNP. This represents a significant increase from a contribution of under 5% in 1986, especially given the rapid expansion of total recorded GNP over the same period. The value to the economy of overseas tourists in 1996 was some £1.45 billion.

Tourism provides around 8% of national employment, at some 102,000 full-time equivalent jobs in 1995; this is expected to increase to 110,000 by end-1997. The *Operational Programme for Tourism, 1994-99* (the *Tourism OP*), is expected to deliver an additional 35,000 full-time job equivalents by 1999. It is likely, however, that this underestimates the total employment impact of the tourism sector, as many jobs which are supported by tourism (for example in the retail and leisure sectors) are recorded elsewhere in the statistics. Tourism is a growing force for employment; the additional 30,000 tourism-related jobs created between 1987 and 1994 represented half of the net increase in employment in that period.[2]

Continued growth in tourism in Ireland is expected in line with the projected annual growth of around 4% per annum for world tourism generally to the end of the century. In particular, Ireland has targeted growth of 9% per annum in overseas tourism revenue. Current trends in international tourism, which provide further strong opportunities for Irish tourism, include a growing environmental awareness and a preference for activity-based holidays. Maintaining the Irish environment and physical cultural heritage, which are recognised as being of high quality, will provide the foundation on which to build sustainable tourism and take advantage of these international trends.

However, it is important that tourism development itself should not become a force which threatens this foundation.

The *Tourism OP* recognises that Ireland's quality natural environment is one of the major strengths of Irish tourism. Ireland offers an ideal setting for a wide range of recreational and leisure pursuits, many of which (such as swimming, fishing, sailing and equestrian pursuits) are critically dependent on the maintenance of a high quality environment. The scope for further development of tourism in these areas must not be limited by deteriorating environmental quality, but neither must tourism be allowed to contribute to any such deterioration.

Ireland's tourism development strategy seeks to promote an image of an uncrowded, relaxed island, of great scenic beauty, with a distinctive heritage and culture, a friendly welcoming people, high-quality facilities and a superb, unspoilt environment for outdoor activity. Ireland must avoid the drift to uniformity, evident in many countries, and concentrate on enhancing competitive image, improving the quality of the tourism product and attracting tourists seeking environmentally-based holidays. Sustainable tourism development is identified as the way to achieve this goal.

Fig 11.2 Key Strengths of the Irish Tourism Product

- superb scenic landscapes
- a quiet island with a relaxed pace of life
- a distinctive heritage and culture
- the absence of mass tourism
- a friendly, welcoming, convivial people
- an excellent location for outdoor activities and sports
- a "green" unspoilt environment

Source: Bord Fáilte[3]

Tourism's Interactions with the Environment

Tourism promotes regional development, as many of the top tourism destinations are located in the less-developed and more remote regions of the country. Almost three-quarters (£1.47 billion) of total tourism revenues (over £2 billion) in 1995 (excluding carrier receipts) accrued outside Dublin.[4] From a sustainability perspective, the management of our tourism assets, to ensure their preservation while continuing to promote viable growth in the sector, is a key issue.

The development of the tourism industry can have beneficial effects on the environment, particularly with a growing realisation of the high degree of inter-dependency between the industry and the environment in which it is rooted. There have been both positive and negative experiences, for example, in the development of facilities and infrastructure, the spread and seasonality of activity, and interactions with the landscape and natural resources. An example of the high level of environmental awareness in the Irish tourism industry was the award, in 1995, of the inaugural EU Tourism and the Environment Prize to Kinsale.[5] Local efforts under the Tidy Towns Competition[6] also provide an impetus to community action supporting environmental and tourism objectives. The *Action Against Litter* campaign[7], which will operate until 1998, is an integrated approach to tackling litter and its negative effect on the "green" image which is so important to tourism.

Land use

Land use planning has a role to play in bringing about the optimum development of tourism. A key issue for tourism is the protection of our natural and cultural landscape. Local development plans must ensure the protection of this landscape, as well as the preservation of views and of the human heritage. The Department of the Environment will take tourism development into account in the preparation of land use policy guidelines for planning authorities, developers and the public.

National tourism policy recognises that Ireland should not aim at becoming a mass tourism destination. Local authorities, in preparing development plans, will make provision for sustainable tourism and, in considering applications for tourism development, must recognise capacity limitations and not permit over-development.

Image and infrastructure supports

Sustainable tourism growth must be underpinned by high quality tourist services, efficient supporting infrastructure and strong management policies to protect natural resources. Infrastructure requirements for sustainable tourism growth include not only sensitively developed amenity and recreational developments, but also basic facilities in terms of accommodation, transport (including roads and parking), water and sewerage, solid waste services, etc.

The potential environmental impacts of this infrastructure must be taken into account to avoid conflict between proposed developments and the environment. The application and enforcement of planning controls in regard to major tourism facilities, including golf courses and interpretative centres, is an important component of this process. The justification for new facilities, which in some cases may duplicate existing facilities or increase environmental pressures, is an important issue for the planning control process. The emphasis of the *Tourism OP* is on the enhancement of existing infrastructure, rather than the development of new facilities, and up to 75% of investment under the *OP* is being directed to this end.

Potential difficulties arise when expanding tourist numbers exceed the carrying capacity of existing environmental infrastructure. Overloading of sewage treatment plants has contributed to some pollution of rivers and lakes; responses to cater for additional loading have included the upgrading of sewage treatment in major tourist centres. Account must also

be taken of the demands placed on infrastructure by concentrated tourist numbers during the peak season - offshore islands can be particularly vulnerable in this respect. Where new services are being provided, modular design may be appropriate.

Overall, however, the carrying capacity of the environment must be respected where tourism planning is concerned. Where large scale expansion of, for example, waste water treatment infrastructure is contemplated to provide for increased tourism, the question must be asked whether tourism activity is sustainable on the scale proposed, or would it in time erode the quality of the tourism product. In general, it is preferable that pressure of numbers be relieved by greater dispersion and a better seasonal profile of tourism.

Tourism related infrastructure should protect and enhance, not detract from, environmental quality. Adverse impacts can include landscape intrusion, erosion, loss of flora, disturbance to wildlife, pollution and littering, noise, disturbance and congestion, undermining the resource upon which tourism depends and altering the character and attractiveness of natural and heritage features. Sustainable development requires a balance between preserving a natural, unspoilt environment and providing facilities which allow tourists - and local residents - to better understand, appreciate and enjoy it. Facilities must be in harmony with the local environment, and reconcile the economic benefit to the local community with the preservation of the natural and cultural environment which underlies economic well-being.

One indication that development actively respects and enhances the local environment would be a tourism eco-label. A pilot project[8] under the EU *LIFE* initiative was launched in 1995 and is now operating in four areas - West Donegal, West Mayo, Galway City/Connemara and the Brandon area of the Dingle Peninsula.

Over a period of three years, a thorough examination of all aspects of the natural, cultural and economic environments in relation to tourism development will be carried out with the participation of the local communities in these areas, with a view to drawing up a set of standards for a tourism eco-label. If successful, the intention is that it will be adapted for use throughout the EU as a universally recognisable "green tourism" label.

Increasing tourist numbers also have implications for demand for transport infrastructure. 60% of current overseas tourist business is related to car touring, either in hire cars or the estimated 500,000 cars brought in by tourists.[9] Both of these sectors are expected to expand with tourist growth and increasing capacity in ports and ferries. The implications for road congestion in peak tourism areas are considerable, and need to be taken into account in addressing the general issue of transport growth. Tourist traffic also requires effective management measures, without overall curtailment of tourism. Greater emphasis will be placed on promoting holidays which can avail of more environmentally-friendly modes of transport such as railways, waterways, cycling and walking. To minimise adverse effects on the environment, the car hire fleet should comprise the most fuel-efficient, least-polluting vehicles available. The use of collective transport, as currently operated in Glenveagh National Park, Co. Donegal, should be expanded where practicable.

High quality Irish goods and consumer services to support the tourism sector are important in enhancing the perception of a quality Irish tourism product. These goods and services need to emphasise the sustainable use of resources and highlight Irish food and other natural products. Suitable training in support of this approach will continue to be provided by CERT, in conjunction with the education sector.

Managing numbers

"In the interests of sustainable tourism development, we must aim to improve significantly the yield from visitors, thus achieving agreed revenue targets with slower growth in visitor numbers."

- Bord Fáilte[10]

The significant growth in tourist numbers between 1984 and 1994 increased the pressures on the Irish environment. In 1984, some 1.7 million overseas tourists visited Ireland. By 1994, this number had more than doubled, and at almost 3.7 million exceeded the resident population for the first time.[11] These increases have continued; overseas visitors in 1996 totalled some 4.6 million.[12] Good management is necessary to sustain this level of growth.

An indication of the increased numbers visiting historic sites under the care of the Department of Arts, Culture and the Gaeltacht is set out in Fig 11.3. While visitor densities are relatively low by international standards, the growing emphasis on cultural/heritage holidays suggests that further increases are likely. The sustainability of increased visitor numbers at particular historical monuments will need careful consideration, especially as such numbers may, in certain circumstances, result in damage to the monuments (e.g. as at Newgrange). Careful management of access to these sites will therefore be increasingly important.

The impact of tourist numbers on towns and other accommodation centres is also described by an index compiled by Bord Fáilte. This shows that in thirteen of the main tourism centres, tourist beds in approved accommodation represent between 10% and 36% of the resident population (see Fig 11.4). Tourist beds in Dublin, by comparison, equate to only 2% of the resident population. The relative pressure of tourist numbers on local communities and local infrastructure is considerably greater in the west and south-west of Ireland, including offshore islands.

Fig 11.3 Visitor Numbers on Historic Sites under the care of the Department of Arts, Culture and the Gaeltacht

Site	Visitors in 1985	Visitors in 1994	percentage increase
Aughnanure Castle	4,268	24,081	464%
Charles Fort	13,901	33,296	140%
Clonmacnoise	31,471	118,157	275%
Derrynane House	10,262	16,673	62%
Dublin Castle	62,674	122,479	95%
Dunmore Cave	22,334	32,391	45%

Source: *State of the Environment in Ireland*[13]

Fig 11.4 Tourist Beds as % of Resident Population

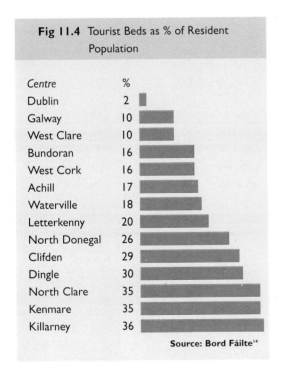

Centre	%
Dublin	2
Galway	10
West Clare	10
Bundoran	16
West Cork	16
Achill	17
Waterville	18
Letterkenny	20
North Donegal	26
Clifden	29
Dingle	30
North Clare	35
Kenmare	35
Killarney	36

Source: Bord Fáilte[14]

Continuing increases in numbers could not be entertained without seriously damaging the capacity of the Irish environment to continue to support the industry. The approach taken in the *Tourism OP* is designed to reduce the impact of tourism on the product, at any given level of revenue, while contributing to improved profitability.

Tourism development policy must leave the physical and the social environment undiminished and, ideally, enhanced as a resource for future enjoyment by domestic and foreign visitors alike. To this end, the carrying capacity of sensitive natural areas and of tourist centres must be identified, and steps taken to ensure that this capacity is not exceeded. This will require a form of control to be exercised over the most highly sensitive areas (possibly, although not necessarily, some form of designation) and the implementation of plans for managing access so as to reduce extremes of pressure. Success in this regard will be indicated by, *inter alia*, a low level of complaint from local communities regarding the impact of visitor numbers on the local quality of life, the numbers admitted to specified areas, and the limitation of damage already being caused to these areas.

Bord Fáilte's plan for developing tourism over the period 1994-99 aims for an "optimal" number of tourists. Optimal is defined as the point beyond which it would not be possible *"to enhance the welfare of additional tourists without making the community worse off as a result"*.[15] Optimisation includes taking account of social as well as economic costs, including environmental damage, congestion, time losses, inconvenience and the disruption of local communities by increased tourism. The "optimal" number can, however, change over time in the light of increased success in improving the seasonal profile, dispersing tourism more evenly around the country, and improving controls on access and behaviour of visitors to sites. Conversely, if pressures on the environment become excessive, the optimal number of tourists permitted may be reduced.

Current policy focuses on increasing the revenue value of tourism rather than the number of tourists. This is a welcome development.

Fig 11.5 Tourist Participation in Environment-related Activities			
Activity	Number of tourists		
	1989	1993	percentage increase
Cycling	100,000	167,000	67%
Golfing	95,000	162,000	71%
Horse riding	42,000	61,000	45%
Sailing	31,000	35,000	13%
Walking	244,000	323,000	32%

Source: Bord Fáilte [16]

Seasonality

At present, 30% of all overseas tourists (over 1.25 million people in 1995) arrive in Ireland in the peak months of July and August. Domestic tourism is almost twice as peaked as overseas tourism in the same months, leading to significant concentration of numbers in this limited period.

Irish tourism policy recognises the need to extend the tourism season more evenly beyond the traditional summer holiday period, in order to relieve the concentration of peak numbers for environmental reasons and also to improve the economic performance of the industry. Better seasonal spread is positively encouraged by the development of "off-peak season" activities and non-weather dependent facilities. The objective under this Strategy, in line with the *Tourism OP*, is to secure a tourism seasonality profile which is fully consistent with environmental sustainability; specifically, to reduce the current high-season load from 30% to 25% of total tourist numbers by 1999. In order to meet this objective, greater attention will focus on the provision and marketing of off-season activities and facilities.

With regard to domestic tourism, other countries have shown that effective ways to improve this situation include staggering school and public holidays. As only one Irish public holiday falls within the peak period, scope for change is limited, and may be unnecessary. The structure of the Irish education system, including terminal examinations, is such that there is no immediate prospect of a change in this regard. However, there is scope for individuals who can do so, as consumers of tourism services, to choose to holiday outside the peak period of July-August.

Sensitive areas and scenic landscapes

"The stability and appearance of the landscape [are] inextricably linked to the prosperity and activities of the community who live in these landscapes."
- Tourism and the Landscape [17]

It is recognised that a small number of sensitive landscapes is already experiencing significant pressure from tourism. These include the Burren, Connemara, the Ring of Kerry, the Dingle Peninsula and the Wicklow Mountains. Several of these areas contain rare flora and fauna which need to be protected, and Killarney National Park has been designated by UNESCO as a biosphere reserve. Protection, however, cannot mean exclusive dedication to tourism/leisure uses, nor the prohibition of development within those areas. Nor should it compromise the economic and social viability of local communities, or the range of activities necessary to sustain a living landscape.

The national network of scenic landscapes proposed by Bord Fáilte in *Developing Sustainable Tourism* would embrace about 25 areas of outstanding scenic beauty, which would be actively managed and selectively promoted. Bord Fáilte has suggested that Comprehensive Area Management Plans are urgently required to address this issue and ensure that these landscapes are protected and preserved from the excesses of tourism. A demonstration project, funded under the EU *LIFE* programme and carried out by Bord Fáilte and An Taisce, has tested the practicality of this proposal in three pilot areas.

It concluded that:

- the integration of tourism and the environment is more likely to be effective and acceptable to the local community through a process of agreement on, rather than designation of, special areas;
- there is a need to shift the emphasis from the idea of sustainable tourism to one of sustainable communities, which requires a total integration of the environment, tourism and other sectors; and
- sustainable activity is promoted through awareness, understanding and consensus rather than through regulation.[18]

Bord Fáilte is now considering the establishment of a pilot Scenic Landscape Forum, as recommended in the study, as a means of taking forward the preparation of an integrated management strategy for a scenic landscapes network.

Inland waterway cruising is a growth area in Irish tourism. The number of boat-weeks sold *per annum* increased from 6,186 to 8,195 over the period from 1988 to 1992.[19] A programme of providing pump-out facilities on inland waterways is continuing to ensure that environmental quality is not threatened by increasing cruiser activity. The Department of Arts, Culture and the Gaeltacht, which licenses hire cruisers, will ensure that all such boats are fitted with appropriate storage and pumping facilities. Local authorities (and the Department of Arts, Culture and the Gaeltacht where canals are concerned) are providing sufficient, and suitably located, shore pumping facilities to cater for cruiser traffic and will ensure that these are properly used and maintained. Cruising may also impact on certain riverine archaeological monuments; the Department of Arts, Culture and the Gaeltacht will develop appropriate management strategies in this regard.

Unsustainable leisure activities

There has been a growth in recent years in certain leisure activities which have the potential to damage or destroy natural landscapes and habitats, as well as causing noise, emissions and general nuisance. Generally minority activities, they include motorcycle scrambling, the use of jetskis, beach buggies and all-terrain vehicles, and horse riding on dune ecosystems. Although not limited to the tourism industry, they may be associated with, or promoted by, it. Their adverse effects can damage tourist perceptions of the Irish environment.

For the tourism industry and the preservation of a characteristic quality of life, it is essential to prevent damage to the environment caused by activities incompatible with the maintenance of a high quality image. To this end, consideration will be given to:

- implementing controls such as the designation of certain sensitive areas, which are either in public ownership or recognised as important heritage areas, as "off limits" for defined activities;
- restricting the number of persons, vehicles, etc., involved in these activities; and
- controlling activities by limiting them to organised events or competitions in particular areas.

The implementation of any such measures would largely fall to local authorities, subject to guidance to be developed by the Department of the Environment, in consultation with the Department of Arts, Culture and the Gaeltacht, the Department of Tourism and Trade, and the Department of the Marine, where appropriate.

Impacts on biodiversity

Irish flora, fauna and their habitats are an important asset to tourism. Their conservation requires a delicate balance to be struck between habitat protection and planned and controlled visitor access.

Where tourist activities are specifically related to natural fauna, as in the case of hunting, shooting or fishing holidays, due regard must be had to the requirements of EU nature conservation Directives, such as the Birds and Habitats Directives, and of national law. Participation limits are enforced by controlling the number of licenses and permits issued in certain areas or seasons, or for certain species which are under pressure. These limits will be kept under continuous review and further restricted, where required, so as not to undermine the regenerative capacity of stocks of wildlife.

Pressures on the Coastal Zone

Tourism and leisure pressures on the coastal zone include the building of holiday homes, caravan parks, and golf courses, the erosion of sand dunes by recreational use such as horse trekking, and the concentration of service facilities such as car parking and picnic areas.

A pilot tax relief scheme for fifteen designated resort areas, which will operate until 1998, will support the renewal and updating of tourist amenities and facilities, including approved accommodation and other tourism-related buildings and structures.[20] In support of this scheme, the Department of the Environment has provided funding to extend and upgrade water and sanitary services in nine of the designated resorts. This will ensure that adequate high quality water and sanitary services are in place to maximise their tourism and development potential.

The annual Blue Flag Awards Scheme[21] for beaches and marinas, administered by An Taisce, encourages the maintenance of high standards in relation to bathing water quality, coastal management, environmental education and information, and the provision of facilities for visitors. Other measures to preserve beach and coastal quality include:
- the continuing full implementation of the provisions of the Foreshore Acts in relation to preventing and penalising damage to beaches, sand dunes and seashore ecosystems; and
- the taking into account, in the authorisation of aquaculture, of implications for other uses of the coastal zone and marine resources.

A coastal zone management policy which will address tourist-related pressures, amongst others, is being developed (see Chapter 13).

Green Housekeeping

"The conservation and sustainable use of resources - natural, social and cultural - is crucial and makes long-term business sense ... The key lies in sound purchasing and procurement and in effective waste management."

- Irish Hotel and Catering Institute[22]

Green housekeeping, or good environmental management, is an important factor for the tourist accommodation sector. Just as industry and domestic consumers must play their part in energy conservation, the efficient use of natural resources (including water) and general good environmental practice, similarly hotels, guesthouses and other providers of accommodation should carry out an environmental audit of their practices to ensure compatibility with high environmental standards. Guidelines to the industry in this regard will be issued by the Department of Tourism and Trade/Bord Fáilte, following the lead of the public sector in relation to promoting green housekeeping (see Chapter 19).

Other tourism-related operations where green housekeeping will be encouraged include:
- the use of energy-efficient floodlighting in historic buildings;
- energy conservation measures in tourist offices and interpretative centres (following the line of the Government programme on Energy Conservation in State Buildings); and
- the use of recycled paper and other goods in marketing and promotion.

 12

SUSTAINABLE TRADE

- supports economic prosperity while protecting the global environment in all its
diversity

- enhances social and economic equity
throughout the world

- takes account of the wider global impact
of national policies regarding imports
and exports

An action programme towards sustainable trade

- Trade policy will be examined to ensure compliance with the objectives of *Agenda 21* in relation to promoting an open, non-discriminatory and equitable trading system, taking particular account of the needs of developing countries.

- Ireland supports the EU consensus on the importance of upholding the validity of multi lateral agreements (MEAs) designed to protect the environment and of ensuring the integration of sustainable development into world trade policies and practices.

- The Department of Arts, Culture and the Gaeltacht will make any amendments to legislation which may be necessary to enable Ireland to ratify the CITES Convention in 1997.

Introduction/Overview

Fig 12.1 Issues in Irish Trade

- Trade accounts for 63% of GNP - the second highest proportion in the EU
- Exports, almost three-quarters of which are destined for the EU, represent 72% of Irish GDP at current market prices
- The value of exports in 1995 was approximately £27.8 billion
- Imports in the same year amounted to approximately £20.6 billion in value giving a trade surplus of over £7 billion

As a small open economy, Ireland is strongly dependent on trade, which accounts for 63% of GNP - the second highest proportion in the EU. Exports, almost three-quarters of which are destined for the EU, represent 72% of Irish GDP at current market prices. In 1995, their value was approximately £27.8 billion. Imports in the same year amounted to over £20.6 billion in value giving a trade surplus of over £7.2 billion. A breakdown of imports and exports, by area of origin, is given in Fig 12.2.

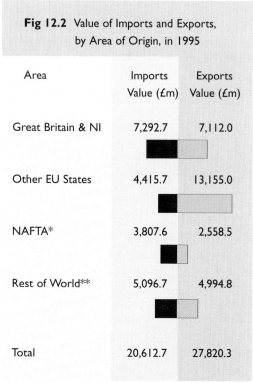

Fig 12.2 Value of Imports and Exports, by Area of Origin, in 1995

Area	Imports Value (£m)	Exports Value (£m)
Great Britain & NI	7,292.7	7,112.0
Other EU States	4,415.7	13,155.0
NAFTA*	3,807.6	2,558.5
Rest of World**	5,096.7	4,994.8
Total	20,612.7	27,820.3

* USA, Canada & Mexico
** including country unknown and unclassified
Source: Central Statistics Office[1]

International trade is growing. The volume of world trade expanded almost four times faster than world output in the period from 1990 to 1994. The rate of growth is also increasing. Trade expansion over the period 1985 to 1989 was only 1.8 times faster than growth in output.[2]

The links between trade and sustainable development have come to greater prominence in international fora in recent years. *Agenda 21* stated that greater coherence between international trade and environment policies is necessary to promote sustainable development, recognising that an open multilateral trading system can facilitate a more efficient use of natural resources, both in environmental and economic terms, and can contribute to lessening demands on the environment.

Many complex issues arise from the interface between trade and environment, including:

- how trade controls can be used to support environmental protection without giving rise to protectionist abuses; and
- how the international trading system can support the sustainable development requirements of developing countries.

Traditionally, trade agreements and controls have been product based. Environmental controls, on the other hand, tend to focus on the processes underlying production, and how these processes impact on the environment. The international community is now trying to address the tension inherent in this difference of focus.

The extent of action which can be taken at national level to increase trade sustainability is conditioned by the international nature of trade. As well as national action, concerted international action is necessary. Principle 12 of the *Rio Declaration*[3] recognises that importing countries should avoid unilateral actions to deal with environmental problems outside their jurisdiction, and that measures to address global or transboundary environmental problems should, as far as possible, be founded on international consensus.

"...world trade and environment policies should be not only compatible but also mutually supportive."

- EU Commission[4]

A number of international fora, including the OECD, UNEP and UNCTAD, are examining linkages between trade and environment, including the implications of sustainable development for trade liberalisation, and vice versa. The central forum, however, is the World Trade Organisation (WTO), which seeks to ensure that trade and economic relations are in accordance with the objective of sustainable development. At the heart of the debate is the need to strike a balance between the dynamic for greater trade liberalisation and the requirements of protecting the environment and promoting sustainable development. The WTO Committee on Trade and Environment,

which commenced work in 1995, has the specific task of analysing the relationship between trade and environmental measures, in order to promote sustainable development, and to make appropriate recommendations on any changes to the multilateral trading system which are necessary to give effect to this objective.

The Committee reported to the first Ministerial Conference of the WTO in Singapore in December 1996, where it was acknowledged that full implementation of WTO Agreements will make an important contribution to achieving the objectives of sustainable development. The Committee will continue working to examine the complex relationship between trade, environment and sustainable development. Ireland shares and supports the EU consensus in favour of having environmental concerns fully integrated into the WTO, with due allowance made for developing countries.

There is now increasing emphasis on defining appropriate links between trade and environment, and a growing environmental consciousness both among individual consumers, governments and international bodies. Green consumerism is increasingly a market reality, which must be accommodated within international trade agreements. Irish trade will need to respond to these challenges on two fronts:

- in relation to **exports**, Irish products and services will have to demonstrate a high degree of environmental awareness and protection in order to secure and retain market share in other economies. Issues in this regard have been dealt with in previous chapters (e.g. Chapter 9). The Forfás report, *Shaping Our Future*, identified the importance for trade development of developing a positive image of Ireland, including the pursuit of high environmental standards;

- where **imports** are concerned, greater attention will have to be paid to the sustainability of the goods and services imported from other countries, especially in terms of the environmental impact on developing economies of Irish import requirements and policies. The concept of ecological footprints, already referred to in Chapter 3, suggests that every effort should be made to ensure that Irish trade requirements and policies have the lowest possible impact on the sustainability of ecosystems in all countries, but particularly in the developing world. Examples of specific trade-related issues are given below.

Specific Trade Issues Related to Sustainable Development

"The development process will not gather momentum ... if the developing countries are weighted down by external indebtedness, if development finance is inadequate, if barriers restrict access to markets and if commodity prices and the terms of trade of developing countries remain depressed."

- Agenda 21[5]

Fair trade

Agenda 21 highlighted the role of trade in promoting sustainable development, in particular in the developing countries. As well as the more general issue of trade liberalisation, it addressed specific areas of importance to those countries. Of particular relevance is the issue of fair trade, including fair pricing for commodities such as coffee, cocoa, sugar and tropical timber (see below), which provide vital export earnings for many developing countries.

Principle 2 of the *Rio Declaration on Environment and Development* recognises the sovereign right of states to exploit their own resources. Where natural resources or agricultural commodities are underpriced in world markets, developing countries may, in effect, be forced into over-exploiting their resources in order to generate sufficient export earnings to support internal social and economic development. The underpricing of their export goods also contributes to the debt burden borne by many developing countries, which constrains their ability to finance the investments necessary for sustainable development.

The White Paper on Foreign Policy[6] (1996) recognised the need for coherence between trade and development issues, including the importance of balance between national, domestic interests and the rights of developing countries in relation to market access. At international level, Ireland will seek to ensure a coherent strategy in this regard. National trade policy will be examined to ensure compliance with the objectives of *Agenda 21* in relation to promoting an open, non-discriminatory and equitable trading system, taking particular account of the needs of developing countries. (see also Chapter 17 in relation to Official Development Assistance policy)

Tropical timbers

Ireland imported 70,000 tonnes of tropical timber (logs, sawnwood, veneer and plywood) in 1994, mainly from Ghana and the Ivory Coast. The value of these imports was £37 million.[7] The increasing emphasis in Irish forestry policy on the planting of broadleaved (hardwood) species may, in time, provide some scope to replace imports of tropical timbers. In the long term, more tropical timber should be available from sustainable sources. However, there will continue to be a demand for many tropical timbers which have specific properties which cannot be met by other timbers.

Action to protect remaining rainforests must be carefully balanced to avoid approaches which, by reducing demand for, and therefore the value of, tropical timber, may simply encourage forest clearance in developing countries and the diversion of land to cash crops. A more sustainable emphasis will be to develop options under which trade in tropical timbers and environmental policies are mutually supportive. This could include, *inter alia*, support for the development and implementation of sustainable forest management policies in developing countries, improving market access and transparency for forest products and services, and the development of full-cost methodologies for forest goods and services. Certification and labelling schemes are one among many possible tools to promote sustainable forest management, but there is no international agreement as to their effectiveness or practicality. It is important to bear in mind, however, that most tropical forest clearance is for agricultural development, that most timber production is for domestic fuelwood, that only a small percentage enters international trade, and that certification is an issue in only a limited number of markets.

The issue of trade and environment, including an examination of the issues of labelling and certification, is among those currently being considered by the Intergovernmental Panel on Forests, established in 1995 by the UN Commission on Sustainable Development.

Trade in endangered species

The 1973 Convention on International Trade in Endangered Species of Wild Fauna and Flora (CITES)[8] aims at protecting wild species of animals and plants, through the use of inventories and monitoring systems for endangered and overexploited species and controls on international trade in endangered species. The Convention applies not only to live animals and plants, but also to derivatives and products - for example, all commercial trade in ivory has been banned under CITES since 1992. Ireland is currently taking steps, which may include amendment of legislation, to allow the ratification of the Convention in 1997. In practice, however, the main provisions of the Convention are already being implemented pending formal ratification.

PART 4 - SUPPORTING THE STRATEGY

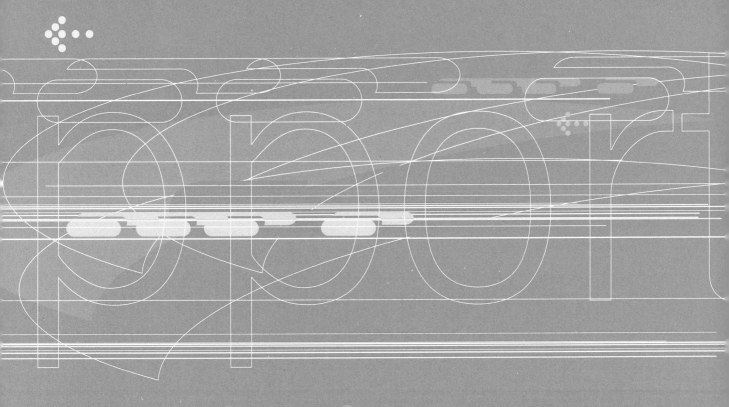

Chapter 13
Environmental Quality

"In general terms, the available data indicate that the quality of the Irish environment is good and compares favourably with most other Member States of the EU. In a period of economic growth, the environment in Ireland requires particular attention to secure its protection and to ensure that development is sustainable."

- Environmental Protection Agency[1]

Introduction

Economy and society are dependent on the natural environment as:

- the source of energy and materials for the production of goods and services;
- the sink for emissions and wastes generated by production and consumption; and
- the provider of services creating basic conditions for human life and the economy, including a stable climate and water resources.

The definition of the quality and quantity of environmental endowments, and the assessment of the pressures placed upon them by human activity, help to determine whether or not development is sustainable. In acknowledging that there is uncertainty about the extent of human-induced change which the global environment can sustain, the European Environment Agency stated that:

> *"a host of warning signals provides us with increasing evidence that the impact of human activities might have already gone beyond the capability of maintaining the integrity and productivity of natural resources."*[2]

The EPA report, *State of the Environment in Ireland*, provides an environmental baseline for this Strategy, and assists the review and analysis upon which policy priorities and responses are developed.

Environmental Quality

Environmental change is caused by natural processes and human activity. With the increasing pace of socio-economic development, human activity is now seen as exerting the greater influence. Modern society enjoys many positive benefits of development, notably in relation to standards of living, health and welfare. It must also address the ability of supporting ecosystems to sustain the demand for natural resources, and absorb the volume of emissions and wastes created by it.

In the light of the major environmental trends and features identified by the EPA, the following sections define strategic objectives for key environmental media and themes, and outline measures which are being, and will be, pursued to achieve those objectives.

Water Resources

Overview

Water is a necessary precondition for all forms of life, and an essential element of ecosystems. Its social and economic uses are extensive, ranging from drinking water supply and industrial and agricultural use, to use as a receiving medium for treated sewage effluents and other waterborne wastes, and as a resource for hydroelectricity, fire fighting, commercial fishing and aquaculture, transport, amenity and tourism purposes.

Ireland has abundant fresh waters and rich marine resources. Although there are wide variations in the availability of water throughout the country, in general, the state of the environment report has shown that quality trends, rather than quantity, are the greater cause for concern. In particular, it is clear that although serious pollution of inland fresh waters is gradually reducing and now affects only 0.6% of river channel length surveyed, the trend towards slight and moderate pollution has increased over the past twenty years[3], and now affects 28% of monitored river channel length. These conditions are brought about by excessive inputs of nutrients (see Chapter 5). Tackling the problem of eutrophication calls for innovative approaches.

Strategic Objectives

A sustainable water policy must be based on protection, management and prudent use of water resources in the interests of optimised environmental quality, and economic performance and efficiency. The objectives of this Strategy for Irish water resources are to:

- protect and improve quality so as to
  - eliminate, as far as possible, serious pollution of rivers,
  - reverse and minimise slight and moderate pollution,
  - reverse and minimise eutrophication,
  - maintain marine water quality generally, in particular abating localised pollution in estuarine and coastal waters,
  - quantify and establish the current quality status of groundwater resources, and
  - ensure that groundwaters may be used, as required, as sources of drinking water supplies and for other beneficial uses;
- manage water resources effectively, allowing beneficial development and use compatible with preservation of good quality; and
- secure the provision of efficient water supply and waste water services of sufficient quality and quantity to protect public health and meet consumer and economic development needs in a cost-effective way.

Actions

The achievement of water quality objectives requires concerted and new action on the part of public authorities and of all users and consumers of water. Many important measures, already being pursued, will be continued in association with new and additional actions under Parts III and IV of this Strategy.

Legislation

Water quality will be protected by enforcement of existing legislation, and the development and implementation of new regulations.

- New regulations will be made in 1997 under the Water Pollution Acts setting water quality standards for a range of polluting substances, including phosphorus. Observance of these standards will be an objective of the effluent discharge licensing control system and will guide local authorities and the EPA in devising and implementing management strategies to deal with diffuse sources of pollution, including those from agriculture.

- New regulations, to be made under the *Waste Management Act, 1996*, will, *inter alia*, apply higher environmental standards to waste disposal facilities which should consequently lead to better protection of water resources.

- The *Fisheries (Amendment) Bill*, when enacted, will establish a streamlined process for the regulation of aquaculture which will ensure that the industry's continued development takes place in accordance with high environmental standards (see also Chapter 7).

- The *Dumping at Sea Act, 1996*, established a strict regime governing the dumping of substances at sea. The Act prohibits the incineration of substances or material at sea, and the disposal at sea of low, intermediate or high level radioactive wastes and toxic, harmful or noxious substances. Disposal at sea of sewage sludge will be prohibited from 31 December 1998. The Act will enable Ireland to complete ratification of the OSPAR Convention in 1997.

- The UN ECE Convention on Protection and Use of Transboundary Watercourses and International Lakes will be ratified in 1997.

Management and Protection

Water quality management plans have for many years been the basic tool for advancing strategic water quality protection requirements at local and regional level. New approaches, as well as reinforcement of existing policies and practices, are now necessary.

- An integrated catchment management initiative will be launched in April 1997, and implemented by local authorities with relevant interests, to reverse deteriorating water quality trends in selected catchments, including water bodies shared with Northern Ireland.

- Supporting the catchment management initiative, Cohesion funding has been approved for an integrated series of projects to improve sewage treatment and collection facilities in towns in the Lough Derg, Lough Ree, Lough Swilly, Lough Erne, River Suir, River Boyne, River Liffey, and River Barrow catchments. Works costing over £65 million have been approved for the first stage of these catchment projects. Cohesion applications have also been submitted for a number of other catchments. Ongoing assessment of the impact of the sewage investment in the catchments, as well as the identification of other point and diffuse sources of pollution, will be carried out through the implementation of monitoring and management programmes, for which Cohesion funding has already been secured for a number of catchments. Provision will be made for the involvement of relevant interests in the preparation and implementation of these projects, so that the necessary cross-sectoral approach will be ensured.

- An updated methodology for the preparation of water quality management plans is currently being prepared by the EPA. This will be utilised to review all water quality management plans over the next five to ten years.

- A thorough review of discharges to waters will be undertaken by the EPA to assess, in particular, discharges of nutrients and of toxic and persistent substances. This will be completed by 1998.

- A national groundwater programme will be established under EPA coordination to quantify groundwater resources, establish their current quality status, and make recommendations for their protection and sustainable use for water supply purposes.

- Marine discharges of all dangerous substances, in particular organohalogens that are persistent, toxic and bioaccumulative, will be reduced by the year 2000 (as required by the OSPAR Commission) to levels which will not harm the marine environment.

- The achievement and maintenance of full compliance with statutory water quality objectives and standards for drinking waters, bathing waters, groundwaters, shellfish waters, freshwater fish and wastewaters will be pursued by public authorities, particularly through legal enforcement.

- R&D activity will be harnessed to increase understanding of natural processes and to study the impact of human activities on water resources.

The above measures will be complemented by action in the agriculture sector, in particular in regard to nutrient management planning, the promotion of the *Code of Good Agricultural Practice to Protect Waters from Pollution by Nitrates*, and adherence to revised phosphorus and nitrogen application rates for grassland to reduce losses contributing to eutrophication (see also Chapter 5).

Water Services

During the 1990s, the Government's objective for the provision of water services has been to ensure that adequate, environmentally well-managed water and waste water services are generally available to domestic users and to support economic development. This objective is being achieved through a significant increase in the annual capital allocation by Government for water services, from a base of £74.5 million in 1992 to an estimated £155 million in 1997, an increase of almost 110%. The allocations for 1998 and 1999 will be significantly higher based on the level of Cohesion Fund commitment remaining to be allocated to water services schemes. The emphasis on the achievement of this objective will be maintained, with a particular focus on cost and environmental efficiency, and on resource conservation. At the same time, it is recognised that the water services capital programme must be progressively increased to provide the infrastructure required into the next century. Investment will be increased to £180-£200 million a year over the period 2000-2005.

- The programme for providing improved services for wastewater collection and disposal and for treatment and disposal of sewage sludge will be continued. This programme is aimed at attaining compliance with the requirements of the Urban Waste Water Treatment Directive[4] and the implementing Regulations.

- Secondary sewage treatment is being provided for all qualifying discharges to rivers, estuaries and coastal waters. Where necessary, the level of treatment will be extended to include nutrient reduction or tertiary treatment, particularly in the case of discharges affecting lakes which are subject to eutrophication. The investment programme will also ensure that Ireland's excellent record under the Blue Flags for Beaches scheme is maintained.

- Alternative sludge treatment and disposal facilities will be provided in Dublin to allow the dumping of sludge at sea to be ended by December 1998.

- Continued improvements in the quality of public and group water supplies will be pursued to further increase the levels of compliance with drinking water quality standards for all health-related parameters.

- Public investment in water supplies will be maintained to meet economic development, domestic and environmental needs. This will include phased implementation of a number of large-scale projects such as the Dublin Water Strategy.[5]

- In recognition of the need for active leakage control, and a more intensive focus on water management and conservation by local authorities generally, the Department of the Environment is developing a programme for the promotion of water conservation. This includes:
  - a requirement for a "water audit" as part of all water supply capital projects;
  - capital funding for water conservation projects including active leakage reduction, infrastructure such as district metering, telemetry, GIS systems, as well as training; and
  - a commitment by all local authorities to long-term active leakage control.

  Guidance on water conservation and leakage detection will be provided to local authorities.

- Pricing policies will be developed to promote conservation by major industrial and commercial water users.

The Coastal Zone

Extent and quality

The coastline of the State, including its islands, is approximately 7,100 km in length. Around 3,000 km are classified as soft, including sandy beaches and glacial cliffs, and some 1,500 km of these are at risk from coastal erosion.[6]

The coastal zone, a highly productive ecosystem, is susceptible to pressure from development and encroachment, pollution, increasing recreational and tourism use, competition for space and over-exploitation of marine resources, as well as erosion. It is an area which requires special attention in order to promote its sustainable use through the balancing of the various demands on coastal resources.

Strategic concerns

This Strategy recognises:

- the ecological wealth and sensitivity of the coastal zone;
- the need for integrated assessment of coastal zone development issues;
- the diversity of habitats, and of development uses, in the coastal zone; and
- potential threats to sustainable development in the coastal zone.

"[This] vital zone ... holds the vast majority of our Important Bird Areas along with 64 species of conservation importance and five Annex I Habitats under the EU Habitats Directive."

- Irish Wildbird Conservancy[7]

Current actions to protect and secure sustainable development of the coastal environment are wide-ranging and include:

- selective investment in coastal protection works under the *Environmental Services OP*[8];
- major ongoing investment in the treatment and disposal of coastal sewage discharges;
- participation in programmes to meet obligations under international conventions (including MARPOL and OSPAR), and bilateral cooperation with the UK in regard to Irish and Celtic Sea issues;
- designation and protection of coastal habitats and biodiversity;
- legislative protection through the Foreshore Acts, which are one of the primary means of ensuring orderly and environmentally acceptable development in the coastal zone; and
- legislative developments, and measures to protect and improve coastal and estuarine water quality, as outlined in the above section on water resources.

"Generally we are not dealing with a single pressure on a resource, but with a mosaic of pressures, some enforcing each other, some cancelling each other out, some combining in a synergistic manner. Yet in our research or management plans, we tend to focus only on one, or a select number of these pressures."

- K. Dubsky[9]

Coastal zone management strategy

The coastal zone is on the one hand relatively fragile, with many resources which are non-renewable, and on the other hand intensively populated and highly attractive to development. There is considerable scope for conflict and competition between coastal zone uses. A coastal zone management strategy study, commissioned by the Departments of the Environment, the Marine, and Arts, Culture and the Gaeltacht to make recommendations for a national policy for the coastal zone, will be completed shortly.[10] There will be a public consultation process, leading to the initiation of a strategic approach to a comprehensive national policy for the sustainable use of the coastal zone, covering such areas as:

- marine environmental protection and resource management;
- development, planning and land use;
- coastal protection; and
- conservation of habitats and biodiversity.

Landscape and Nature

Key Considerations

In Ireland, as elsewhere in Europe, few areas of truly natural habitat remain, as the landscape and ecosystems have been altered by centuries of human activity, affecting the survival, condition and distribution of plant and animal species. Increasing development throughout the 20th century has placed greater pressure on environmental resources and put in question the balance between resource use and conservation. Sustainable development now requires a new relationship between human activity and the natural world.

The EPA has assessed Ireland's record in protecting its natural heritage over the past decade as *"satisfactory but with room for improvement"*.[11] There are many threats, including those from pollution, over-exploitation, destruction of habitats, erosion, drainage, the location and nature of development activity, urbanisation, and conflict related to sporting and recreational uses. Key

concerns now are to:
- define a comprehensive policy with regard to natural heritage and biodiversity;
- protect the quality of landscapes, ecosystems, habitats, species and genetic resources;
- achieve better integration between natural heritage concerns, physical planning and sectoral development policies; and
- improve knowledge and information on the quality and condition of endowments and on nature protection and conservation requirements.

In meeting the above concerns it is important to recognise that:
- nature extends beyond boundaries; while the designation of areas for special protection purposes fulfils an essential function it should be complemented by wider protection and conservation activity;
- some impacts are unavoidable, but can be minimised by
  - applying sustainable development principles,
  - securing sustainable use of resources,
  - promoting a full appreciation of what is rare and priceless in the natural world, and
  - use of the precautionary principle; and
- the natural heritage is everyone's heritage, and its protection and conservation depend on action by, and the behaviour of, communities and individuals, as well as Government, public authorities, and economic actors.

Promotion and appreciation of the national heritage is now reinforced by the functioning of the Heritage Council, established under the *Heritage Act, 1995*.

Actions and priorities

The primary statutory support for habitat and nature protection has been the *Wildlife Act, 1976*. The *Fisheries Acts, 1959 to 1995*, also play a significant part in the protection of fish species. A Wildlife (Amendment) Bill, currently being drafted, will be introduced in 1997 to update national law, and in particular to provide a statu-

tory basis for Natural Heritage Areas (NHAs). The Department of Arts, Culture and the Gaeltacht has prepared draft NHAs which will be taken into account by planning authorities when considering planning applications in/adjacent to NHAs, and which are included in REPS, allowing increased grant-aid to applicants whose lands are within the NHAs.

Council Directive 92/43/EC on the protection of natural and semi-natural habitats and of wild flora and fauna has also been transposed into Irish law by the *European Communities (Natural Habitats) Regulations, 1997*. The Regulations will allow for the definition and protection of approximately 400 proposed Special Areas of Conservation (SACs), covering 550,000 hectares or some 5% of land area. Irish SACs will form part of the European-wide programme *Natura 2000*, which seeks to protect the best remaining examples of national and European natural heritage. Areas in the Burren, blanket bogs, heaths and upland grasslands account for over two-thirds of the land area to be included in SACs. The areas involved will be farmed in a sustainable manner, with certain restrictions related, for example, to stocking levels and the prevention of drainage, and with appropriate compensation to farmers for loss of income and additional costs. Many sites have also been designated as Special Protection Areas required under the Birds Directive for the conservation of certain bird species and their habitats, and further sites will be designated.

A new National Parks and Heritage Bill will be published in 1997, to provide statutory recognition for national parks, national historic parks and national gardens. Policy and objectives in these areas are being reviewed and management plans for their sustainable development and use are being prepared.

Many programmes for the conservation of biological diversity are already in place. Ireland ratified the UN Convention on Biological Diversity in March 1996.[12] A National Biodiversity Plan to reflect its requirements on the conservation and sustainable use of biological diversity, and draw together all of the policies and programmes which already contribute to its objectives, is being prepared by the Department of Arts, Culture and the Gaeltacht. This will reinforce sectoral integration requirements, and make specific recommendations for national action to conserve biological diversity and use its components in a sustainable manner. Some examples of threats to biodiversity are indicated in Fig 2.1. The Plan will be published in 1997.

Measures under physical planning legislation are also critical in the protection of scenic landscapes and natural features. Planning authorities should give wider consideration to the desirability of making Special Amenity Area Orders (SAAOs) in appropriate cases, to protect areas of outstanding natural beauty, of special recreational value, and in the interests of nature conservation. An SAAO outlines a planning authority's reasons for protecting the area in question. Many developments which are exempt under the Local Government (Planning and Development) Acts and regulations require planning permission in an SAAO. The Department of the Environment will issue planning guidelines on the protection of high amenity landscapes.

While ongoing research and information activities are outlined in *State of the Environment in Ireland*, significant gaps are also identified. Knowledge is fundamental to the sustainable management and use of the natural heritage and the conservation of biological diversity. This information base depends, among other things, on:
• good inventories of ecosystems, habitats, species and genetic diversity, and linkage of these to environmental and sectoral data systems;
• understanding of ecosystem structure and functions, and of the impacts of human activity;
• assessment of carrying capacity for habitats

and scenic areas; and
• long-term monitoring of biodiversity trends and identification of early warning signs of unsustainable trends.

These issues will be more fully dealt with in the Biodiversity Plan, which will identify priorities in that area and provide appropriate funding mechanisms.

Waste Management

"While the generation of waste is an inevitable consequence of domestic and economic life, it is now well recognised that the quantities of waste produced by developed countries, including Ireland, are unsustainable."
- Environmental Protection Agency[1]

Waste management policy and instruments
Irish waste policy, in line with the EU approved hierarchy of waste management options, seeks to promote waste prevention, reuse and recycling, and to apply high environmental standards to waste disposal activities. A range of instruments and measures has been developed to promote a more sustainable approach to waste management, including:
• the *Waste Management Act, 1996*, which
  - provides a comprehensive statutory framework for the management of waste,
  - places an obligation on agricultural, commercial and industrial operators to take all reasonable steps necessary to prevent or minimise waste arising from their activities or products, including steps to be taken at design stage of a product,
  - provides for a wide range of measures to be applied to promote and support waste recovery,
  - prohibits the holding, transport, recovery or disposal of waste in a manner which causes or is likely to cause environmental pollution,
  - provides for the establishment by EPA of a Toxics Release Inventory, and
  - provides for penalties of up to £10 million and 10 years imprisonment and for liability for clean-up costs;

- the introduction of Integrated Pollution Control licensing under the *Environmental Protection Agency Act, 1992*, which applies to certain waste activities and places emphasis on waste minimisation for all licensable activities;

- the adoption of a Government Strategy *Recycling for Ireland*[14] in 1994, which established targets for waste recovery up to 1999;

- the establishment of REPAK[15], an industry sponsored initiative for the coordination and financing by industry of systems for recycling packaging waste (see also Chapter 9);

- the provision of £18.4 million in grants, cofinanced by the EU under the *Environmental Services OP*[16], to assist better waste planning and the provision of facilities for waste recovery and hazardous waste management; and

- publication of a report by the ESRI on the economics of solid waste management.[17]

Strategic objectives

"....our growing waste mountains are in many ways a reflection of the considerable economic growth of recent decades but they are not a necessary part of industrial progress."

- John Dunne, Director General, IBEC[18]

Waste is one of the most problematic areas of modern environmental management. The issues associated with its generation and disposal are inextricably linked with present-day economic activity, industrial development, lifestyle and consumption patterns. In working towards more sustainable practices, the acceptance of appropriate responsibility on a shared basis of all sectors of society will be a major general objective. Particular objectives will include:

- a stabilisation and reversal of the growth in waste production; there is some evidence that waste quantities in Dublin have already stabilised - in the short term, to 1999, the goal is to stabilise municipal waste arisings generally at 350 kg/year *per capita,* and in the longer term, to 2010, to reduce these wastes by 20%, for example, by regulation and cost internalisation;

- reuse and recycling activity will be intensified as far as is practicable, both through application of producer responsibility (as evidenced,

for example, by REPAK) and measured actions by public authorities (see Fig 13.1) - the current overall objective of diverting 20% of municipal waste from landfill, by recycling, by 1999 will continue to be pursued, and higher targets will be established for subsequent years, including an increase from 27% by 2001 to at least 50% in the recovery rate for packaging waste by 2005;

- the improved planning and organisational arrangements, provided for in the *Waste Management Act, 1996*, will be implemented quickly;

- higher environmental standards will be applied to landfill and other waste disposal operations by a new licensing system to be operated by the EPA; this will be commenced from 1 May 1997 and applied progressively;

- better waste statistics will be compiled (a process already underway with the publication in 1996 of the EPA *National Waste Database*) to provide more reliable baseline data and to measure performance in future years;

- greater emphasis will be placed on the scope for action by all consumers to minimise waste, and to use recyclable products; and

- the use of economic instruments to reduce waste, promote reuse/recycling, and increase management efficiency will be explored; already a deposit refund system is to apply to the sale of farm plastics.

Fig 13.1 Alternative Waste Disposal

As an example of the options available, Limerick Corporation is developing a system to direct organic waste (some 40% of municipal waste) from landfill to composting. The system will involve the operation of a segregated waste collection system and a major composting facility. Grant assistance from EU Structural Funds for capital expenditure is being funded under the *Operational Programme for Environmental Services, 1994-99*.

Current Government policies in respect of hazardous and clinical wastes will be continued:

- primary responsibility for proper treatment of hazardous waste will continue to lie with the holder and/or producer of the waste;
- EU co-financed assistance will be provided for hazardous waste management facilities which are available to multiple users; however, as already announced, Government assistance will not be provided for contract hazardous waste incineration facilities;
- non-incineration facilities will replace older incinerators for healthcare risk waste; and
- planning, enforcement and other functions in relation to hazardous waste are assigned to EPA under the *Waste Management Act, 1996*.

Waste has also been identified as a priority area for the development of indicators to measure progress in prevention, reuse/recycling and safe disposal. Taking account of EPA recommendations in this regard, some waste production and disposal trends are identified in the tables in Appendix I.

Waste management and BSE

Major challenges were presented to the meat industry in 1996 arising from concerns associated with BSE. Waste management implications have been assessed, so that the arrangements for control of rendering and, in particular, of specified risk material (SRM) (comprising the brain and spinal cord from cattle and sheep and representing some 8% of total offal), are satisfactory in relation to environmental protection.

The waste management strategy in relation to offal includes the following elements:

- all rendering plants which produce meat and bone meal (MBM) for use in animal feedstuff are to be upgraded urgently to operate high-pressure batch systems;
- all SRM will be processed into MBM at a dedicated rendering plant; this MBM can be safely stored without risk to public health or the environment pending destruction;

- in the short-to-medium term, MBM containing SRM will be held in secure storage in Ireland pending disposal in appropriate facilities abroad; and
- the cost of removing and destroying SRM is expected to be met by the meat industry.

Strategic waste management requirements will continue to be assessed in light of the developing situation and of new information emerging in relation to treatment of this waste stream.

Air Quality

"Given Ireland's small population and lack of heavy industry, the level of pollutant emissions is low compared to most European countries. Irish emissions of those pollutants receiving most attention, e.g., SO_2, NO_x, and CO_2, account for typically one percent of the respective totals for EU countries as a whole. Trends in emissions in Ireland are broadly similar to those in other countries and there is general compliance with emission limits imposed by a variety of international emissions reduction agreements."

- Environmental Protection Agency[17]

Overview

State of the Environment in Ireland and the EPA's *Air Pollutants in Ireland, 1984-94*, have provided an up-to-date assessment of air quality in Ireland, concluding that:

- national emissions of some pollutants and greenhouse gases, including carbon dioxide (CO_2), are increasing, but there have been notable reductions in the case of others, such as sulphur dioxide (SO_2), carbon monoxide (CO) and smoke;
- there has been very little overall change detected in annual mean deposition of air pollutants over recent years; and
- road traffic has become potentially the greatest source of air pollution generally, and attention must focus on traffic related pollutants as a new challenge in terms of air quality control. This is notwithstanding the fact that Ireland is relatively unaffected by transit traffic which is a significant factor in increasing vehicle emissions in countries of continental Europe.

Strategic objectives

Good air quality is essential to human health and well-being. Air quality and emissions are also important influences on the condition of ecosystems and on the built environment. While substantial national legislative controls are in place, the transboundary and global impacts of air emissions require that many abatement strategies must be pursued by international cooperation. As part of this Strategy the Government will:

- maintain, and if possible improve, local air quality, particularly in urban areas, so as to minimise any health risk to the urban population and improve the quality of urban living; and

- ensure that Ireland meets international obligations on air quality and is active in support of international action in relation to climate change, ozone depletion and transboundary air pollution.

These objectives will be addressed substantially through strategic action in the energy and transport sectors. The following measures will supplement that action.

Urban smoke control

Apart from transport, the major threat to urban air quality has been the burning of coal for domestic heating purposes. Serious smoke pollution in Dublin, with regular breaches of air quality standards, led Government in 1990 to ban the sale, marketing and distribution of bituminous coal in the built up area of Dublin. While no other urban area has developed air pollution problems to this degree, a similar ban was extended to the Cork City area in 1995 when it became clear that air quality standards were being approached, though not exceeded.

The Minister for the Environment, in association with the EPA and the relevant local authorities, will continue actively to respond to threats to air quality deriving from the use of coal. The monitoring process will be maintained, and all necessary measures taken to address any developing air quality problems.

Low level ozone

Low level, or tropospheric, ozone is formed via a photochemical oxidation process; nitrogen oxides (NO_x) react with volatile organic compounds (VOCs) in the presence of sunlight to produce ozone. The ozone precursors (NO_x and VOCs) are emitted during fossil fuel combustion and various industrial processes. Transport and power generation are the main sources of NO_x while transport and solvent use are the main sources of VOCs.

Low level ozone is now monitored at six sites nationally, and arrangements are in place for the issuing of public warnings by Met Éireann during ozone pollution episodes.[20] Marginal exceedances of the EU population information threshold of $180\mu g/m^3$ occurred at three stations (Cork, Monaghan and Kilkenny) in the untypical hot summer of 1995, but there were no exceedances of the population warning threshold of $360\mu g/m^3$.

The meteorological conditions which can lead to enhanced production of ozone in Ireland also favour the transport of ozone and its precursors from other parts of Europe. Because of this, in developing abatement measures, strategic attention centres on international actions in both EU and UN ECE frameworks to reduce precursor emissions, mainly from transport and power generation.

In addition, eight countries in North-Western Europe, including Ireland, have agreed to cooperate on forecasting, public information and advice, and on a range of short and long-term precursor abatement measures to deal with the particular circumstances of ozone formation in their countries. As part of this agreement, Ireland and the UK will share ozone monitoring sites, exchange monitoring data on a real time basis and cooperate in forecasting ozone episodes.

Acidification

Sulphur dioxide (SO_2) and nitrogen oxides (NO_x) are the main precursors of acid rain. The deposition of these pollutants is low over most of Ireland, but significant in some eastern areas.

Acidification is not, so far, an appreciable problem overall in Ireland, and there is little change in annual mean deposition amounts of emissions. There is an identified need for more study of the impacts of acidifying depositions, and this is being taken into account in the EPA's new national air quality monitoring programme. Under the *Environmental Services OP*, a research project on the determination and mapping of critical loads for sulphur and nitrogen, as well as critical levels for ozone, is also being undertaken.

As in the case of ozone, acid deposition has a considerable transboundary aspect. At least 50% of the annual deposition of sulphur and up to 90% of nitrate are imported into Ireland from other countries. Ireland, therefore, will continue to participate actively at EU and UN ECE levels in the development of abatement strategies.

Ambient air quality

An EU framework Directive on ambient air quality has now been adopted. This Directive will lead to a series of subsidiary Directives which will not only impose stricter standards for pollutants, e.g. NO_x, already the subject of regulation, but will also, over time, extend regulation to a wide range of other pollutants (see also Chapter 10).

Ireland is supporting the development of these new air quality standards and, in parallel with this process, the EPA is preparing a national air quality monitoring programme.

The new Directives are likely to feature a requirement that the public be informed when certain pollution levels occur, as happens already in relation to low level ozone. This will represent a significant strengthening of public involvement in air quality issues.

Chapter 14
Spatial Planning and Land Use

"Land is subject to many competing uses or functions and, being a finite resource, conflicts often arise between them ... The way that land is used has a primary influence on the type of pressures which are allowed to act on the environment."

- European Environment Agency[1]

Role of Land Use Planning

Urban and rural landscapes are constantly changing as a result of the interaction between the natural world and human developments. Spatial planning and land use policies, which of necessity have long time frames, seek to promote orderly development to:

- ensure that the use of land as a resource has regard to the common good;
- meet the needs of society for housing, food and materials, economic and social infrastructure, places of work, amenities and recreational facilities;
- support socio-economic policies concerned with, for example, balanced regional development, social integration, urban renewal and the maintenance of strong rural communities; and
- balance competing needs and prevent and minimise adverse impacts of human activities on the environment.

Land use planning can support the objectives of sustainable development in a number of ways:

- efficiency in the use of energy, transport and natural resources may be encouraged through the careful location of residential, commercial and industrial development, and controls on the shape, structure and size of settlements;
- the planning process can also promote the most effective use of already developed areas;
- the protection and enhancement of the natural environment, including unique or outstanding features, landscapes and natural habitats can be secured; and
- new development needs can be accommodated in an environmentally sustainable and sensitive manner.

The pattern of land use and the shape of the landscape are being influenced by many forces, including changing agricultural practices, increased afforestation, the continuing expansion of urban settlements, one-off rural housing, increasing private car ownership, increased tourism activity, new forms of commercial and business development, coastal erosion and mineral extraction. Visual amenity is also being affected by many forms of development and the location of infrastructure, including electricity transmission, telecommunications masts and new renewable energy generation methods such as wind farms.

Sector specific issues associated with the integration of sustainable development concepts and land use policy are discussed in the relevant sectoral chapters of this Strategy. In addition, however, it is important that this Strategy should ensure that planning and sustainable development policies are consistent and mutually reinforcing.

The Development Plan

Physical planning policies and controls have in fact a longer established history in Ireland than environmental regulation and remain one of the principal instruments of environmental protection. The very title of our physical planning legislation - the *Local Government (Planning and Development) Acts, 1963 to 1993* - foreshadows the concept of sustainable development by acknowledging the need for development in equilibrium with the local environment. The physical planning system has also been extremely important in Ireland in encouraging and facilitating public awareness of environmental issues and public participation in them.

The statutory framework for land use planning involves a responsibility on each local authority (County, County Borough, Borough and Urban District Council) for the determination of policy in its area through the development plan, and for applying that policy, through planning control, in deciding on planning applications and enforcing planning decisions.

The development plan is intended as the main policy instrument for ensuring proper planning and development. While considerable scope already exists for reflecting sustainable development objectives in the development plan process, a new sense of direction and stronger policy integration are needed. The following initiatives will support and complement the implementation of this Strategy:

- planning and development legislation will be amended to require planning authorities expressly to take account of sustainable development considerations in the elaboration of their development plans. The amendment will be designed to exert a practical influence on the delivery of sustainable development policies in the economic sectors and in respect of the built and natural environment;

- to promote understanding of national policy priorities, encourage consistency of approach and raise awareness, the Department of the Environment will continue the publication of its series of Land Use Guidelines for planning authorities, developers and the public. Guidelines on the planning aspects of wind-farms[2] and of telecommunications antennae and support structures[3] were finalised in 1996. Draft Guidelines on forestry development[4] were published in January 1997, for public consultation, and further drafts on high amenity landscapes, the scope and content of development plans, and archaeology will also be issued for public consultation in 1997. Priorities for further Land Use Guidelines will be kept under review and will include the operation of development control and enforcement, and protected habitats;

- in forthcoming Guidelines on the scope and content of development plans, planning authorities will be encouraged to take a more

strategic view of settlement patterns, development needs and major infrastructural services, combining, in an appropriate manner, the statutory five yearly review of the development plan with a coherent longer-term rolling plan. State funding for infrastructure development will not be provided in the event of overzoning, to avoid excessive suburbanisation and inefficiencies in the use of land, energy and transport;

- under the Programme for reform of local government, *Better Local Government - A Programme for Change*[5] (1996), Regional Authorities will be assigned a role in setting out strategic planning guidelines to be respected by the constituent local authorities in drawing up their development plans. This process is intended to start with the Dublin and Mid-East Regions; and

- greater recognition will be given to the quality and character of the countryside. Sustainable development of rural areas involves respect for nature and natural systems, conservation of habitats, species and features of ecological interest, and protection of the environment, as well as the creation of economic opportunity and the maintenance of social fabric. The relationship between the development plan and other forms of special designation, such as Natural Heritage Areas or Special Protection Areas, will be clarified in the forthcoming Bill to amend the *Wildlife Act, 1976*.

Development Control

The development control functions exercised by planning authorities and An Bord Pleanála impact on land use management on a day to day basis. The system is designed to ensure timeliness, good quality decisions, public participation, openness and proper enforcement. The system must, however, remain responsive to change and in this regard, a review of development currently exempted from development control will be carried out.

The use of land for agriculture or forestry is, in general, exempted development under the Local Government (Planning and Development) Acts and therefore not subject to planning permission. However, a development for which an Environmental Impact Assessment is required - at present, afforestation exceeding 70 hectares - requires planning permission. Certain types of smaller agricultural buildings are also exempt subject to conditions regarding restrictions on size and distance from public roads and from houses, schools and churches.

Agricultural activities have been one of the main determinants in shaping the landscape in terms of field patterns, walls, hedges and woodland. While it would not be feasible to bring day to day agricultural activity within the development control system, it will be appropriate to review the exemption for agricultural activities to ensure that its extent and scope are compatible with sustainable development. For example, the physical planning implications of agri-tourism need to be considered to ensure that, where necessary, such developments are brought under planning control.

Environmental Impact Assessment

Environmental Impact Assessment (EIA) for major developments is now an integral and valuable part of development consent and land use management procedures. In transposing the EU Directive on EIA[6], Ireland established thresholds for all project categories (whether mandatory or discretionary in the Directive) at levels which reflect national environmental conditions and are comparatively stringent in EU terms. In addition, with very limited exceptions, the planning authority has power to require EIA for projects which fall below the stated thresholds where the authority considers that a development would be likely to have significant effects on the environment.

The exceptions referred to above are afforestation, peat extraction and intensification of agriculture, which, if not subject to EIA, are exempted development under the Planning and Development Acts. While the overall approach has resulted in significantly higher numbers of EIAs being carried out in Ireland per head of population than in other EU Member States, it is recognised that in relation to afforestation and peat extraction the thresholds originally fixed were too high. The threshold for forestry was therefore reduced with effect from October 1996 and it is also intended shortly to reduce the peat extraction threshold.

EIA will continue to play an important part in the approach to sustainable development, through its identification of concerns in the interaction between development and environment and its role in reconciling the socio-economic aspirations of society with the ability of the natural environment to sustain them.

Efforts continue to be made to improve the quality of Environmental Impact Statements (EISs) and of assessment generally. The EPA, in 1995, published *Draft Guidelines on the Information to be Contained in Environmental Impact Statements* and accompanying *Advice Notes on Current Practice*.[7] Following a two-year period of review and evaluation in day-to-day practice, it is the intention of the EPA to issue the Guidelines formally under Section 72 of the *Environmental Protection Agency Act, 1992*. In the meantime, they are of practical use to all involved in preparing and evaluating EISs by providing an agreed basis for determining the adequacy of EISs, within the context of established development consent procedures.

EU Environment Ministers have now reached agreement on a common position on a draft Directive to clarify and strengthen the provisions of the 1985 EIA Directive. It is envisaged that the new Directive will come into force at the end of 1997. The draft Directive provides for the alignment of the Directive, with regard to transboundary environmental impacts, with the *Convention on Environmental Impact*

Assessment in a Transboundary Context[8] - the "Espoo Convention". Ireland will shortly ratify this UN ECE convention.

Strategic Environmental Assessment

The term Strategic Environmental Assessment (SEA) is used to describe the environmental assessment of plans and programmes and can be extended to include the assessment of policies. SEA is, by its nature, a more general assessment than that carried out in EIA which is project specific (see also Chapter 19).

A proposal for a Council Directive on the assessment of the effects of certain plans and programmes on the environment was published by the European Commission in December 1996. The proposal covers land use plans and programmes, including sectoral land use plans in sectors such as transport, waste management, water resource management, industry, telecommunications, tourism or energy. The Department of the Environment is currently assessing the proposal for a Council Directive in consultation with other relevant Departments and intends to adopt a constructive Irish position.

Integrated Pollution Control

Land use planning alone cannot deal with all of the issues relating to the environmental impact of industry and mineral extraction. The increasing complexity of major industrial activities and processes - and of corresponding environmental control possibilities and techniques - have underlined the need also for a more specialised approach to activities involving complex industrial processes or otherwise involving potentially significant impact on the environment. Given the relatively small number of such activities, it was appropriate that specialised expertise for addressing them should be developed nationally through the Environmental Protection Agency, established in 1993, and its Integrated Pollution Control (IPC) licensing system. This approach is now being extended (under similar provisions of the *Waste*

Management Act, 1996) to the licensing of major waste management facilities.

The separation of planning and environmental control functions in respect of activities which require an IPC/waste licence avoids, as far as possible, duplication of effort between regulatory authorities, and gives developers flexibility in regard to the timing of the relevant applications for new development. The arrangements also ensure that the highest standards are applied in controlling potential pollution from new and existing development and they allow a consistent approach to these activities throughout the State.

Unavoidably, however, the separation of planning and IPC/waste licensing procedures may sometimes create an artificial divide when dealing with a project as a whole. It also clearly separates land use considerations, properly a function of planning authorities, from environmental pollution considerations, which, for the relatively small number of complex activities concerned, need more specialist consideration. The operation of these complementary procedures will be kept under review and further adapted, as appropriate, in the light of experience.

Territorial Integration of Sustainable Development

Above all, it should be the function of the physical planning system to achieve integration of sustainable development on a territorial basis. The need for territorially integrated sustainable development is recognised, for example, in the European Commission's Sustainable Cities Project, and the European Sustainable Cities and Towns Campaign supported by major European networks of local authorities, as well as in coastal zone management (see Chapter 13), as a leading strategy for spatial planning in littoral areas. Support for these and other integrated approaches will be provided through the Irish physical planning system.

Chapter 15
The Built Environment

"The overall human settlement objective is to improve the social, economic and environmental quality of human settlements and the living and working environments of all people ... Urban settlements ... generate 60% of gross national product and, if properly managed, can develop the capacity to sustain their productivity, improve the living conditions of their residents and manage natural resources in a sustainable way."

- Agenda 21[1]

Introduction

The built environment both affects and is affected by the natural environment, using water, energy, land and materials, providing goods and services, and, as settlement intensifies, generating increasing wastes and emissions, traffic and noise, and potentially diminishing the quality of life. Urban settlements, however, also offer potential economies of scale, and can achieve environmental and social sustainability, with good planning and design, balanced development and lower consumption of resources. The impacts of economic activity on human settlements are addressed, as appropriate, in the sectoral chapters of this Strategy. This chapter focuses on sustainable development issues associated with the built environment, including urban policy, conservation, quality design, construction and housing.

"We must make, and remake, our built environment so that to shelter, light, heat and cool ourselves does not destroy our planet."

- Architects' Council of Europe[2]

Ireland was one of up to 200 UN Member States and organisations represented at the HABITAT II conference in Istanbul in June 1996, which was devoted to the agreement of a common agenda for the attainment of the objectives of **adequate shelter for all** and **sustainable human settlements in an urbanising world**. The conference gave expression to its agreement through the adoption of the comprehensive **HABITAT Agenda**. The Government is committed to ensuring that its policies in relation to housing and the urban environment take full account of the provisions of this Agenda, and will also work in this regard with EU partners to agree common approaches, where appropriate.

Urban Development

"To avoid unbalanced, unhealthy and unsustainable growth of human settlements, it is necessary to promote land-use patterns that minimise transport demands, save energy and protect open and green spaces. Appropriate urban density and mixed land-use guidelines are of prime importance for urban development."

- HABITAT Agenda[3]

Urban development dynamics have greatly changed in Ireland. In addition to the migration of people from the country to the town, the centres of cities and towns have been subject to depopulation with a consequent fraying of the urban fabric. The trends towards less intensive urban patterns together with the consequent increasing separation between home, work and town centre have exacerbated the growth in private car traffic. This has led to increased energy use and emissions of air pollutants, and has militated against the effectiveness of public transport networks. The following actions will counteract these trends and promote more sustainable development patterns.

- There will be closer coordination of transport and land use planning so as to increase the use and efficiency of public transport, rather than private cars, particularly in the larger cities. The Dublin Transportation Initiative (DTI) noted that:
  "cities which have little or no influence on land use development policies beyond their administrative boundaries experience difficulty in providing high quality and accessible public transport systems within their catchment areas."[4]

- The Department of the Environment will take an initiative to promote higher residential densities, particularly in redeveloping brownfield sites and in proximity to town centres, public transport nodes and access points, in consultation with local authorities, the architectural, planning and auctioneering professions and the house building industry. There has been in recent years an increased emphasis on infill and inner city social housing and the urban renewal incentives have promoted private sector development in designated inner city areas.

- The proposed Department of the Environment guidelines on development plans (see Chapter 14) will stress the need to ensure a clear demarcation between urban and rural land use, to help prevent urban sprawl, encourage more sustainable development patterns in larger settlements, and help maintain the rural landscape.

- Local Agenda 21 initiatives by local authorities can bring together many critical urban policies, which influence sustainable development of urban settlements, including those on housing, environmental servicing, traffic management, open space and parks and recreational and amenity services.

The **Tidy Towns Competition**, for which the Department of the Environment assumed responsibility in 1995, represents a practical opportunity for local people to promote the sustainable development of towns and villages. Following an in-depth review the competition has been given a wider focus to encompass the totality of the urban environment, including wildlife, natural amenities, and landscaping. The Department of the Environment has in 1997 begun to provide a range of support services to assist Tidy Towns Committees in addressing the new criteria.

Urban Regeneration

"The challenge of urban sustainable development is to solve both the problems experienced within cities and the problems caused by cities, recognising that cities themselves provide many potential solutions."

- European Commission, Expert Group on the Urban Environment[5]

The principles of sustainable urban development dictate that there must be continued evolution of policies which seek to bring redundant and derelict land and buildings back into active use.

Returning land and buildings to active use in itself meets sustainable objectives: it reuses available resources, contributes to energy efficiency, sustains the urban fabric, reduces the need to develop greenfield sites, and protects the countryside. Sustainable urban regeneration must go further than this by promoting uses that are supportive of urban life as a whole. Policies for achieving sustainable urban regeneration will have as key elements:

- **Integrated strategic economic and social planning** to link measures and programmes for urban renewal on an integrated basis to address the physical, economic, social and environmental regeneration of urban areas.

- **Ecological principles** will be applied in developing measures for more efficient use of water, heat, energy and light in buildings and to separate and recycle/reuse waste effectively, with increased emphasis on adequate open space for outdoor recreation and on planting and landscaping.

- **Improving accessibility** of areas in need of regeneration which tend to be isolated from mainstream activities in cities and towns: good public transport linkages are particularly important in this regard.

- **Environmental upgrading**: under the Urban and Village Renewal Sub-Programme of the *Operational Programme for Local Urban and Rural Development, 1994-99*[6], investment will continue in a range of measures to promote the rejuvenation of towns and villages, rehabilitate the built environment and restore and conserve important heritage buildings.

- **Design flexibility** so that buildings are designed or adapted in a way which allows for as many uses, and as much flexibility of use, as practicable. Sustainable urban regeneration also requires a high degree of flexibility in the application of zoning and planning policies to encourage a greater range of leisure facilities in town centres, the use of upper storeys for residential purposes and the conversion of out-moded buildings to new uses, e.g. obsolete commercial buildings to residential use. The *Guidelines on Residential Development in Designated Tax Incentive Areas*[7] were aimed at promoting significant improvements in this area. These will be reviewed by the Department of the Environment in the light of experience.

- **Open spaces**: within cities the main justification up to now for retaining open spaces has been to fulfil social functions such as the provision of meeting places, recreation areas, sports and entertainment facilities and general amenity value. While the need for these facilities will continue, open space can also fulfil various environmental functions in terms of surface water management, maintenance of biodiversity and improved air quality. Accordingly, from a sustainability perspective, there is need for a new emphasis on the environmental and ecological, in addition to the traditional social and amenity, roles of open spaces within the urban fabric.

- **Mechanisms and resources to overcome critical barriers** so that planned urban regeneration objectives can be achieved.

- **A partnership approach** involving cross-sectoral consultation and participation between local authorities and business and community interests and representative organisations.

A Consultancy study on the impact, effectiveness and cost of the tax-based urban renewal schemes in designated areas was completed in 1996.[8] The study recognised the value, in terms of sustainability, of renewing inner urban areas. While concluding that the schemes have been highly successful in directing investment towards the renewal of such areas, it recommended an approach to future policy based on the key elements referred to above. A consulta-

tion process in relation to the study has concluded and proposals for future action are being developed.

Following the enactment of legislation by the Oireachtas, the Dublin Docklands Authority is to be established on 1 May 1997, to lead the social and economic regeneration of the Docklands Area of Dublin.

Urban-Generated Housing in Rural Areas

Although the predominant demographic characteristic of many rural areas is one of population decline, leading to vacant dwellings, there is, in some areas, severe pressure of demand for one-off housing to meet the needs of people working in nearby towns and cities. There is also demand to build tourist housing in scenic areas.

Growing demand for housing in the countryside from people working in cities and towns is generally unsustainable because:

- being separated from all other activities which the householder normally has resort to, such as work, shops, schools and entertainment, one-off housing is a large utiliser of energy;
- most one-off houses are served by individual septic tanks, raising concerns for groundwater protection;
- there are increased roads and transport costs; and
- there is a negative impact in terms of the urban fabric of towns.

In general, there must be a presumption against urban-generated one-off rural housing adjacent to towns. The Planning Acts enable local authorities to grant permission for dwellings for certain categories of person whose occupation requires them to be rurally based, thereby catering for genuine needs. However, certain principles should apply to all such development. These include:

- development along national primary and secondary roads should not be allowed for traffic safety reasons;

- the need to preserve outstanding landscapes and views of special importance should be recognised;
- the ability to integrate one-off housing into the landscape should be emphasised, through good design, good use of site and use of appropriate building materials;
- the site should be suitable for sewage disposal and drainage; and
- rehabilitation of derelict houses should, in certain instances, be encouraged as a more sustainable option than the construction of a new dwelling.

Conservation of the Architectural Heritage

As with the natural environment, there is now much greater awareness of the value of conserving our built environment. The refurbishment of older buildings, while ensuring the retention of detail and character, revitalises cities and towns, supporting their aesthetic value and giving them a distinctive identity.

The report of the Inter-Departmental Working Group - *Strengthening the Protection of the Architectural Heritage*[9] - was published in September 1996. The report contains a comprehensive set of recommendations for the protection of the architectural heritage, including recommendations relating to legal, administrative and financial aspects. The Minister for the Environment:

- is now preparing extensive new legislative proposals along the lines recommended in the report; and

- is working with the Minister for Arts, Culture and the Gaeltacht on a joint package of administrative and financial measures to create a fully effective framework for protecting the built heritage.

The proposed legislation will include:
- an obligation on local authorities to maintain a formal record of protected buildings as part of the development plan;
- using the National Inventory of Architecture as a resource for local authorities;
- ensuring that, where a building is protected, the whole of the building, including interior and curtilage, is safeguarded;
- an active role for local authorities in ensuring that protected buildings are not endangered by neglect; and
- provisions in relation to special streetscapes and other features of interest which need to be protected.

The conservation and restoration of urban architecture and heritage buildings has also been addressed in the Urban and Village Renewal Sub-Programme of the *Operational Programme for Local Urban and Rural Development*. The Conservation Measure of this Sub-Programme provides financial support of up to 50% to local authorities, civic trusts and conservation groups to promote various urban conservation measures in towns throughout the country. The series of conservation booklets published by the Department of the Environment in 1996 is proving to be a valuable resource in terms of giving advice on a wide range of conservation issues and setting out principles of best conservation practice.

Following the recent review, additional flexibility in relation to the design and construction of buildings is being incorporated into the Building Regulations. As a result, designers will have the freedom to adopt more sympathetic and appropriate approaches to the refurbishment or conversion of existing buildings. This will, in particular, facilitate the refurbishment or adaptation of architecturally valuable buildings for new uses.

Building Design and Construction

"The basic principles of sustainable design are quite straightforward: minimise artificial lighting, heating and mechanical ventilation; avoid air-conditioning; conserve water; use site and materials wisely; recycle where possible. A great deal can be achieved by intelligent design and without using untried technologies."

— GREEN DESIGN: *Sustainable Building for Ireland*[10]

Buildings consume land, energy, water and materials, and create waste. Sustainable building:

- optimises energy performance and reduces CO_2 emissions through, for example, location to maximise use of natural light and heat, good thermal insulation, and energy-efficient space and water heating;
- uses renewable materials, reduces use of non-renewable materials, and avoids use of synthetic materials which affect indoor air quality or comfort;
- promotes lower consumption of resources through the use of efficient components and fittings, such as low water consuming flush toilets, and water recycling systems in industrial premises;
- is designed flexibly to facilitate adaptation to changing uses in the interests of maximising lifespan; and
- encourages reuse of existing buildings, and of demolition spoil.

The Minister for the Environment launched a wide-ranging strategic review of the construction industry in March 1996. As part of the review, the Minister asked the Strategic Review Committee (SRC) to consider how the industry can optimise its contribution to the goal of sustainable development. Success in this respect will involve balancing the short-term perspective of market forces by the longer-term considerations associated with sustainability. Sustainability principles must underlie the implementation of future strategy for the construction industry.

Energy Efficiency in Buildings

The Building Regulations and the associated Technical Guidance Documents contain advice on how energy conservation requirements should be met. Since the introduction of the Regulations in 1992, insulation levels are estimated to have increased by up to 50%. Overall energy use in new buildings is estimated to have been reduced by up to 20% as a result, generating annual savings of up to £100 (1996 prices) for the average house. It is also estimated that, by the year 2000, the new standards will result in a reduction of about 2% in CO_2 emissions arising from the heating requirements of buildings generally.[11] Further amendments to be made in regard to insulation standards arising from the recent review of the Regulations will yield additional savings in the order of 5% of energy use for space heating in respect of buildings.

The revised Technical Guidance Document will, for the first time, incorporate an optional Energy Rating System for new houses. This provides a measure of the energy requirement for space and water heating for standard conditions of usage and is expressed in terms of the energy requirement per unit floor area. In addition to showing compliance, this rating can be used to convey to house-buyers the advantages of levels of energy efficiency which surpass the requirements of the Regulations. Where the development provides additional insulation, the effect will be clearly shown in an improved rating. Thus, the enhanced energy efficiency is made transparent, providing meaningful information to the potential purchaser and a marketing advantage to the developer. The Irish Energy Centre which was set up to take a lead role in Ireland's energy programme is developing a software package to facilitate the design professions in using the Energy Rating System.

Fifty-eight houses have been completed and a further 500 are to be built as part of a project supported by the EU Thermie initiative to encourage the use of energy-efficient and environmentally friendly building practices.[12] The project involves local authority, voluntary and private housing. The houses are innovative energy-efficient homes, built to give maximum comfort to the occupants and to cause minimum pollution of the atmosphere by incorporating tried and tested modern technologies.

Housing authorities were requested in 1996 to assign a high priority to energy conservation within their housing programmes and to develop and implement an effective energy conservation programme for their housing stock.

Complementary Measures

In order to promote water conservation, the Department of the Environment will formally request the National Standards Authority of Ireland (NSAI) to revise the existing Irish Standard (I.S. 70:1970 - Water-Closet Cisterns for Domestic Use) to make provision for a flush toilet water cistern involving substantially lower water consumption. Following consultation at national and EU level, the revised standard should be operational by the end of 1999.

Ensuring sustainability in the long-term will require the use of a range of measures to complement the regulatory approach and reinforce or, where necessary, correct short-term market forces. In particular, within the framework of this Strategy, measures to be pursued will include:

- encouragement of voluntary codes of practice;
- use of voluntary, or mandatory, environmental performance assessment;
- improvement of scientific and technical knowledge; and
- use of fiscal instruments.

As pointed out in *GREEN DESIGN*[13], *"design for durability is superior to design for recycling. And recycling is superior to waste."*

Sustainable Housing

"The design of the built environment is recognised as having an impact on people's well-being and behaviour and, thereby, on people's health. Good design in new housing and in upgrading and rehabilitation is important for the creation of sustainable living conditions."

- HABITAT Agenda[14]

The basic principles of sustainability in building, referred to above, increasingly inform policy decisions in regard to:
- the design, quality and location of new housing; and
- the maintenance, refurbishment and improvement of the existing housing stock.

In the housing context, the concept of sustainability has a social as well as an environmental dimension. Positive measures to counteract social segregation and to promote tenant participation and involvement contribute to this social dimension.

Fig 15.1 Major Redevelopment for Ballymun

In March 1997, the Minister for the Environment and the Minister for Housing and Urban Renewal announced a major redevelopment of the Ballymun housing estate, costing about £180 million. This will be the central element in an integrated strategic plan for the economic and social development of Ballymun. The tower and spine blocks of flats will be demolished progressively over eight years and replaced with a self-sustaining urban centre for the 20,000 people who will continue to live in, and around, the area. The plan will include arrangements for consultation with, and involvement of, the local community in its implementation.

New Housing

The current high level of house building consumes an estimated 2,000-2,300 hectares of serviced land annually. In recent years, the greater emphasis on infill developments and increased apartment building in the private housing sector has resulted in higher density developments and a considerably more intensive use of land by the housing programme. Apartments currently represent about 20% of new housing completions and around 40% of completions in Dublin.[15] Nevertheless, much of the land absorbed by the housing programme is good agricultural land located on the fringe of urban areas or in rural areas. Housing demand is likely to remain at a high level as, relative to Western European norms, the housing stock is small in relation to the population. Future development must be as prudent as possible in the consumption of land and demand for services.

Local authorities have been requested by the Department of the Environment to develop, as far as possible, infill sites for local authority housing to enable new housing to be integrated with existing communities. This has fundamentally changed the nature of the local authority housing programme.

Existing Local Authority Housing

A number of schemes exist to assist local authorities to improve substandard housing and upgrade the physical environment in certain older local authority housing estates. The most significant of these, the Remedial Works Scheme introduced in 1985, enables local authorities to carry out major improvement works to substandard elements of their rented housing stock, certain pre-1940 dwellings and inner city flat complexes. Since 1985, some 6,500 units have been improved, with capital investment of some £155 million by 1996, and a further £18.7 million has been provided for the programme in 1997.

An Estate Improvement Programme, with £3 million in funding over two years, has been introduced in 1997 arising from the first report of the Ministerial Task Force on Measures to Reduce the Demand for Drugs. This Programme will assist local authorities in tackling environmental and related problems of severely run-down urban housing estates and flat complexes. It will help to eliminate or modify certain undesirable aspects of the design and layout of estates, carry out improvement work to enhance the living environment for tenants and establish

improved estate management arrangements. This new Programme will be focused on "priority areas" in Dublin - both City and County, and in the Cities of Cork and Limerick.

There are a number of important sustainability aspects to these schemes:
- the quality of existing substandard housing is improved and its lifespan expanded;
- environmental improvement works are carried out in conjunction with the structural works to the dwellings, to renew and improve general living conditions and the visual attractiveness of the estate; and
- there is consultation with tenants at every stage of the project and they have a continued participation in management of the improved estate.

The Social Dimension

A strategy to counteract social segregation in housing was first set out in *A Plan for Social Housing*[16] (1991). The policy was to replace the traditional, almost exclusive, reliance on the local authority house building programme as the response to social housing needs with a range of options, including an expanded voluntary housing sector and new measures to assist marginal home owners, such as the shared ownership system.

In order to mitigate the extent and effects of social segregation in housing and to improve social mix, local authorities are encouraged to provide new housing in smaller developments and, where possible, to avoid adding to existing large scale local authority housing estates. They have been requested to:
- consider purchasing existing or new houses, as an alternative to new building by the authority;
- avoid large concentrations of single class houses and encourage the achievement of a good social mix; and
- make existing lands owned by authorities which are suitable for housing available to individuals, voluntary bodies and co-ops.

These policies were further accentuated in the latest housing policy document *Social Housing - The Way Ahead*[17] (1995).

As indicators of the success of these policies:

- less than 10% of new local authority housing built in 1994 and 1995 was on greenfield sites; and
- the purchase of existing housing accounted for over 16% of the total housing programme in 1994, and 23% in both 1995 and 1996.

Fig 15.2 Social Integration in Practice
Housing at South Douglas Road, Cork

A recent housing development at South Douglas Road, Cork, is a good example of how local authorities can influence the creation of communities with a mix of housing tenures.

Cork Corporation, with the National Building Agency, carefully planned the development of a sixty acre site to illustrate the range of housing options that can be successfully achieved in a single location. The northern edge of the site was bounded by existing private housing and new private housing was built on Corporation land to the west. At the southern extremity of the lands, the Corporation provided housing sites at low cost to a voluntary housing agency to develop 30 houses and a community centre. The Corporation developed 104 local authority houses, in four phases, catering for a range of needs by providing two, three and four bedroomed houses, a number of which were specifically designed for people with disabilities. The Corporation also provided low-cost housing sites to persons in housing need and arranged for the construction of 16 houses for sale under the shared ownership system.

Apart from the range of housing to meet different needs, the Corporation provided sites for Nemo Rangers Gaelic Football Club, a running track for Tramore Athletic, public open space, and a playing pitch for the local community school in this location.

Tenant Participation

Sustainability in housing requires tenant participation and empowerment. Good housing management must convey to tenants that they have a genuine stake in their home and in their neighbourhood. Tenant participation has been a notable feature of the voluntary housing Rental Subsidy Scheme since its introduction in 1991. Local authority housing management now involves a greater emphasis on tenant and staff training, and tenant participation, in order to help foster strong communities in local authority housing estates.

A Housing Management Group comprising senior officials of local authorities and the Department of the Environment has been established to identify and promote best practice in the housing management area. This Group has already established a consultation process to enable tenants to contribute to its work. The Group's first Report[18] (December 1996) specifically endorsed the potential benefits of tenant involvement and set out general guidelines on best practice in this area.

Future Housing Policy

For the future, housing policies should continue to develop in a direction which promotes more sustainable settlement formation and building practices, encourages housing that is closer to the centre, which is more amenable to public transportation options and which achieves greater social integration.

Chapter 16
Public Action and Awareness

"For consumers, concern for the environment now transcends the physical surroundings of where they live, to include the food they eat, the products they use, where they go on holiday, and the sort of world their children and grandchildren will inherit."

-Forfás *Shaping our Future*[1]

Introduction/Overview

Individual members of the public often express concern about environmental problems, both national and international. Growing awareness of the implications of climate change and other global environmental issues is paralleled by concern about national developments such as:

- increasing production of waste and the difficulties involved in its disposal;
- the pollution of inland waters by agricultural or industrial emissions;
- the use and depletion of natural resources; and
- the problems of road congestion with resultant air pollution and noise caused by increasing vehicle numbers.

Public concern about the natural environment, and unsustainable practices which threaten or damage it, is well developed in Ireland. However, this concern is not always translated into action at individual and consumer levels to support solutions to these problems.

Large problems are often the sum of individual actions and choices, and can be ameliorated by small, incremental steps which change individual consumer behaviour (e.g. minimising and recycling household waste, leaving the car at home, conserving water and energy). Encouraging and educating consumers on how to take these steps is an objective of Government policy on sustainable development.

"It is on the level on which we lead our daily lives - in the distance and way we must travel to work, in the amount of rubbish we generate - sustainability will stand or fall. And it is to this that we should turn our attention."

- An Taisce West Cork[3]

Fig 16.1 Europeans and the Environment, 1995[2]

Is protecting the environment and fighting pollution an immediate and urgent problem?
- 76% of Irish people said Yes (up from 70% in 1992)

Which should get priority - economic development or environmental protection?
- 68% of Irish people said that while economic development must be ensured, the environment must also be protected (up from 59% in 1992)

"Serious environmental damage", according to Irish concerns, was caused by
- factories which release chemicals into the air and water (68%)
- storage of nuclear waste (48%)
- oil pollution of seas and coasts (44%)
- industrial waste (43%)
- excessive use of herbicides, insecticides and fertilisers in agriculture (37%)
- rubbish in the streets, in green spaces and on beaches (29%)
- sewage (28%)
- air pollution from cars (24%)

Fig 16.2 Consumer Interactions with the Environment

General consumption/purchasing
- consumer demand has the potential to influence significantly the market and production

Energy consumption
- the domestic sector accounts for 28% of energy consumption in Ireland, second only to transport (31%)

Emissions to air
- the domestic sector accounts for one-third of national energy-related CO_2 emissions

Water consumption
- the growing household demand for water, particularly in urban areas, has led to occasional shortages of supply

Transport
- increasing transport volume, including over 990,000 private cars, contributes to traffic congestion

Waste production
- total household waste production is estimated to be over 1,300,000 tonnes per annum - 11.5% of the total non-agricultural wastes in 1995

Consumer Interactions with the Environment
Sustainable consumption

"In a world with finite resources and environmental limits, affluent consumers will need to use less of the world's resources, so other consumers may claim their rightful share of the Earth's resource wealth. Consumption patterns in the Northern Hemisphere need to change so that consumer standards are maintained or improved, while less resources are used and less waste and pollution are created."

- Erna Witoelar, President, Consumers International[4]

The concept of sustainable production and consumption has been referred to in Chapter 9, largely in the context of production. It is, however, also relevant to domestic consumption and consumer demand. Maintaining the choice of a wide variety of goods, available all year round (even if this means importing seasonal foods from the far side of the globe, with significant transport implications) feeds the industrial production cycle. Advertising and marketing strategies suggest that ever more consumer goods are essential for the modern home. Against this background, the purchasing power of the "green" consumer has the potential to be a significant force for sustainability.

Individual action in response to growing awareness of the environmental implications of lifestyle has included the development of **green consumerism**, i.e. discrimination on the part of the consumer in favour of environmentally-friendly products and services. This is particularly evident in northern European countries, where consumers are prepared to pay more for greener (or organic) products or services. The 1995 survey *Europeans and the Environment* concluded that *"changing consumption habits is a step that Europeans are prepared to take to curb or even stop the deterioration of the environment"*.[5] This consumer willingness provides economic opportunities for companies whose products or services have perceived environmental advantages.

The informed consumer can exert considerable pressure on producers, suppliers and retailers regarding the type of goods produced for sale, including their content and method of production, packaging and facilities for disposal. This pressure can affect many sectors of the economy, including agriculture (through demand for organically-produced food), and industry (by demand for longer-life and energy-efficient household appliances, less use of toxic chemicals in products and processes, and less packaging). Consumer pressure can affect services as well as goods, including repair and conversion, transport and tourism. Other areas where consumer behaviour and preferences can influence more sustainable consumption and production include:

- demanding and supporting goods which are less materially-intensive, e.g., products which are eco-efficient in their design and manufacture;
- using durable rather than throwaway products, repairing and recycling goods where possible; and
- leasing, instead of buying, large household appliances, and buying services rather than purchasing goods.

Production and consumption are at the core of present day economic activity, and are the driving forces of modern lifestyles. Ultimately, the end consumers of goods and services can create a major impetus for sustainable development by informed and aware choices. To improve information on the environmental impacts of goods, and reinforce opportunities to choose the most environmentally-friendly goods, the Government will ask the Director of Consumer Affairs to consider new arrangements for providing full and authoritative environmental information to consumers. The Office of Consumer Affairs will also be asked, in consultation with the Departments of Enterprise and Employment and the Environment, to prepare a **Code of Practice** on green marketing, to which producers and retailers may voluntarily subscribe.

The EU Eco-label Scheme was introduced under a 1992 Regulation as an information aid for consumers, setting criteria for categories of products which establish their environmental credentials. To date ecological criteria have been set for 12 product groups: washing machines; dishwashers; soil improvers; toilet paper; paper kitchen rolls; laundry detergents; double-ended light bulbs; single-ended light bulbs; bed linen and T-shirts; copying paper; indoor paints and varnishes; and refrigerators. The EU is committed to the concept as a visible sign to consumers that manufacturers are taking environmental issues into account. The Eco-label Scheme is currently under review and the possibility of extending it to the services sector is being examined.

Energy consumption

The implications for sustainable development of Ireland's increasing energy consumption have already been analysed in Chapter 8. The contribution of the residential sector, at 28% of total energy consumption in 1993, makes it second only to transport as the largest sectoral consumer of energy.[6] The residential sector (including emissions from electricity generation which is consumed in the sector) accounts for approximately one-third of national energy-related carbon dioxide (CO_2) emissions. In effect, Irish homes represent the single biggest contributor to emissions of CO_2, a major factor in global warming and climate change.

The financial costs of domestic energy consumption are illustrated in figures prepared by the Irish Energy Centre; the average household energy bill is estimated at £675 per year (1995 prices), which indicates a total annual energy cost for the 1.15 million Irish homes of over £750 million. The Centre also estimates that average energy costs in an uninsulated house are £2.80 per day, or over £1,000 a year. Simple conservation measures which can save energy, and thereby reduce these costs are outlined in Fig 16.3. The message is clear; energy wasted is money wasted.

Fig 16.3 Examples of Home Energy Conservation Measures

Measure	Typical cost	Typical payback period
Hot water cylinder insulation	£10	2-4 months
Draught-proofing (average house)	£55	1-3 years
Attic insulation (150 mm.)	£135	approx. 3 years
Cavity wall insulation	£300-£500	3-5 years

Source: Irish Energy Centre[7]

The potential for Irish consumers to save energy in the home is also highlighted in an ESRI study on energy conservation in the home, published in 1993.[8] This showed that:

- only 66% of households had attic insulation (described by the Irish Energy Centre as one of the most cost-effective ways of achieving energy savings in the home);
- only 59% had lagged their hot water tanks (which can save 30% of the energy used to heat water); and
- only 32% had double glazing.

While these figures represented an improvement over the position reported by An Foras Forbartha in a previous (1985/86) survey[9], they demonstrate that there is still significant scope for further savings in domestic energy consumption. The savings benefit the consumer financially, while the environment benefits from the effects of reduced energy consumption, including lower CO_2 emissions.

Water consumption

Domestic water requirements are increasing throughout most of Europe. This increase is partly associated with changes in household structure and in living patterns (e.g. the trend is towards smaller households, which tend to be less resource-efficient). Increased availability and use of domestic appliances such as washing machines and dishwashers, arising from improved economic conditions, results in a greater volume of water used and of sewage/waste water produced. Greater emphasis on personal hygiene leads to increased use of water in baths and showers. Gardening practices such as the use of hosepipes and sprinklers also increase pressure on water resources, particularly during summertime when these resources are at their most limited.

"Domestic and commercial water requirements, in urban areas, amount to approximately 250 litres per person per day."

- Environmental Protection Agency[10]

Water losses through leakage and other faults in the supply system have been identified as a major factor in shortages and ability to meet growing demand, as well as an inefficiency in the economics of water supply and treatment. The domestic contribution to these water losses is often underestimated, yet a dripping tap or leaking water fitting can waste many thousands of litres of water in a year. It has been estimated[11] that domestic losses in the greater Dublin area, for example, amount to approximately 5% of total supply. While modest in the overall context of water losses, this represents some 60 litres per property per day. Distribution losses are being addressed by the public authorities concerned. Individual consumers can save water by simple measures such as fixing leaks and dripping taps, choosing more water-efficient washing machines/dishwashers when purchasing these appliances, and economising in the use of water for gardens.

Questions are being raised in a number of countries and organisations - particularly by environmental NGOs - about the possibility of using either untreated or "grey" (recycled) water within the domestic setting. While all water supplied to households meets the high standards specified for drinking water quality, only a small percentage of this water is actually used for drinking or cooking. Most is used for bathing, washing clothes and other goods, flushing toilets and other miscellaneous uses such as washing cars and watering gardens. A dual supply system, which would allow the use of untreated or recycled water for these latter purposes would have the potential to save water and also economise on both the costs of treatment and the use of chemicals. However, a duplicate system would be expensive to install, and might not be economically justifiable. In all likelihood, this is not an option in the short-term. A more practicable alternative would be for consumers to recycle water within their households, for example, by using rainwater and water from washing for garden purposes or for car washing.

Transport

"A cyclist can travel 1,600 miles on the energy equivalent of one gallon of petrol."

- Global Action Plan Ireland[12]

People, as consumers of transport, also have a significant impact on growth in the transport sector and its environmental implications, including energy consumption. With over 990,000 private cars registered at the end of 1995 and car sales in excess of 100,000 units during 1996, private transport is placing increasing pressure on the environment and sustainability, in terms of air pollution, congestion, noise, etc., as detailed in Chapter 10.

Consumer action to ease these pressures can take many forms; transport volume growth can be curbed by the use of alternatives to private cars. These may include:

- **using public transport**, where this is an option. This Strategy places emphasis on better public transport options and traffic management measures, particularly in urban areas;

- **choosing to walk or cycle**, especially for short journeys; where safe cycling facilities are not available, consumers can actively seek them, for example, by participating in the local planning and development process. The Dublin Transportation Initiative set out criteria for the development of cycle facilities and emphasised the importance of creating an efficient and convenient network of such facilities; the basis of their approach was that the overall aim of cycling policy should be to increase the share of travel undertaken by bicycle; and

- **making car-pooling arrangements** with colleagues for commuting to work, with neighbours for school runs or shopping trips, with friends for social occasions; this cuts down on the number of cars on the roads and increases the efficiency of car transport.

Where cars are used, there is also considerable scope for consumers to use unleaded, rather than leaded petrol, and, when buying new cars, to choose more efficient and less polluting models.

Waste

"Almost everybody in Ireland contributes to the growing waste stream and so must bear a share of responsibility for what is produced."

- Environmental Protection Agency[1]

While the contribution of the domestic sector to the overall waste stream, at 11.5% of total non-agricultural wastes, is relatively modest, it is part of the noticeable trend of increasing amounts of waste produced by Irish society. Domestic waste is biogenic in composition and has, therefore, a potentially greater impact on the environment than more inert wastes, such as construction wastes. Domestic and commercial waste increased

by around one-third over the past decade.

A continuing increase in waste production is not sustainable. Improved recycling rates and better disposal practices can reduce environmental impacts, but volume is the first issue for sustainability. Waste minimisation/reduction at source is paramount, followed by recovery, reuse and recycling, with disposal as the final resort.

Previous chapters have addressed wastes produced by the main economic sectors, principally agriculture and industry. However, the role of individual consumers and households in, firstly, minimising waste production, and secondly, reusing and recycling waste material, is also important. At present, only a very low proportion of domestic waste is recycled; the vast bulk of consumer waste goes directly to landfill.

"... it is estimated that, theoretically, between 70 and 80 per cent of the household and commercial waste stream is either recyclable or re-usable. This figure reduces to about 60 per cent when the practical problem of contamination is accounted for."

- Environmental Protection Agency[1]

The national recycling strategy *Recycling for Ireland* (1994) focuses on the possibilities of recycling domestic and commercial waste, and will divert 20% of this waste to recycling by 1999. Government policy is to provide for the supporting infrastructure to meet this target; this includes expanding the number of collection points to a total of 500 multi-material sites, including 20 civic amenity sites for this purpose in the short-term and 75 in the medium-term. Consumers must play their part in availing of the opportunities provided. This consumer support is evident in relation to existing recycling schemes, such as Kerbside in Dublin which now involves some 42,000 households.

Past surveys of public attitudes to the environment have identified litter as a major concern, possibly because it is the most widespread and visual example of waste production. The Government launched the national *Action Against Litter*[15] campaign in 1996, and is committed to sustaining it over the next two years. The campaign is an integrated approach to a key environmental issue which is readily amenable to individual and community action. It includes the promotion of awareness of, and a more responsible attitude to, litter to motivate the public to tackle the problem. Local and national voluntary groups are being invited to participate actively in the campaign, which will also target measures at specific groups such as motorists, shoppers, public transport users and leisure groups.

Legislation will be strengthened; a new Litter Pollution Bill, which will replace the *Litter Act, 1982*, is progressing through the Oireachtas and when enacted, will be vigorously implemented. This will broaden the powers of local authorities to deal with litter polluters and place a renewed emphasis on the responsibility of individual citizens for litter control. Penalties for litter polluters will also increase. Clear goals will be agreed for improving local authority performance in preventing and controlling litter with a strong emphasis on effective enforcement of legislation.

Fig 16.4 Europeans and the Environment, 1995

Within Ireland, the greatest concerns of the respondents were

1. *pollution of rivers and lakes; pollution of seas and coasts; and industrial waste*
2. *harm caused to animals, plants and the natural habitat; pollution of agricultural origin (insecticides, pesticides, slurry, etc.); and risks connected with the use of nuclear power*
3. *air pollution; and possible risks for the environment from the development of biotechnologies*

In the respondents' immediate environment, the greatest causes of complaint were

1. *the amount of traffic*
2. *waste disposal*
3. *drinking water quality*
4. *air pollution*
5. *damage to landscape*

Supporting Consumer Responsibility for the Environment

There is an ongoing need to increase public sensitivity to environment and development problems and at the same time to encourage individual involvement in their solution. Personal environmental responsibility must be encouraged to create greater motivation and commitment towards sustainable development. To achieve these aims, *Agenda 21* set as an objective:

> *"to promote broad public awareness as an essential part of a global education effort to strengthen attitudes, values and actions which are compatible with sustainable development".*[16]

theatre and competitions. The aims of the campaign include raising awareness of local environmental issues, particularly in relation to waste minimisation, recycling and waste management, and serving as a catalyst for permanent changes in attitudes and behaviour. The annual event also helps to instil respect for the environment in participants and can make the introduction of more sustainable policies and practices, such as recycling, more acceptable to consumers.

Fig 16.5 Europeans and the Environment, 1995

What did/would Irish respondents do to protect the environment?

- *avoid dropping paper and waste on the ground (89%)*
- *save energy, e.g. by closing doors/windows and using less hot water (60%)*
- *buy environmentally friendly products, even if they were more expensive (43%)*
- *save tap water (42%)*
- *sort household waste for recycling (39%)*
- *use less-polluting transport than a private car (28%)*

The GAP Household ECOTEAM Programme

... is designed to guide and support individuals in taking effective action for the environment through:

- reducing waste;
- improving water and energy efficiency;
- improving transport efficiency;
- becoming eco-wise consumers; and
- empowering others through home, workplace and community action.

The role of community and environmental groups

Growing environmental awareness reflects local concerns about environmental quality and resources, growing media coverage of the environment and the campaigning activities of community and environment groups. Advances in the understanding of environmental sciences, increased material prosperity and a level of globalisation which underlines the interconnectedness of environmental systems and resources have also contributed to this heightened environmental awareness, which encompasses world environmental issues such as climate change as well as local concerns more directly amenable to individual action.

The *Clean Up The World Campaign*[17] was developed in Australia in 1989, and has operated in Ireland since 1993 under the coordination of the Dublin Healthy Cities Project. Based on the principle of "Think Globally - Act Locally", this initiative unites people in over 1,000 cities around the world in carrying out a simultaneous clean-up of their local environs on one weekend each year. Activities undertaken to date in Ireland have included the clean-up of rivers, woods, beaches and local areas, as well as graffiti removal, tree planting, exhibitions, street

Global Action Plan (GAP) originated in the United States in 1990 to help householders to adopt sustainable lifestyles. The central principle is that individual action can make a difference, and that the actions of individuals are greatly enhanced by teamwork and the provision of proper support structures. People work together in teams of 4 to 10 households and, with guidance, learn simple and practical ways of reducing their impact on the environment by taking action at home and in their community. Teams estimate their impact on the environment before and after the programme by conducting a household audit. GAP is now operating in the United States, the Netherlands, Sweden and the United Kingdom and is being developed in Canada, Belgium, Finland and Poland. The GAP approach has now been launched in Ireland, with the assistance of the Department of the Environment and a number of local authorities, as a practical contribution towards the achievement of Local Agenda 21 objectives.

Local authorities should support similar individual and community activities within their functional areas, which can contribute to enhancing consumer awareness and action achieving sustainable development. The Department of the Environment will develop innovative mechanisms to continue support for specific environmental projects carried out in partnership, including a new Environment Partnership Fund(see Chapter 19).

Environmental awareness and education

"The sustainable future of our cultural and physical life depends upon the education of the public".

- An Taisce West Cork[18]

Progress in solving environmental problems depends fundamentally on the values, attitudes and behaviour of individuals in relation to their environment. These, in turn, can be formed and informed by processes of awareness and education.

Access to environmental information

Environmental education and awareness must be viewed in the broadest context, which includes access to information and the dissemination of information to the public. The informal and non-academic aspect of enhancing environmental awareness in this way embraces the whole population, not just those in formal education. An essential element in encouraging people to change their behaviour is to make information readily available. This will promote understanding of the long-term benefits of environmentally-friendly behaviour maximising the sustainability of our natural resources.

The *Access to Information on the Environment Regulations, 1996,* implement a number of improvements in the statutory guarantee of access to environmental information. In line with Government commitments to improve access to information generally, these Regulations will be reviewed in the context

of the new Freedom of Information legislation. In particular, a system for appeals in cases where access to environmental information is refused will be implemented by the end of 1997. The Department of the Environment will prepare a **Code of Good Practice on Issuing Environmental Information**, for implementing authorities.

The publication in 1997 of the first Pollution Emissions Register, and the making of regulations under the *Waste Management Act, 1996,* to provide for a Toxics Release Inventory (see Chapter 9) will provide additional sources of information relating to the environment. In addition, the forthcoming publication by the Department of the Environment of a comprehensive list of public rights to information from local authorities (in accordance with the commitment in *Better Local Government*) will further enhance access to information.

"The successful implementation of recommendations arising from the Strategy will require the full involvement of the general public. In this regard, the Strategy should lead to the production of a concerted programme of education, training and awareness raising."

- Earthwatch/Friends of the Earth Ireland[19]

ENFO - The Environmental Information Service

Over 345,000 people have visited the headquarters of ENFO since its establishment by the Department of the Environment in 1990.[20] Increasing attendance levels and the volume of queries received are indicators of increasing awareness of environmental issues in the community as a whole and of the success of ENFO.

ENFO provides information to its target groups - the general public, schoolchildren, students, NGOs, and industry and business interests - in a variety of ways, including a query-answering service, information leaflets, a video-lending service, exhibitions, lectures and other activities. The facilities available at the ENFO centre are comprehensive and include an extensive reference database with on-line access to international databases. On-line connections to the ENFO database are also now in place in 36 public libraries, spread over 26 counties, where they are available for use by members of the public. ENFO has also established a site on the Internet.

ENFO will continually review its services, in consultation with its organisational and individual customers, so as to maximise their value and impact. The Department of the Environment will continue to support and develop the role of ENFO as a core resource in the area of environmental awareness building. Measures to be taken in this regard will include:

- accelerating development of the ENFO Internet service, through the further development of an integrated site to include access to the ENFO database and links with the EPA and the European Environment Agency;

- enhancing linkages between ENFO and the County Library Services, replacing the current on-line database access with an Internet-based service and also providing a CD-ROM database service; and

- inviting local authorities to appoint environmental information officers and to draw on ENFO as a key resource in the provision of environmental information.

Environmental education

"Environmental education should be included in, and should run throughout, the other disciplines of the formal education curriculum at all levels - to foster a sense of responsibility for the state of the environment and to teach students how to monitor, protect and improve it."

- The World Commission on Environment and Development[21]

The formal education system also has a crucial role in promoting environmental awareness. The potential of the education system to inform attitudes and behaviour from an early age can be a major force in support of consumer understanding and acceptance of sustainable development.

Environmental education not only promotes more responsible citizens by making them aware of problems but can provide them with the skills to participate in environmental management. This will be assisted by a more practical, dynamic and operational approach to environmental education. The overriding objectives should be to lay the foundations for a fully informed and active participation of the individual in the protection of the environment and the prudent, rational use of natural resources.

Education will continue to play a vital role in protecting the environment and all stages of the formal education system should contain an environmental component. Environmental education can provide a sound basis for sustainable development and it should be integrated into all educational systems. To achieve this the objective should be to:

- make environment and development education available to people of all ages;

- work such concepts into all educational programmes with analyses of the major issues; and

- involve schoolchildren in local and regional studies and activities on environmental issues, and the environmental and economic impacts of resource use.

Even simple activities such as nature walks and nature study tables can be developed to encompass broader issues such as improvements to school premises, gardens and parks, energy saving and recycling. These local projects can be run with the support, financial and otherwise, of the local authorities. In addition, each educational institution should carry out an internal eco-audit.

"In order to ensure the future wellbeing of our total environment, natural and man-made, it is necessary to enlist the support of our children. It is they, and future generations, who will one day inherit the overall responsibility of caring for our environment."

- Report of the Inter-Departmental Working Group on Environmental Awareness[22]

The need to develop identification with sustainable development in children from an early age is recognised. The education system has a key role to play in this process, both in terms of developing a fully integrated environmental dimension across the curriculum and in terms of promoting responsible environmental behaviour among young people in the school and its environs.

A *Green Schools* award scheme is being introduced to Irish schools in 1997 by An Taisce; this is part of a European-wide programme coordinated by the Foundation for Environmental Education in Europe (FEEE). The scheme, which is being run in Ireland in conjunction with local authorities, will be judged on a combination of a school's commitment to environmental education and the greening of the school itself. The Department of Education will, in consultation with the Department of the Environment, support the awards scheme which recognises schools that make a particular effort to support sustainable living.

At the higher educational levels, environmental education can also be effectively implemented through integrating environmental education concepts, skills and strategies throughout the existing general curriculum. This has a two-fold advantage:

• firstly, integration of environmental education would enhance existing programmes without competing for limited curriculum time and resources; and

• secondly, environmental education shares subject content and intellectual processes with many other disciplines such as the sciences, sociology and communications.

The third level sector has demonstrated a strong commitment to maintaining and enhancing environmental quality and a keen interest in responding to the needs of industry in the area of environmental protection and design. Positive action and awareness, understanding, and the protection of the environment are integral to many other areas of study (e.g. CERT and tourism related courses). The sector is also active in the field of environmental research.

The Departments of Education and the Environment will further strengthen bilateral contacts on environmental education matters and will set up a liaison committee to discuss matters of mutual interest. Consideration will be given to appropriate measures relating to curriculum, teacher training (both pre- and in-service) and provision of appropriate resources. In particular, Education Boards and schools will be directed by the Minister for Education to include in their Education Plans and School Plans, required by the new Education Bill, an environment policy statement in relation to the content of educational programmes and the management of facilities. ENFO will be promoted as a key resource and schools will be invited to capitalise on growing IT facilities by linking into ENFO's developing Internet service. Greater links between ENFO and the Regional Education Centres (formerly Teachers Centres) will also be developed.

Corporate citizenship

The need for heightened public awareness of environmental threats and opportunities is as relevant to the corporate as the individual citizen, to Government as to the private sector. All organisations create an environmental impact as corporate citizens of their communities which is distinct from any licensable emissions which may result from their core activities. It is essential, therefore, that awareness of environmental effects among organisations and employees is not confined to the private lives of individuals but extends into their corporate lives. So, for example, awareness of the need to conserve, to reuse and to recycle should be promoted so that it is seen to be as relevant in the workplace as in the private lives of employees. Details of the approach being adopted by Government in relation to its own staff are given in Chapter 19.

Chapter 17
Ireland in the International Community

Introduction

Recent decades have seen intensified international cooperation in relation to the environment; this is now reflected, *inter alia*, in some 180 international conventions relevant to the environment and sustainable development. This international cooperation is driven by increasing concern about global problems (such as climate change, ozone layer depletion, deforestation and loss of biological diversity), as well as by the transboundary dimension of many environmental problems. The environmental impacts of the increasing globalisation and liberalisation of trade (see Chapter 12) also underline the need for global cooperation in relation to environmental protection and sustainable development.

There is a growing emphasis on environmental issues in the work programmes of international organisations, including the United Nations (UN), the Organisation for Economic Cooperation and Development (OECD) and the World Trade Organisation (WTO). Environment policy and legislation have been developing at European Union level for the past 25 years and exert a major influence on environmental standards and objectives at Member State level. In addition, the EU, acting alongside its Member States, plays an influential and progressive role in wider international fora such as the UN Commission on Sustainable Development and OECD.

Active participation in international cooperation for the environment is now an integral part of Irish foreign policy, as set out in Chapter 13 of *Challenges and Opportunities Abroad*[1], the White Paper on Foreign Policy published in 1996. In accordance with the *Declaration on the Environment*[2] adopted by the European Council meeting in Dublin in June 1990, Ireland participates fully in efforts at UN and EU level to combat regional and global environmental problems and to advance sustainable development. Ireland is committed to cooperating in the use of world resources in a manner which benefits both the global environment and the economies of the developing countries.

United Nations

Ireland was one of some 130 countries which participated in the UN Conference on Environment and Development (UNCED) held in Rio de Janeiro in June 1992. At UNCED, agreement was reached on:

- the *Rio Declaration on Environment and Development*, a charter of basic principles for sustainable development;
- *Agenda 21*, a global plan of action to address the challenge of sustainable development into the 21st century, which calls on countries to follow practical action programmes in their own environment and development policies;
- two major new international conventions on Climate Change and Biological Diversity;
- the commencement of negotiations for a convention on Desertification (subsequently adopted, and signed by Ireland); and
- a *Statement of Principles on Forests*, which outlined a number of principles for conservation, management and sustainable development of all types of forests.

Framework Convention on Climate Change

This Convention seeks to address the global threat of climate change, and to develop concerted action to mitigate its adverse environmental, economic and social consequences. All parties to the Convention are required to undertake general commitments, including the preparation of national inventories of greenhouse gas emissions and the adoption of national programmes for mitigating climate change. These obligations have been fulfilled by Ireland, which is also participating in current efforts to strengthen its provisions (see Chapter 8). The Convention entered into force in 1994.

Convention on Biological Diversity

This Convention, which has been ratified by Ireland, aims at protecting global biodiversity. One of the major commitments required of parties to the Convention is the preparation of national plans for the protection of biological diversity; Ireland's plan is currently being prepared by the Department of Arts, Culture and the Gaeltacht and will be completed by end-1997.

Forestry Principles

The statement of principles on forestry, outlined at Rio, is being developed internationally by an intergovernmental panel, established at the third session of the Commission on Sustainable Development. At European level, progress is largely being advanced through the Helsinki process, which commenced at the 1993 Ministerial Conference on the Protection of Forests in Europe (see Chapter 6). Ireland is participating actively in this process.

UN Commission on Sustainable Development

The Commission on Sustainable Development (CSD) was established to promote and monitor effective international follow-up to the Rio agreements. Its work includes international cooperation in such sectors as trade, the environment and sustainable development as well as cooperation in the transfer of environmentally sound technologies. The Commission meets annually to review progress on the objectives agreed at Rio.

Ireland originally attended meetings of the CSD as an observer, but was elected to full membership in 1996, and commenced a three-year term of office on 1 January, 1997. This will enable Ireland to play an important role in formulating policy on the protection of the global environment, and in particular, to participate fully in the preparations for the UN General Assembly Special Session to be held in June 1997 to review progress since UNCED.

Global Environment Facility (GEF)

The GEF is the primary funding mechanism for environmental measures having global environmental benefits, including the areas of climate change, biological diversity, international waters and ozone depletion. It will act as the interim financial mechanism for the Conventions on Climate Change and Biological Diversity. Ireland is committed to subscribing £1.64 million to GEF over the four years which began in 1996.

Other UN developments

Many of the objectives of UNCED have been paralleled and enhanced since 1992 by other major UN conferences which have focused, in particular, on the social aspects of sustainable development. These included the Conference on Population and Development (Cairo, 1994), the World Summit for Social Development (Copenhagen, March 1995) and the Fourth International Conference on Women (Beijing, September 1995). More recently, the Second International Conference on Human Settlements (HABITAT II), held in Istanbul in June 1996, also addressed many related issues. Ireland has participated in all of these conferences, which reflect a growing international awareness of the interdependence of social, economic and political issues and of the links between these issues and sustainable development.

Ireland also participates in **Environment for Europe**, a pan-European cooperation process involving 49 countries, coordinated by the UN Economic Commission for Europe (ECE). Under this process, an Environmental Programme for Europe seeks to improve environmental conditions throughout Europe, and to promote the convergence of environmental quality and policies. At the request of the first Conference of Ministers, held in Dobris Castle in the then Czechoslovakia in 1991, a comprehensive assessment of the pan-European environment was carried out by a Task Force led by the European Environment Agency. Their report, *Europe's Environment: The Dobris Assessment*, published in 1995, assessed the pressures and human activities impacting on the European environment, and analysed prominent environmental problems of concern to Europe as a whole. The next Ministerial Conference in the **Environment for Europe** process will be held in Denmark in May 1998.

Development Cooperation

"It is increasingly recognised that development assistance alone is not enough; development policy must take account of a range of factors including human rights, trade and investment, the arms trade, debt, the role of women, population and the environment."

- White Paper on Foreign Policy[1]

Ireland is currently working towards the UN target of increasing development assistance to 0.7% of GNP.[4] In 1996, Ireland's Official Development Assistance (ODA) programme amounted to £122 million, or 0.31% of GNP. While still below the UN target, this is above the OECD country average of 0.27% of GNP.[5] It also represents a doubling of the Irish aid programme, in relation to GNP, since 1992, when it stood at 0.16% of GNP. The Government is committed to increasing ODA by 0.05% each year in order to meet the UN target.

Ireland's development cooperation objectives are:
- to reduce poverty and promote sustainable development in some of the poorest countries of the world;
- to assist in establishing and maintaining peace in developing counties by fostering democracy, respect for human rights, gender and social equality and protection of the environment;
- to respond promptly to emergencies and humanitarian disasters, both natural and human-made, as they occur, and to support preventive measures so that such emergencies may, so far as possible, be avoided; and
- to contribute to building civil society and social solidarity.

These objectives reflect an overriding concern about sustainability in its widest sense (environmental, economic, financial institutional and administrative). The strong emphasis on the concepts of partnership and participation, with a preference for making the maximum possible use of locally-available resources, is also in accordance with the tenets of *Agenda 21*. The basic objective of these programmes is to enhance the quality of life and productivity of poor people, thereby empowering them to deal with their problems. A key concern is that activities initiated with ODA support should be capable of being integrated into, and sustained by, the local environment. Ireland also supports the efforts being made in international financial institutions to resolve the problems caused by the heavy burden of debt carried by many developing countries.

In 1996, 61% of Irish ODA allocations were targeted to bilateral aid, and 35% to multilateral (including EU) aid; the remaining 4% was accounted for by administration costs and other items.

Bilateral aid

Some 42% of bilateral aid, or approximately one-quarter of Ireland's total ODA, is targeted towards six priority countries (Ethiopia, Lesotho, Tanzania, Uganda, Zambia and Mozambique). This helps to give the ODA programme a clear poverty focus, supporting basic needs (primary health care, basic education and rural infrastructure) and capacity-building at national, regional and, increasingly, at local levels.

Multilateral aid

A significant part of Ireland's ODA is allocated in the form of mandatory contributions to multilateral development and finance organisations; these include the EU, the World Bank Group and the UN agriculture and food agencies. In the case of the EU, Ireland contributes both to the European Development Fund (the funding mechanism for the developing countries of Africa, the Caribbean and the Pacific (ACP) under successive Lomé Conventions) and through the General Budget of the Community to other EU aid activities. Voluntary contributions are also made to various UN development agencies and programmes. Ireland takes a direct interest in the work of these multilateral agencies in order to ensure that they perform effectively and that their funds are used in the most efficient manner possible.

Promoting food security and sustainable agriculture

In 1995, the Irish Aid Advisory Committee (IAAC) initiated a project towards the development and establishment of an agreed policy for Irish Aid in the areas of Sustainable Agriculture, Rural Development and Food Security. In its September 1996 report to the Minister for Foreign Affairs, *Irish Aid and Agriculture*, IAAC recommended, *inter alia*, that the following be adopted as a strategy statement for Irish Aid:

> *"The strategic objective of Irish Aid in relation to food security and sustainable agriculture is to develop programmes and policies in partnership with developing countries so as to contribute to increasing the effective and sustainable use of natural resources in such a way that the food security and livelihoods especially of the poorest in those countries are enhanced; and to develop such programmes in a way that is empowering for the beneficiaries."*[6]

The Government has accepted this recommendation as being in line with official policy.

Countries in transition

Ireland also supports and participates in programmes providing finance and technology transfer to countries in transition, in particular, the PHARE and TACIS programmes. The PHARE programme aims at supporting Central and Eastern European countries to the stage where they are ready to assume the obligations of membership of the EU, by financing environmental and nuclear safety projects. The TACIS programme fosters the development of the New Independent States and Mongolia; it requires the integration of environmental considerations into all sectors, and encourages environmental institutional capacity-building in these countries.

The European Union

The *Treaty on European Union* (the Maastricht Treaty), which entered into force in November 1993, considerably strengthens the capacity of the Union to deal with environmental problems and to promote sustainable development.

The EU has developed a comprehensive policy on environmental protection and sustainable development. The Fifth Action Programme on the Environment, *Towards Sustainability*, adopted in 1993, set out a programme of action, including integration of environmental considerations into all other policy areas, particularly the five key areas of agriculture, energy, industry, tourism and transport, and a broadening of the range of instruments used for environmental protection.

Following the publication of a progress report in January 1996, the EU Commission submitted a proposal for co-decision by the Environment Council and the European Parliament on an Action Plan to intensify the Programme. This was a priority during the Irish Presidency of the EU, and political agreement on the proposal was reached at the Council of Environment Ministers in December 1996.[7]

Intergovernmental Conference

The question of strengthening the environment provisions in the Treaty on European Union (*TEU*) has arisen in the context of the Intergovernmental Conference (IGC), which commenced in March 1996. Both nationally and in its recent Presidential role, Ireland has taken a supportive stance on the strengthening of the *TEU* to improve both the Union's response capacity to challenges to the environment, and its ability to integrate environmental considerations into other policy areas.

Draft texts in this regard were prepared under the Irish Presidency of the EU and were submitted to the Dublin Summit (December 1996). The proposed text would, *inter alia*, make the achievement of sustainable development an explicit objective of the Union. This includes balanced and sustainable economic development, as well as a high level of protection of the environment and improvement of its quality, among the tasks of the Community, and highlight the need to integrate environmental protection requirements into the definition and implementation of all Community policies. Formal negotiations to conclude agreement on revision of the *TEU* are continuing under the Dutch Presidency.

European Environment Agency

The European Environment Agency (EEA), was established in October 1993 to provide objective, reliable and comparable information at the European level, to support policymakers and to provide better environmental information to the public.

Ireland is represented on the Agency's Management Board, and on its Scientific (advisory) Committee. The Environmental Protection Agency acts as the national focal point for the EEA, and has an important coordinating role between the EEA and national networks. Ireland also participates in a number of the European Topic Centres established by the EEA. Teagasc is co-leader of the European Topic Centre on Soil, which was established in 1996. The Environmental Protection Agency is a partner in the Topic Centre on Inland Waters. In addition, Forbairt is a member of ENERO (the European Network of Environmental Research Organisations) which is included in the Air Emissions Topic Centre.

OECD

As part of the Organisation's work, a programme of environmental performance reviews was instituted in 1992, whereby member countries submit themselves for peer review of their environmental policies and performance. While Ireland has assisted in the performance review of other countries, it has not yet been the subject of review. Ireland will invite this OECD review for 1998, if this can be accommodated within the work programme of the Environmental Performance Review Group.

PART 5 - IMPLEMENTING AND MONITORING THE STRATEGY

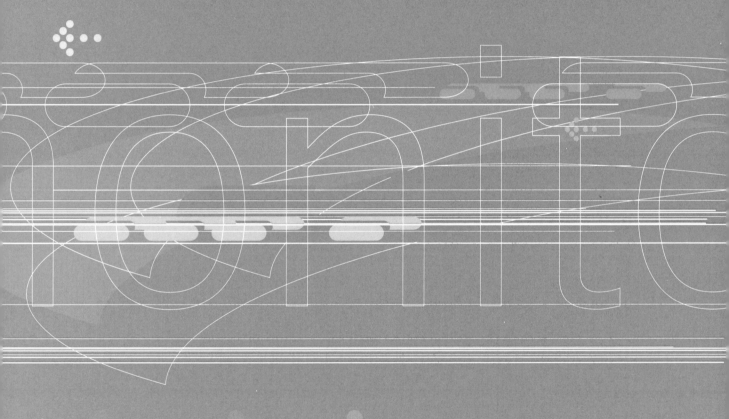

Chapter 18
Monitoring and Indicators

"It is very difficult to derive widely acceptable definitions as to when sustainability has been achieved. But it is possible to identify performance indices which can tell us whether we are moving away from, or in the direction of, sustainability."

- F.J. Convery, "Assessing Sustainability in Ireland - a Synthesis"[1]

Introduction

Sustainable development indicators are a means of measuring progress over time towards, or away from, sustainability. The *Policy Agreement for a Government of Renewal* states the Government's commitment to work towards a new set of indicators of sustainable economic development, taking account of environmental and social factors, and to be used alongside existing measures of economic activity such as GDP.

In declaring this commitment, the Government recognised that conventional measurements of national economic activity and wealth do not consider the environmental implications and impacts of development. There are two aspects to the task set by the Government:

• suitable indicators must be devised; and

• they are intended in the long-term to qualify, from a sustainable development perspective, the standard information of traditional National Accounts.

Both aspects will be developed within the framework of this Strategy.

The Purpose of Indicators

Indicators are a means of assimilating information to improve communication and enable trends to be understood. Several kinds of indicators may be used to fulfil particular functions and measure the quality/quantity of environmental resources:

• state of the environment indicators reflect environmental quality;

• stress indicators reflect development effects; and

• performance indicators may be used to evaluate long-term achievements in environmental management and protection.

Sustainable development indicators introduce a new dimension to the provision of information, in that they seek to describe and measure key relationships between economic, social and environmental factors. In all cases, indicators both quantify and simplify information, thereby making it more accessible to policy-makers and the public.

International Context

Agenda 21 recognised that *"in sustainable development, everyone is a user and provider of information".[2]* Despite the wealth of data and information already in existence, *"finding the appropriate information at the required time and at the relevant scale of aggregation"[3]* was a difficult task. *Agenda 21* acknowledged that institutional capacity to integrate environment and development, and to develop relevant indicators, was lacking at both national and international levels, and advocated that the concept of sustainable development indicators should be further progressed.

Substantial work on the development of indicators has been under way for some time in the OECD, and more recently within the EU, the UN Commission on Sustainable Development and the World Bank. The OECD has identified a Core Set of Indicators on the State of the Environment. Attention is now focusing on the means of defining and measuring indicators which will link economic growth and physical environmental impacts. No single conceptual framework has yet emerged. The UN is seeking to build international consensus on a suitable range of indicators for purposes of *Agenda 21*. While a standard approach would facilitate comparison across countries and maintain a global perspective, indicators must also address national development frameworks, and add value to policy and action in the appropriate environmental and socio-economic contexts.

Alongside this work, it is increasingly recognised that national accounts, which measure the national income from economic activity and do not take account of the environmental implications of that activity, cannot illustrate whether economic growth is sustainable or not. There are, however, substantial difficulties in producing environmentally adjusted, or "green" accounts.

National Context

Apart from national accounts aggregates and standard macro-economic variables, such as GDP, inflation rates, employment levels and balance of payments figures, use of indicators is not well developed in Ireland. Environmental monitoring systems provide quantitative and qualitative information clearly identifying some unsustainable trends in current growth patterns. But a systematic framework within which environmental trends can be evaluated and key conclusions widely communicated has not yet been devised.

An important development, however, has been the inclusion of a series of macro-development, sectoral and environmental indicators in the *CSF*. It is a primary objective of the *CSF* to enhance economic performance through sustainable growth and development. The indicators are being measured having regard to quantified forecasts for 1999, and they represent a first attempt to make the relationship between structural funds' assisted economic growth and environmental sustainability more tangible. Their measurement, therefore, has significance in the context of this Strategy as well as for purposes of the *CSF*. Indicators which are relevant in a sustainable development context include:

Agriculture, Forestry and Rural Development[4]

	unit	1992	1999
serious pollution from agricultural waste	km of river	32	28
number of fish kills due to agriculture	recorded kills	22	15
gross forestry output	IR£m 93 prices	108	185

Fisheries[5]

	1993		1999	
	value IR£m	volume tonnes	value IR£m	volume tonnes
fish landings	98.0	254,300	118.0	301,000
aquaculture production	40.4	27,060	103.1	69,140

Tourism[6]

	1993	1999
visitors in the off-peak periods	70%	75%

Transport[7]

	1993	1999
rail passenger numbers	7.90m	8.70m

Energy[8]

	1993	1999
energy intensity (TPER/GDP)	80%	75%
primary energy supply by source %		
- coal	21[1]	18
- peat	14[1]	10
- oil	49[1]	53
- natural gas	15[1]	17
- renewables/hydro	2[1]	2
Energy supplied from renewables	-	+75(MW)

[1] 1992 Figures

Environment[9]

	1993	1999
compliance with EU standards in relation to public or group water supplies based on the drinking water Directive (80/778/EEC)	94%	100%
proportion of urban waste water being treated in accordance with the requirements of the urban waste water treatment Directive (91/271/EEC)	20%	80%
dumping of sewage sludge at sea	40%	0%
recovery rate for packaging waste	10%	25%
level of recycling of municipal solid waste	8%	15%

The above indicators were identified for objectives which lend themselves to quantification; where this was not possible they were supplemented by qualitative goals in Operational Programmes. It was also recognised that external factors could influence the indicators and that they should be kept under review and amended if necessary. Certain trends, indicating a basis for amendment, have now been identified in the EPA's *State of the Environment in Ireland* and some new targets have resulted from specific policy developments since 1993. For example:

- agricultural activities now account for some 31%, or 24 km, of recorded serious water pollution;
- the number of fish kills due to agriculture was 18 in 1996;
- over 100 MW of electricity from renewable energy sources will be installed by the end of 1999; and
- the rate of recycling of packaging wastes will be increased to 27% by 2001.

As part of the mid-term evaluation of all structural fund operations, which commenced in the second half of 1996, a detailed examination of indicators in each Operational Programme is being undertaken to examine how well they serve their purpose and whether they need alteration or amendment.

Approaching the Development of Indicators

In approaching the development of indicators, it is important to identify the characteristics of good indicators, as well as the limitations associated with their use. These are only partly attributable to current gaps in information.

Successful indicators are readily understandable, representative of key environmental policies and concerns, and capable of illustrating trends over time. They must be scientifically valid, analytically sound, measurable and verifiable. They depend significantly, therefore, on the availability of adequate, good quality data which is updated at regular intervals. Methods for aggregating data and composing indicators needs to be clear and unambiguous.

There are many difficulties involved in preparing sustainable development indicators; so far, most attention has focused on environmental indicators, where the OECD Pressure-State-Response (PSR) framework provides a widely accepted model. This recognises cause and effect relationships; human activities exert pressure on the environment, and change its state in terms of the quality and quantity of natural resources. Society then responds to these changes through environmental, economic and sectoral policies.

The PSR framework provides a means of grouping information on the environment; there is much similarity in the choice of environmental themes at international level, and EPA has advised on prioritisation of themes in an Irish context in *State of the Environment in Ireland* (see below). Experience suggests that data is most readily available for pressure indicators and least available for response indicators.

Environmental indicators do not adequately measure progress towards or away from sustainability. Interrelationships between environment, economy and society are more complex than the linear PSR framework allows; this is now being further amplified by a closer focus on economic driving forces as the anterior cause of environmental pressures.

ESRI Study on Indicators

In 1995, the Department of the Environment requested the ESRI to advise on the issues and options arising in connection with the Government commitment to the preparation of sustainable development indicators. The resultant study was published by the ESRI in April 1996.[10] It contains separate essays on environmental and social indicators as an integrated

approach to these areas has not yet emerged. While there are difficulties with information and monetary evaluation, three main types of environmental indicators are discussed.

Environmental indicators for individual themes

Most international work has focused on this area, forming a foundation for the development of more sophisticated indicators in the future. The indicators can be expressed in physical terms and the choice of themes may reflect environmental aims and priorities at national, regional or local levels. The OECD's core set of indicators[11], and ongoing work by Eurostat on Pressure Indices, use individual themes; many such indicators could be assembled for Ireland.

Environmentally-adjusted (or green) national income

This would extend the measurement of national income to take account of important environmental considerations. National income is a measure of economic activity rather than well-being. It ignores the depletion of natural assets and the negative impact on welfare of environmental damage which has not been remedied. It also reflects "defensive expenditure", i.e. expenditure to prevent or correct pollution - and maintain the status quo environmentally - as output rather than costs.

There are no easy ways to adjust national accounts. Monetary valuation of depletion and degradation, judgement on whether/the extent to which human-made capital can substitute for natural assets, and methodologies for dealing with defensive expenditures in an integrated framework are still largely at an experimental stage.

National sustainability indicators

These are related to green national income and have similar data requirements, but go further in terms of estimating national change in assets over time. The national savings rate adjusted for depletion and degradation of environmental assets would be the appropriate national sustainability indicator to use alongside GDP. Where the change in assets, measured by the adjusted savings rate, is positive when averaged over a period of years, society is on a sustainable path. However, the difficulties of measurement associated above with green national income also arise here. In both cases, measurements which rely on monetary valuation cannot easily include aspects of environmental sustainability which have no price.

As the Government intends that sustainable development indicators should take account of social as well as environmental factors, the ESRI addressed the issues associated with the selection and quantification of social indicators. National income does not adequately measure welfare; the essential purposes of social indicators are to focus on the distribution of economic resources, and to extend traditional economic measurements to include non-economic aspects of social life.

While a comprehensive set of social indicators would require considerable additions to existing data sources, a List of Social Indicators developed by the OECD[12] provides a useful starting point for the development of social indicators for Ireland. This contains 33 indicators covering health, education, employment, quality of working life, distribution of income and wealth, leisure, physical environment, social environment and personal safety. It is broadly applicable across developed countries and generally feasible in measurement terms.

A Work Programme towards Sustainable Development Indicators

The Government will now build on the work already undertaken and in train to develop sustainability indicators for purposes of the monitoring and implementation of this Strategy. In doing so, it will take account of the recommendations made by the ESRI and EPA, and the output of the National Sustainability Indicators Forum[13] (April 1995). The Department of the

Environment, the Department of Finance and the CSO, as appropriate, will participate in related work at EU, OECD and UN Commission on Sustainable Development levels, with particular reference to the developing EU framework for the integration of environmental and economic systems and the preparation of environmental accounts as a satellite to national accounts.

A phased approach will begin with the preparation of a series of national environmental quality indicators, to be developed by EPA by 1998. This will take account of the EPA's conclusion, in *State of the Environment in Ireland*[14], that initial priority be given to three themes - eutrophication, the urban environment and waste. In the meantime work will proceed on the longer-term areas including research, data assembly, methodology development and monetary valuation necessary to approach the measurement of sustainability indicators and the preparation of satellite environmental accounts. Progress will be reported annually as part of the annual review of the Strategy.

It is clear that the quality of underlying data will determine the quality of indicators, and that the availability of data in a number of areas is an immediate constraint. Equally, to fill gaps efficiently, and ensure that the environmental data collected meet national requirements for economic policy analysis and monetary valuation, there is a need for good liaison between the agencies involved. The EPA has primary responsibility for the coordination of environmental data, while the CSO has overall responsibility for statistics, in particular, economic and social statistics and national accounting data.

The CSO, following consultation with EPA, the Department of the Environment and the ESRI, has assessed requirements arising from a Eurostat project on the integration of environmental accounts in a national accounts matrix. It will commence a work programme in 1997 to formulate a methodology for the preparation of satellite environmental accounts in a national accounting framework. This will have regard to the emerging work at EU level.

Given their existing responsibilities, EPA and CSO will have a primary role in the collection and coordination of environmental data and official statistics to develop suitable indicators and, ultimately, satellite environmental accounts. The overall work programme will be coordinated by the Department of the Environment, which will be assisted by a Steering Group, with representation from EPA, CSO, relevant Government Departments, ESRI and the research community. The Group will be convened in 1997.

A preliminary series of economic and environmental trend tables, reflecting the priorities of this Strategy and the recommendations already referred to above, is included in Appendix I, for illustration and discussion. Work towards the definition of indicators will be refined as information systems and methodologies are developed, and as consensus grows internationally about the choice of themes for international comparisons.

Chapter 19
Implementation and Review

Introduction

Achieving sustainable development will involve:

- the active engagement of economic actors and society;
- support at all levels of Government and in the Oireachtas; and
- participation by the public at community and individual levels.

It will also be facilitated by good spatial planning, and the inclusion of sustainability concerns in urban and built environment policies.

This chapter identifies the approaches to be pursued, and the instruments to be developed, by Government and public authorities generally, and by socio-economic sectors, in support of sustainable development. These will be designed to:

- reinforce the new directions provided by the Strategy;
- emphasise the need for leadership and exemplary action at all levels of Government;
- create a foundation for good partnerships with non-governmental interests;
- create new, innovative opportunities for sustainability initiatives; and
- support a comprehensive and long-term process of conversion to a sustainable development path.

Structures

Joint Oireachtas Committee on Sustainable Development

The Government will propose that the Joint Oireachtas Committee on Sustainable Development should become a standing Committee of the Oireachtas to oversee relevant policy development and the implementation of this Strategy. New terms of reference will be prepared to broaden the remit of the Committee in this regard, and, in particular, to enable it effectively to discharge a supervisory and monitoring role. The Committee should regularly hear from Ministers and Departments/Agencies about their progress in implementing the Strategy and

will develop its own assessments and reports. It will retain its current powers to send for persons, papers and records; engage specialist services; publish evidence and related documents; invite submissions; and discuss and draft proposals for legislative changes.

National Sustainable Development Council

The Government will establish a National Sustainable Development Council to facilitate participation by economic, social and environmental interests in the achievement of sustainable development, and to promote better consultation and dialogue on key sustainability issues. The Council will be independently chaired, and will include wide representation from the social partners and NGOs. Relevant Government Departments and Agencies, as well as Regional and Local Authorities, will also participate. The Council's work, which will begin in 1997, will be supported by the Department of the Environment, which will provide necessary back-up services.

The Sustainable Development Council will:

- generally advise Government on the implementation of policies and actions under this Strategy, and assist with the Strategy monitoring and review arrangements;
- review reports prepared periodically by Task Managers appointed to operationalise the Strategy at sectoral level;
- review implementation of Agenda 21 and the Rio Agreements, and prepare/contribute to national reports to the UN Commission on Sustainable Development;
- promote information exchange and dialogue among the participants to reinforce the national commitment to sustainable development; and
- increase public awareness and work towards the creation of a sustainable development ethos throughout society.

In discharging its functions, the Council will join a growing network of national councils or similar entities within the EU and at a wider international level, with mutually beneficial interaction in the pursuit of sustainable development.

Management and organisation

".... many of the most pressing issues which must be addressed require the expertise and commitment of a variety of Departments and Agencies in order to achieve a successful outcome."

- Strategic Management Initiative: Delivering Better Government[1]

The Government's Strategic Management Initiative (SMI) emphasises the need to go beyond traditional structures to achieve more effective delivery of policies. In developing SMI, more appropriate mechanisms were examined for cross-Departmental action on a number of issues; these involved the long-acknowledged need to integrate consideration of the environment into Government decision-making at all relevant levels.

International experience of environmental integration shows it to be a complex task, still in its formative stages. No definitive structural or institutional solutions have so far been identified internationally. However, it is clear that the capacity of Government to formulate environmentally-sustainable economic and social development plans and programmes should be enhanced and supported. Environmental integration will therefore be designated as a "Strategic Result Area" in the context of SMI.

Strategic environmental assessment (SEA) is becoming a recognised means of advancing integration of environmental considerations into key policy areas. The Government recognises its potential as an integration tool, and a means of strengthening preventive rather than remedial action. Accordingly, in addition to supporting SEA of land use plans and programmes (see Chapter 14), proposals will be brought forward within three years to develop an SEA system for major plans and programmes, likely to have significant environmental impacts, in the sectors covered by this Strategy.

The Government will designate relevant Government Departments as Task Managers to lead in the development of the more detailed processes and measures necessary fully to operationalise the Strategy across the economic sectors discussed in Part III. The EPA will be designated as Task Manager to monitor and report on environmental quality trends in the context of strategy implementation, and the Department of the Environment (which will coordinate the reporting programme overall) will have a similar role in respect of the balance of the Strategy, including spatial planning, the built environment and the development of sustainable development indicators.

The role and functioning of Departments as Task Managers, and the better internalisation of environmental considerations into their work, will be supported by:
* **Environment Units** to be maintained or provided in all Departments and Agencies, whose remit has significant, or potentially significant, environmental implications; and
* further development of the **Green Network of Government Departments**[2], to be undertaken under the coordination of the Department of the Environment, so as to deepen cross-departmental awareness of the environmental agenda.

A timetable for progress reporting by Task Managers will be set out by the Department of the Environment, in consultation with the National Sustainable Development Council, having regard to the annual reporting agenda of the UN Commission on Sustainable Development and other international requirements. All reports will be provided to the Council for comment; together with any such comments this will provide a basis for periodic review by Government, and the re-direction, rebalancing or updating of the Strategy as appropriate. Task Managers may also be requested to discuss progress on relevant aspects of the Strategy with the Council at any time.

Annual review of the Strategy, as envisaged by the *Programme for a Government of Renewal*[3], will be addressed through the process outlined above.

Better Environmental Practice in the Public Sector

There is a special obligation on the public sector to demonstrate good environmental performance as part of the services which it delivers.

"The public sector will lead the way in demonstrating best environmental management practice. This will include formulating environmental management plans incorporating waste minimisation, green purchasing and recycling policies."

- Policy Agreement for a Government of Renewal[4]

The public sector is a major consumer of natural resources. Adoption of green housekeeping in the interests of environmental sustainability can also enhance the quality of service to the public and produce administrative savings. The *Green Government Guide*[5] (published in 1996) is designed to:

- promote a progressive approach to the environmental management of each Government Department;
- integrate green housekeeping into each Department's management strategy; and
- demonstrate a basis for extending the concept of green housekeeping to the wider public sector and the private sector.

The office environment is demanding on many resources, including energy, water, paper, equipment and consumables for this equipment. Green housekeeping is directed primarily at realising benefits for the environment through reductions in the consumption of natural resources, emissions/discharges and waste generated. But Departments can also expect progressively to increase savings in their administrative costs, e.g. energy costs, paper and other materials costs, reduced storage requirements, etc. **Green housekeeping involves taking conservation and demand management as central**

principles, so that quantities used are always the minimum consistent with the efficient running of the office. A key element of this initiative involves Government Departments formulating environmental management plans for their organisations.

The proposals for green housekeeping are complementary to the measures recommended in the Government's Programme for *Energy Conservation in State Buildings*.[6]

Good environmental management in Government Departments must serve as a model for the extension of green housekeeping to the wider public sector. In the longer term, it will also allow Departments to progress to a more formalised system of environmental management and audit along the lines of the EU's voluntary Eco-Management and Audit Scheme (EMAS). This would involve the carrying out of an environmental audit, preparation and publication of an environmental statement, on-going reporting on, and the improvement of, environmental performance, together with independent verification and review.

The public sector can exert a positive influence on the production of environmentally-friendly goods and services through the integration of environmental considerations in public procurement policy. A range of purchasing policies to minimise waste and emissions, save energy and give preference to environmentally-responsible suppliers and products is outlined in the *Green Government Guide*. The Government will examine what further steps should be taken, by 1999, to develop a policy for environmentally-sustainable public procurement.

Local Government

A major programme for the renewal of local government, *Better Local Government - A Programme for Change*, was launched by the Minister for the Environment in December 1996. Setting a path to the new millennium for the progressive renewal and revitalisation of local government, the Programme is based on core principles of

- enhancing local democracy,
- serving the customer better,
- developing democracy, and
- providing proper resources.

It *"seeks to move progressively towards a system which provides efficient services; embraces local development in all its forms; has an input to other public bodies whose actions impact locally; and the strength of which lies in its local democratic mandate and genuine partnership with the local community".*[7]
A reformed local government system will support this Strategy by enabling local authorities at regional and local levels, in terms of the efficiency of their structures and operations, and their leadership of and interactions with local communities, to participate more effectively in the achievement of sustainable development.

Regional Authorities

The Regional Authorities, established on
1 January, 1994, provide a focus for regionally based coordination

- between different areas and sectors,
- between local and other public authorities/ agencies, and
- in the provision of public services.

The membership of the Regional Authorities consists of county/city councillors from the region, who are appointed by the constituent local authorities. Each Regional Authority has established an Operational Committee, which includes the relevant county and city managers and executives of various public agencies. In addition, for EU purposes, a wide range of interests is represented on a special monitoring committee to assist the Regional Authority in reviewing the implementation of EU Structural and Cohesion Fund programmes in its area.

This Strategy places importance on the regional dimensions of sustainable development. Previous chapters have referred, for example, to regional coordination of land use policy and development planning, the need for a catchment based approach to water pollution, regionally balanced economic development, the implications of dispersed population and economic activity for transport policy, and regional impacts of tourism and forestry development. A number of structural measures are identified in *Better Local Government* to provide better supporting systems and increase the level of commitment of public bodies, including local authorities, to the work of the Regional Authorities. These measures will help to underpin the coordinating and representative roles of the Regional Authorities[8], which will be relied upon to:

- provide a regional perspective on environmental issues and resources, including strategic waste management, regional water quality and coordination of water services, groundwater resources, the coastal zone, uplands and scenic landscapes;
- promote coordination among existing organisational and institutional structures to help secure the most beneficial, effective and efficient use of resources; where development pressures threaten the sustainability of environmental resources, the Regional Authorities may provide appropriate fora for achieving the best balance regionally between development and sustainability;
- promote partnership between service providers on the Operational Committees, semi-State bodies, and business and development organisations to secure a unified vision regarding sustainability targets at the regional level; and
- review local authority Local Agenda 21 initiatives to ensure consistency across the region and monitor implementation actions.

Having regard to the framework of the Strategy and the findings of *State of the Environment in Ireland*, and building on Local Agenda 21 initiatives in their areas, Regional Authorities, in cooperation with the various interests represented on the Operational Committee, will also be asked to:

- identify and define sustainability priorities for their regions within the framework of this Strategy;
- recommend appropriate implementation mechanisms based on the involvement of bodies at regional level; and
- assist in the development of regional sustainability indicators relevant to conditions in their regions.

To start promoting action on these lines, a series of Regional Sustainability Fora, involving the Regional Authorities, will be organised in 1997 by An Taisce, with funding from the Department of the Environment and the European Union. Effectively, Regional Authorities will have ongoing responsibility for the regionalisation of this Strategy. Local authorities will be asked to report regularly to the Regional Authorities on the implementing and supporting actions taken by each authority.

Local Authorities

Better Local Government emphasises that local authorities have an important role both as environmental protection authorities and as agents for sustainable development. As to the former, the role of local authorities in providing and managing infrastructure services, implementing environmental regulations, monitoring, and providing information is now balanced in important respects by that of the EPA. Formal supervision by EPA will make local authorities more transparently accountable for the proper environmental management of the services they provide. Implementing *Better Local Government* will involve the following actions, underway or planned, in addition to those already identified elsewhere in this Strategy:

- increased emphasis on the provision of support and training services to improve the management and maintenance of water services;
- consolidation of responsibility for water and waste water services at county/city level;
- intensification and improvement by local authorities of their environmental perfor-

mance, in particular under guidance being developed by EPA;
- adoption of environmental management plans and development of information policy statements as a commitment to openness and transparency in providing environmental information;
- provision of more accessible and user-friendly monitoring data; and
- continued promotion of environmental awareness activities and campaigns, where appropriate jointly with community/NGO interests.

Local Authorities and Local Agenda 21

"Building on the strongly representative character of the local government system, on its key functions ... and on the opportunities for coordination offered by the regional authorities, Local Agenda 21 can give new emphasis and direction towards the goal of sustainable development."

- Minister's Foreword: *Guidelines on Local Agenda 21*[1]

In 1995, the Department of the Environment prepared Guidelines on Local Agenda 21 for local authorities, inviting them to develop this process further in their own functional areas, building on existing policies, plans and programmes and bringing forward appropriate initiatives. The Guidelines offered recommendations for the development of an environmentally responsible ethos throughout local government organisations, the incorporation of Local Agenda 21 aims in current policies and actions, and the development of information, consultative and participative arrangements in the community.

Better Local Government acknowledges the Local Agenda 21 process as an important means by which local authorities can promote sustainability in their areas with the involvement of local communities. There is no single, prescribed response to Local Agenda 21; however, the Guidelines recommend:
- leading by example; local authorities should "green" their own performance and operations through, for example, pursuing green housekeeping measures and adopting environmental management systems;

- integrating sustainability considerations into policies and functions, for example, in regard to planning, urban development, housing and traffic management; and
- leading and facilitating action in the community, through the provision of information, and dialogue and partnerships with business/industry and voluntary/NGO interests to promote sustainable development.

The Government is now requesting all local authorities to complete a Local Agenda 21 for their areas by 1998. This can be advanced by, for example, building on the suggestions made in the Guidelines, or participating in the European Sustainable Cities and Towns Campaign (by adopting and signing the Aalborg Charter (1994)) or in other Local Agenda 21 initiatives by the International Council for Local Environmental Initiatives (ICLEI). The role of local government in the achievement of sustainable development will be supported by:

- the development, by the Department of the Environment in consultation with local authorities, of an Eco-Management and Audit System for local government; and
- advice and assistance from the Environmental Protection Agency.

Non-Governmental Organisations

Ireland has many highly committed non-governmental organisations (NGOs), who provide a focus for public involvement in environmental protection, and support socio-economic development nationally and internationally. The NGO movement is an effective contributor to environmental action and, like Government, is committed to the pursuit of sustainable development policies. Voluntary groups also play a key role in local environmental action, maintaining dialogue with local government, State agencies, business and industry, promoting environmentally responsible behaviour throughout communities, and encouraging change by households and individuals.

There are numerous separate organisations of different scale and range, and with different agendas. However, NGOs are also forming and participating in networks which promote shared involvement and increase the effectiveness of action.

Government will continue to act in, and develop, partnership with the NGO movement. In particular, a new Environment Partnership Fund will co-fund sustainable development projects to be undertaken by local authorities and NGOs in partnership at local level.

Ongoing action will include, as appropriate:
- sponsoring NGO organisations/networks to undertake national, regional and local environmental protection campaigns;
- improving the flow of information on environment and development issues;
- providing for inclusion of NGO representation in national delegations to major international fora; and
- increasing NGO representation in national and official fora concerned with environment and development issues.

"Non-governmental organisations ... possess well-established and diverse experience, expertise and capacity in fields which will be of particular importance to the implementation and review of environmentally sound and socially responsible sustainable development ..."

- Agenda 21[10]

Instruments

The Need for New Approaches
Sustainable development requires conditions where economy and society can more fully share responsibility for the environment. In creating those conditions, a balance must be achieved between traditional (mainly regulatory) controls and new approaches which may have the potential to meet environmental objectives more flexibly and cost-effectively.

Regulation
Irish environmental policy has traditionally relied heavily on legislative instruments for purposes of implementation. This position is rein-

forced by the need to give effect to the extensive body of EU legislation; EU derived provisions are estimated to comprise some 80% of the environmental legislation of Member States. Major developments, such as the enactment of the *Environmental Protection Agency Act, 1992*; the establishment of the Agency in 1993 and the commencement of integrated pollution control licensing in 1994; and the enactment of the *Waste Management Act, 1996*, have substantially updated environmental legislation. For activities with significant polluting potential integrated, rather than single medium, controls are in general preferable.

Strong emphasis will continue to be placed on regulations which offer clear and reliable means of defining and maintaining standards for environmental and public health protection, as well as the quality and quantity of emissions to environmental media. Short-term priorities include:
- the completion of detailed regulations under the *Waste Management Act, 1996,* to implement waste licensing and support recycling activity;
- the complete phase-in of integrated pollution control licensing of activities scheduled under the *Environmental Protection Agency Act, 1992*, and the amendment of that Act to give effect to the European Council Directive (96/16/EC) on Integrated Pollution Prevention and Control; and
- the enactment and vigorous implementation of the Litter Pollution Bill.

Within this overall emphasis, Government will also have due regard to the relationship between regulation and competitiveness, and to the commitment in *Partnership 2000* in regard to the development of a national strategy to improve the quality of regulation and reduce the administrative burden.

Legislation must also be effectively enforced. The Government will continue to resource the Environmental Protection Agency to support and supervise local authority statutory environ-

mental functions, and to advise Ministers of the Government, as appropriate, for the purposes of environmental protection. It will also support efforts at EU level to improve the implementation of Community environmental law. Penalties for breaches of environmental regulations will be regularly updated.

Economic Instruments
However reliable in the definition of standards and other environmental objectives, traditional forms of regulation control rather than prevent pollution. Because it must be clearly and widely prescribed, regulation may lead to inefficiencies in some instances.

Conservation of the environment must be internalised both in economic sectors and the fiscal

"New economic instruments are ... emerging which are more sensitive to environmental needs; new approaches to regulations are emerging that are more flexible (and thus more cost-effective). The result is that the emphasis will increasingly be on finding combinations among economic and regulatory instruments, rather than choosing between them."

— OECD[11]

regime, while maintaining the competitiveness of the economy. Means and methodologies for such internalisation are largely at a developmental stage, but are driven by a range of considerations, including:
- concerns about the cost-effectiveness and inflexibility of environmental regulation;
- growing recognition of the cost and other efficiencies which may be associated with economic instruments, which create an incentive to better environmental performance and can promote technological innovation;
- rising estimates of environmental externalities and their economic impacts;
- the revenue raising potential of environmental taxes and charges, which may be used to fund further environmental improvements, or reduce other taxes, including taxes on labour; and
- increasing realisation that a mix of policy instruments (environmental and economic) may offer the best long-term approach to achieving environmental goals.

As noted in *State of the Environment in Ireland*, several economic instruments for environmental protection (including taxes, charges and subsidies) have been in operation in Ireland for some time, although, in general, the use of such instruments is not widespread here. The Government is now developing a more concerted approach to the use of economic instruments in the interests of sustainable development and application of the polluter pays principle. This will increase the use of economic instruments where this can achieve efficiency gains without compromising environmental and economic policy objectives.

Internationally, tax policy has become a common route for applying economic instruments. In the context of the 1996 and 1997 Budgets, the Government has given a new recognition to the key role of the taxation system in environmental policy. Taxation measures with environmental advantages were adopted in the 1997 Budget:
- excise duties on petrol and diesel were increased;
- the VRT refund scheme for car scrappage was extended to the end of 1997; and
- a three-year improved capital allowance for farm pollution control was announced.

Green taxation policy is of growing relevance worldwide, and the European Commission is developing framework proposals for a Community-wide energy tax regime. Against this background, an Environmental Tax Group in the Department of Finance, with representation from relevant Departments and Agencies, is undertaking a complete examination of possible options for environmental taxation for purposes of future budgets. This will develop a medium to long-term policy on environmental taxation and seek to structure a progressive shift in taxation from labour to polluters. It will involve two approaches:
- removing anomalies or distortions in the current system of taxation and subsidies, including those which hinder labour-intensive environmental activities, to ensure that the structure of existing arrangements does not have significant adverse effects on the environment; and
- developing new measures to secure more environmentally-friendly behaviour across economic sectors.

An economic approach to environment policy must have a broader focus on market-based as well as fiscal instruments. In the light of implementing policy elsewhere, and developing EU policies, strategic options will include pricing of resources and services, emissions trading and product and emission charges. In the design of instruments for application, particular attention will be paid to issues related to environmental effectiveness, economic efficiency and public acceptability.

Appendix I
Some Economic, Social and Environmental Trends

Strategic Framework

Economy

1 General Government Deficit and General Government Deficit as a Percentage of GDP

2 Consumer Price Index

3 General Government Debt as a Percentage of GDP

4 Trends in Gross Domestic Product (GDP) and Gross National Product (GNP)

5 Percentage change in GNP and GDP (Volume change)

6 Unemployment

Population and Housing

7 Population in Ireland

8(1) Annual Infant Mortality Rate

8(2) Birth Rate

9 Life Expectancy

10 Population Living in Towns of 1,500 or Greater

11 Housing Completions

12(1) Housing Stock (Dwellings)

12(2) Dwellings per 1,000 Population

Strategic Sectors

Agriculture

13 Land Cover in Ireland (excluding Northern Ireland)

14(1) Gross Agricultural Output

14(2) Commodity Value as a Percentage of Gross Agricultural Output, 1995

15 Livestock Numbers

16 Trend in P fertiliser use and soil P availability

17 Consumption of nitrogenous fertilisers

Forestry

18 Afforestation

19 Broadleaves and Conifers in EU National Forest Estates

20 Broadleaf Afforestation

21 Timber Production

Marine Resources

22 Bathing Water Quality Monitoring Results for Sea Water Bathing Areas

23 Total Allowable Catch

24 Growth in Aquaculture Production

Energy

25	Energy Demand and Economic Growth (GDP)
26(1)	Energy Consumption
26(2)	Energy Intensity
27	Fuel Mix in Total Primary Energy Requirement
28	Total Final Energy Consumption by Sector

Transport

29	Vehicle Numbers
30	Heavy Goods Vehicles
31	Ratio of Road Travel to Population
32	Estimated Millions of Vehicle Kilometres of Travel in Ireland, 1995

Tourism

33(1)	Overseas Tourist Numbers
33(2)	Overseas Tourism Revenue
33(3)	Overseas Tourists by origin
34	Employment Sustained by Tourism (full-time job equivalents)
35	Domestic Tourism Numbers

Supporting the Strategy

Environmental Quality

Water

36	River Water Quality (recent trends)
37	River Water Quality (long-term trends)
38(1)	Lake Water Quality
38(2)	Lake Water Quality (by surface area)
39	Bathing Water Quality Monitoring Results (Freshwater Bathing Areas)

Waste Management

40(1)	Household and Commercial Waste collected by, or on behalf of, Local Authorities (Landfilled)
40(2)	Quantities and Composition of Waste in 1995
41	Recycling Rates for Materials Recovered from the Household and Commercial Waste Stream
42	Estimated Hazardous Industrial Waste Arisings

Air

43	CO_2 Emissions
44	SO_2 Emissions
45	NO_x Emissions
46	VOC Emissions
47	CO Emissions
48	Smoke Emissions

Table 1 **General Government Deficit and General Government Deficit as a Percentage of GDP**

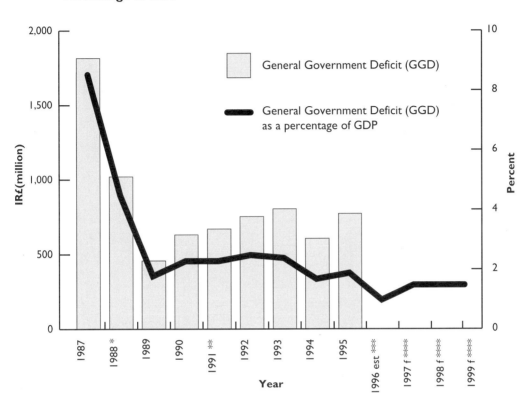

*   Exclusive of once-off tax amnesty receipts
**   Excluding £270 million received from the floatation of Irish Life plc.
***   Dept. of Finance estimate of GGD as a percentage of GDP is 1% for 1996.
****   Budget forecasts

Source: Department of Finance, *Economic Background to the Budget, 1997*, p. 3.

The General Government Deficit (GGD) is a measure of the Government's annual borrowing and a measure of its fiscal policy.

Maintaining the GGD at a level at or below 3% of GDP is one of the Maastricht Treaty criteria for participation in Economic and Monetary Union. Strong growth rates, low inflation and buoyant tax revenues in recent years have ensured that Ireland's fiscal position meets this criterion. With the 1996 GGD outturn estimated at 1.0% of GDP, this was the eighth consecutive year in which Ireland satisfied the 3% reference value. A GGD of 1.0% in 1996 compares with 8.6% in 1987. The Exchequer Borrowing Requirement (EBR) in 1996 was £437 million or 1.2% of GNP - £292 million below the £729 million targeted in the 1996 Budget. Fiscal stability over the long-term is Government policy. The 1997 Budget was designed to maintain fiscal discipline while facilitating the economy's potential for sustainable economic growth in the medium and long term. GGD is forecast at 1.5% of GDP for each of the years 1997-1999. (These figures include a contingency provision to be included in government finances under the new Multi-Annual Budget process). A buoyant economy, including a resurgence in employment, is likely to yield total tax revenues ahead of Budgetary expectations and therefore should not pose a constraint on government policy.

Table 2 **Consumer Price Index**

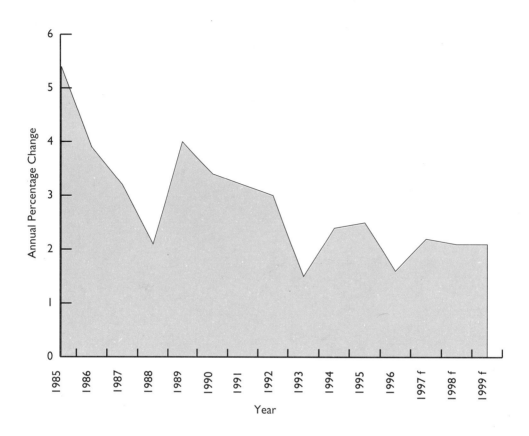

Sources: CSO Statistical Releases and *Economic Background to the Budget, 1997, p. 4.*

Irish inflation averaged 1.6% for 1996, down from 2.4% in the previous year. Measured by EU Interim Index of Consumer Prices (IICP), inflation averaged 2.2% last year, compared with 2.5% in 1995. The annual percentage change in the Consumer Price Index for the year to January rose by 0.9%, with the percentage change for the period November 1996 to January 1997 showing a drop of 0.5%.

Over the past decade, Ireland's inflation rate has remained at or below 4%. Inflation is relevant to sustainable growth as economies work most effectively when inflation is low and stable.

High inflation rates tend to distort economic decisions and the allocation of resources. A consistently low inflation rate indicates that the economy is on a sound sustainable growth path. Maintaining inflation below the 3% level is one of the Maastricht criteria for participation in Economic and Monetary Union. Inflation is likely to remain moderate over the coming years as inflationary pressures worldwide remain subdued. Low inflation will allow the economy to continue on a sustainable growth path over the coming years, facilitating sustainable development.

Table 3 **General Government Debt as a Percentage of GDP**

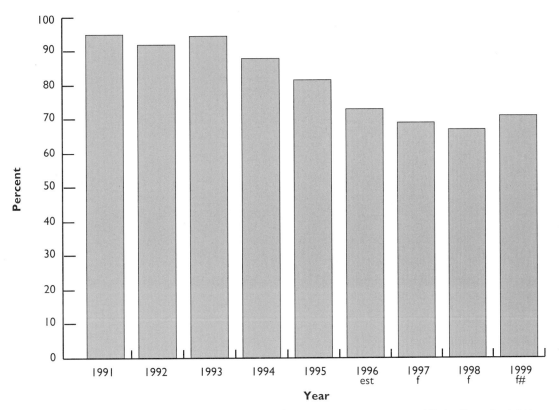

\# These percentages take account of new measurements of debt service, debt and GDP in 1999 for Maastricht definition purposes. The measurements have the effect of adding 0.4% to the General Government Deficit calculation in 1999. They also increase the General Government Debt measure by 7% of GDP in 1999.

Sources: National Treasury Management Agency, *Report and Accounts for the year ended 31 December, 1995*, p. 13, and Department of Finance, *Economic Background to the Budget, 1997*, p. 3.

The ratio between General Government Debt and national output has declined significantly over recent years. Apart from a temporary increase in the ratio in 1993 as a result of the currency crisis, the trend has been on a long-term downward path. 1996 saw a fall of almost £300 million in the national debt in absolute terms, reflecting the relative strength of the Irish pound. This was the first time a reduction had occurred in the national debt in almost forty years. The policy of keeping the Debt/GDP ratio on a downward path increases budgetary flexibility and is in keeping with key factors affecting future budgetary positions, in particular Economic and Monetary Union. The decline in the ratio is expected to continue in 1998 and 1999 on an underlying basis. The above table is based on definitions of Maastricht debt criteria and GDP.

Table 4 **Trends in Gross Domestic Product (GDP) and Gross National Product (GNP)**

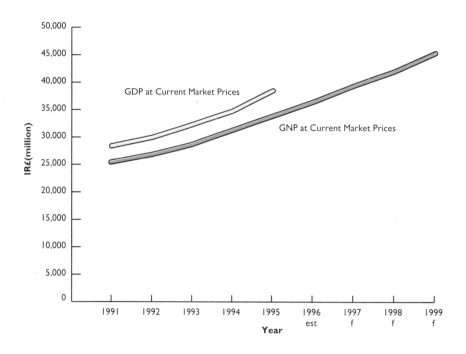

Sources: CSO, *National Income and Expenditure 1995*, p. 3 and *Economic Background to the Budget, 1997*, p. 3.

The rate of growth of GDP/GNP is the main indicator of how fast the economy of a country is expanding. If growth is sustainable over time, the well-being and living standards of citizens will increase. However, the relationship between growth and sustainable development is complex. It is Government policy to promote economic growth, but not at any cost. Higher growth reflected in standard growth measures may be the result of increased investment in pollution control or may involve a depletion of natural resources. On the other hand, there is much activity to improve the environment which is not registered in the growth figures. The growth figures which have been published to date reflect monetised transactions and do not give a true picture of social well-being.

Traditional national income as set out in the national accounting framework does not take account of the depletion of natural resources or the impact on welfare of environmental damage which has not been repaired. The measure is also potentially overstated by expenditures by gov-

ernment and households which are made to remedy environmental damage caused by the production process. The weaknesses in traditional accounts have led to attempts to develop "satellite environmental accounts" to integrate environmental considerations into the traditional national accounts framework. Satellite environmental accounts are intended to qualify, in the long term, the standard information of traditional national accounts and to provide a better measure of total welfare. There are, however, substantial difficulties which need to be addressed in their production. Monetary valuation of environmental depletion and degradation, judgment on whether human-made capital can substitute for natural capital and methods for integrating defensive expenditure into the national accounts framework remain at an experimental stage. A EUROSTAT project towards a matrix for the integration of environmental accounts into the national accounts framework, to be carried out by the CSO, is commencing in 1997.

Table 5 **Percentage change in GNP and GDP (Volume change)**

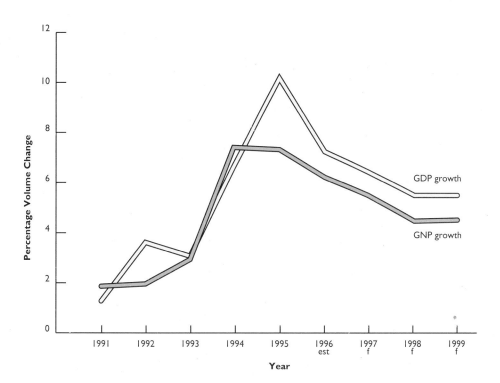

Sources: CSO, *National Income and Expenditure Accounts, 1995* and *Economic Background to the Budget, 1997*, p. 3.

Strong economic growth continued in 1996. Gross Domestic Product increased by an estimated 7.25% with Gross National Product rising at an estimated 6.25%. The difference between the two measures of growth is net factor income from the rest of the world. Principal among outflows are profit repatriation by multi-national enterprises and repayment of interest on the foreign element of the national debt. Principal inflows are from European Union funding and direct investment by multi-national firms. Manufacturing output is estimated to have grown by approximately 9%, with significant production increases being recorded in the computer and pharmaceutical sectors.

Since the end of 1994, GNP has grown by over 15% with a very substantial expansion of domestic demand and exports. Ireland's GDP per head has risen from 76% of the EU average in 1991 to approximately 100% in 1996. GNP per head however, a more appropriate measure of economic well-being for Ireland, is still significantly below the EU average. Low interest rates and inflation, combined with modest wage increases and tax concessions, have led to increased growth and hence increased real disposable incomes. More balanced international growth has also contributed to the improvement. Consumer expenditure has risen by more than 10%, a strong indication of improved living standards. The strong growth record has translated into a substantial increase in the number of people at work.

The pattern of low-inflationary growth is set to continue with GDP forecast to increase by about 6.5% in 1997. This would constitute a very strong performance by international standards with average growth in EU and OECD countries expected to be around 2.5%. GNP is forecast to grow by 5.5% in 1997, and 4.5% in both 1998 and 1999. As in 1996, the domestic economy is expected to make a greater contribution than the external sector to overall growth this year. Real disposable incomes are forecast to rise by 5% for the year.

Table 6 **Unemployment**

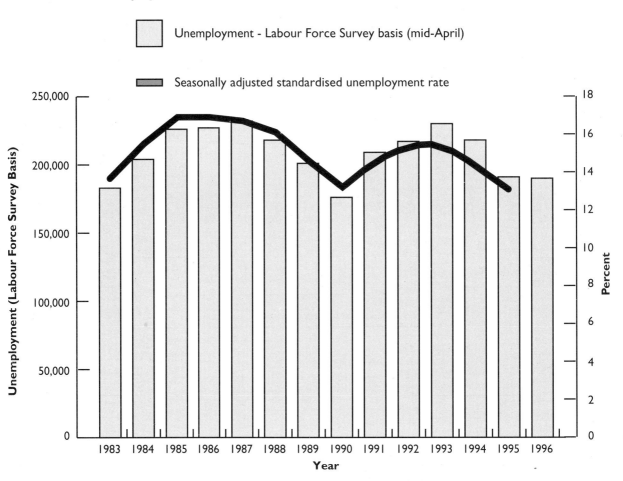

☐ Unemployment - Labour Force Survey basis (mid-April)

▬ Seasonally adjusted standardised unemployment rate

Sources: CSO, *Labour Force Survey, 1996*, p. 24 and CSO, *Statistical Bulletin*, Vol LXXI No. 4, pp. 765-766, 772-773.

Exchange is the basis of all economic activity, which generates employment. The workforce in Ireland has increased from just over 1.3 million in 1988 to 1.475 million in 1996.

The results of the 1996 Labour Force Survey published in January 1997, show that employment increased by 46,000 between April 1995 and April 1996 to a figure of 1,285,000, the highest number of people at work in the history of the State. For 1996 as a whole, it is estimated that total employment grew by 50,000. Taken in conjunction with other macro-economic indicators, this, the third year of substantial growth in numbers at work, is a sign of the current strength of the Irish economy. Budgetary forecasts indicate that total employment may rise by approximately 45,000 in 1997 and on average by 35,000 *per annum* over the years 1997-99. These increases will result from a continuation of the strong growth of recent years which has seen employment rise by over 100,000 since the end of 1994.

Unemployment, as measured on the Labour Force Survey basis, fell to 190,000 as at April 1996, a reduction of 28,000 since 1994. Unemployment on the Labour Force Survey basis is estimated to have been 182,000 for the calendar year 1996 and is forecast to fall to 175,000 in 1998 and 168,000 in 1999.

Table 7 **Population in Ireland**

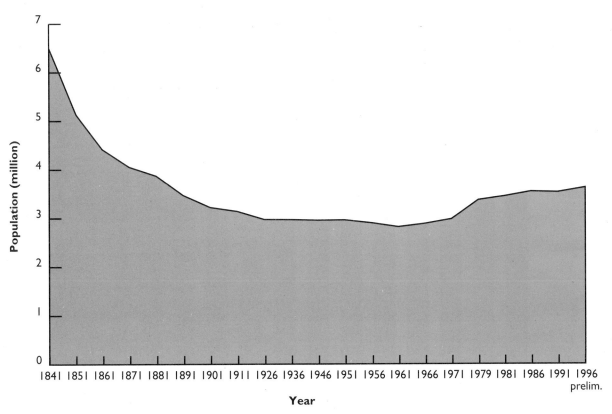

Source: CSO, *Census 96 (Planning for the Ireland of tomorrow) - Preliminary Report*, p. 6.

The above table illustrates population change from 1841 to date. After a long period of decline up to the 1960s, the population rose substantially during the 1970s. The population growth rate has now slowed. However, preliminary 1996 Census figures indicate a total population of 3,621,035, the highest figure since the foundation of the State.

Average population density of 51 persons/sq. km is low in comparison with other EU countries. The population density varies from 100 persons per sq. km in parts of the east and south to less than 25 persons per sq. km in many parts of the west. Population distribution trends over the past century have seen a decline in population in rural areas and an increase in urban populations, both as a result of emigration and of migration to towns. In 1991, 57% of the population lived in towns with 1,500 inhabitants or more compared with 28.3% in 1901 (see Table 10).

Table 8(1) **Annual Infant Mortality Rate**

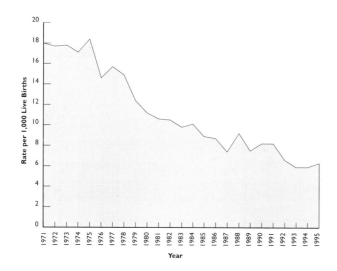

The infant mortality rate in Ireland was 18 per thousand in 1971. By 1995, this had fallen to 6.3 per thousand, a drop of 65%. Current infant mortality levels are amongst the lowest in Europe although lower rates in Finland and Sweden show that there is further potential for improvement.

Birth rate per 1,000 population has also declined considerably since 1971, falling by over 40%. The trends in birth and fertility rates indicate that in the future, Ireland's age profile will generally converge towards the European average. The proportion of the population in the 0-14 age group is above the European average with the proportion in the working age group of 15-64 years being below the EU-15 average. The increase in the average age of the population due to take place over the next 15 years as a result of the decline in fertility rates will enable convergence of Irish living standards with the EU-15 average.

Table 8(2) **Birth Rate**

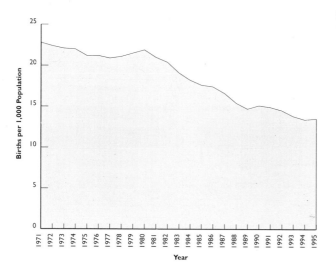

Source: CSO, *Statistical Bulletin*, Vol LXXI No. 4, pp. 796-797.

Table 9 **Life Expectancy**

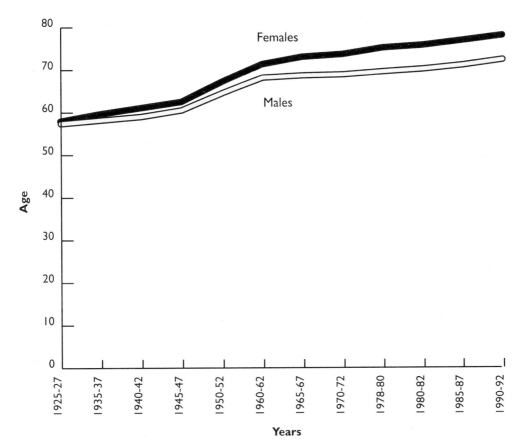

Source: CSO, *Irish Life Tables, 1985-1987 and 1990-1992.*

Advances in medical treatment and improvements in standards of living have contributed to significant changes in life expectancy. This is an indication of a healthier population but it also has many social, economic and environmental implications. More people living longer means a larger population of elderly people relative to those of working age.

Average life expectancy in the period 1970-72 was 68.8 years for men and 73.5 for women, a difference of 4.7 years. By the period 1990-92, life expectancy had increased to 72.3 years for men and 77.9 years for women, increases respectively of 5% and 6%. Greater longevity still is predicted in future years. Increasingly, the period during which individuals can expect to live healthy, independent lives is being seen as a more important indicator than total life expectancy. The definition and quantification of healthy life expectancy is a matter of future development.

Table 10 **Population Living in Towns of 1,500 or Greater**

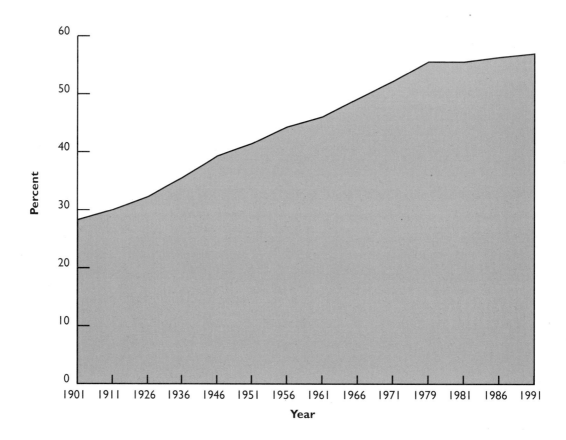

Source: CSO, *Census 1991, Volume 1 - Population classified by area*, p. 10.

The many changes in legally defined boundaries of towns and the practice since the 1961 Census of including the population or environs in determining town size, make it difficult to give comparable population figures extending back over a long period of years for areas defined in the 1991 Census as aggregate town or aggregate rural. In the above table, figures are given for each Census date for aggregate town and aggregate rural areas as they are defined at the Census date in question. The practice over the recent past has been to give strictly comparable figures for the immediately preceding Census only, with the exception of the 1981 Census where comparable figures are available for both 1971 and 1979. Despite the lack of strictly comparable figures, there is a clear pattern of increasing concentration of population in towns of 1,500 and over in the period 1901-1991. In 1901, only 28.3% of the total population was in aggregate town areas whereas by 1936 this proportion had risen to 35.5%. At the 1991 Census, 57% of the population lived in aggregate town areas.

Table I I **Housing Completions**

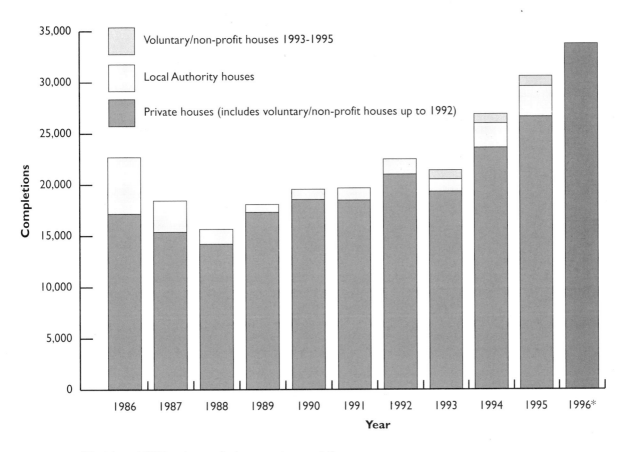

* Breakdown of 1996 figure between the three categories not available.
Footnotes:
(a) The local authority figures include demountables and pre-fabricated houses.
(b) Local authority house completions for the years up to and including 1992 include a small but unquantified number of houses acquired by the
authorities. The local authority house completions from 1993 onwards do not include houses acquired by them.
(c) The figures for private houses from 1993 onwards are not directly comparable with those for previous years which contained an unquantified
number of "voluntary/non-profit houses".
(d) "Voluntary/non-profit houses" consists of completions under the rental subsidy and capital assistance schemes.

Source: Department of the Environment, *Housing Statistics Bulletin, September Quarter, 1996*, p. 9.

Department of the Environment figures for 1996 indicate a continued strong performance in housing activity. Housing completions for the year at 33,721 increased by 10% over 1995, and represent the highest number of annual completions ever recorded in Ireland. The lead indicators for private housing output during 1996 showed strong growth compared with the corresponding periods in 1995. Continuing demand for housing constitutes a significant pressure on land for development. The re-use of land in urban areas for housing and commercial development can contribute to a reduction in pressures on the countryside to accommodate new development. Current levels of house building consume an estimated 2,000-2,300 hectares of serviced land annually. In recent years, greater emphasis on infill developments and increased apartment building in the private housing sector has resulted in higher density developments and a considerably more intensive use of land by the housing programme. In 1994 and 1995, less than 10% of new local authority housing was on greenfield sites.

Table 12 (1) **Housing Stock (Dwellings)**

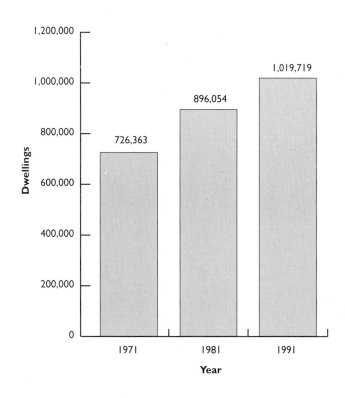

The housing stock increased by 40% over the period 1971 to 1991, an average percentage increase of 1.7% *per annum.* Over the same period, the population increased by 18.4%. Increased longevity, changes in household size and changes in social preference have also had an effect on housing demand. Forecast trends in population and household size will continue to exert pressures for new housing into the next century and will increase total dwelling numbers.

Table 12 (2) **Dwellings per 1,000 Population**

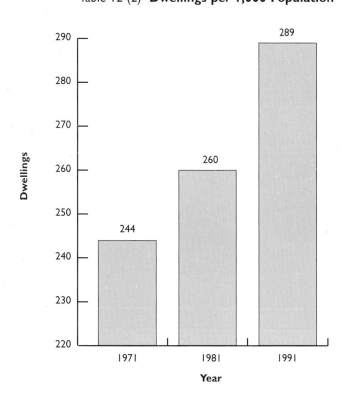

Source: Department of the Environment

Table 13 **Land Cover in Ireland (excluding Northern Ireland)**

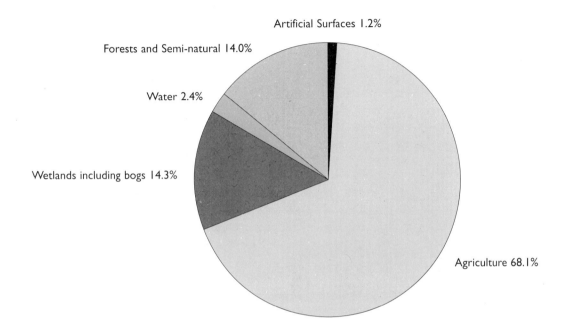

Source: CORINE Land Cover Statistics for Ireland (1989/90), excluding Northern Ireland (O'Sullivan, 1994)

Land cover statistics reflect a range of factors including geological history, national climate, and land usage. Land cover statistics have changed over time. By the start of the twentieth century, once extensive forest cover had been virtually eliminated. Forestry now represents 8% of the land cover, and is increasing at a rate of 0.33% per year. Agriculture remains the primary land use with 68.1% of land cover.

Table 14(1) **Gross Agricultural Output**

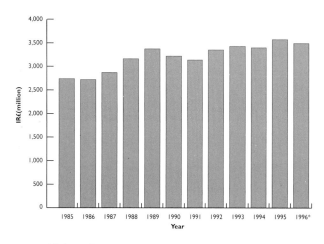

* Preliminary Estimate

Sources: CSO, *Preliminary estimate of output, input and income in agriculture 1996* (January 1997 estimate); CSO, *Statistical Abstract 1996*, p. 76; and EireStat, the Data Bank of the CSO, Ireland.

Gross Agricultural Output (GAO) is the sum of final sales of livestock, livestock products and crops from the "National Farm" and includes the increase or decrease in livestock numbers over a year. The increases in livestock numbers experienced in recent years have been one factor contributing to the steady growth of GAO. However, CSO figures (February 1997) on GAO indicate that while there was an overall increase in the volumes of output in 1996 (+1.9%), which included increases in the volume of pigs (+7.2%) and of cereals (+8.5%), there was a decline in the overall value of GAO by an estimated 2.2 %. This arose particularly from declines in prices experienced in the cattle and cereals sectors during the year.

The breakdown of the 1995 GAO figure indicates that livestock related agriculture including dairying, meat and poultry production accounts for approximately 87% of total GAO. Gross Agricultural Product at market prices (i.e. GAO minus inputs of materials and services) for the year is estimated to have dropped by 7.8%.

Table 14(2) **Commodity Value as a Percentage of Gross Agricultural Output, 1995**

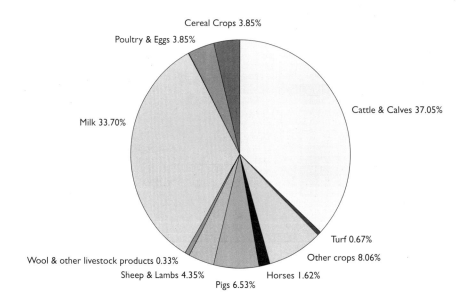

Source: CSO, *Statistical Abstract 1996*, p. 76.

Table 15 **Livestock Numbers**

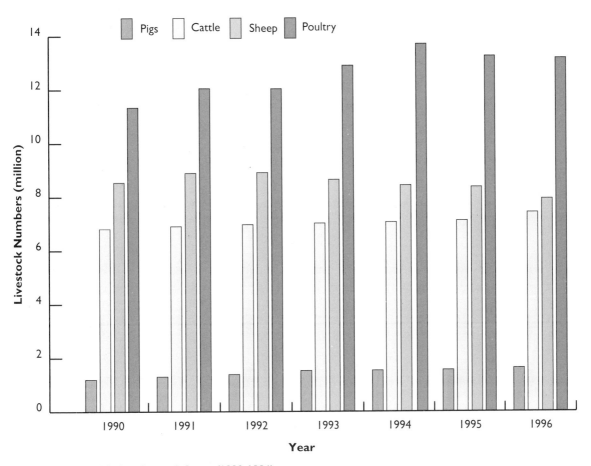

Source: CSO, *June Livestock Survey* (1990-1996).

There have been changes in recent years in farm livestock population. During the period from June 1995 to June 1996, cattle numbers rose by 4.2%. The number of cattle in the country is now similar to the herd levels of the mid-1970s. There was also an expansion in the Irish pig herd, with a rise of 4.5% in pig numbers between June 1995 and June 1996.

The sheep flock declined by 5.2% over the same period, continuing the reduction from the peak in numbers of the early 1990s. Overstocking of sheep occurred in the 1980s and early 1990s affecting the environmental quality of peatlands, heaths and wildlife habitats.

Poultry numbers changed little between June 1995 and June 1996 (-0.6%) reflecting the continued high consumption pattern displayed by this sector. When aggregated, total animal numbers over the four sectors have increased in recent years. The changes in numbers between sectors have occurred in response to EU measures designed to restrict expansion of surplus production sectors. The continued expansion in animal numbers over time has resulted in increased pressure on the environment.

Table 16 **Trend in P fertiliser use and soil P availability**

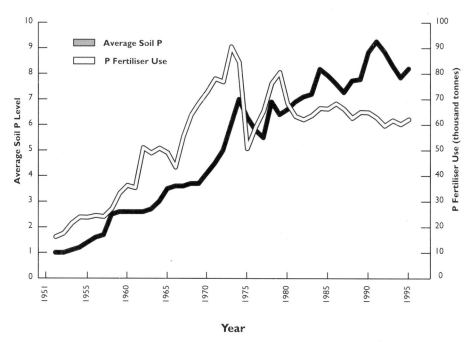

Note: Fertiliser year calculated on a July to June basis for the period 1951-1992, thereafter it is calculated on an October to September basis.

Source: Teagasc

One of the principal environmental impacts of agriculture is the eutrophication of inland waters by Phosphorus (P) from organic (animal wastes) and anthropogenic (chemical fertiliser) sources. P is a requirement for both plant and animal growth, but its application in the form of mineral fertilisers and as manures/slurries has important consequences for water quality. National trends show a steady increase in soil P levels between 1950 and 1991 when the average P level increased from 0.8 mg/l to 9.3 mg/l. Since 1991, the average P appears to have dropped to about 8 mg/l and to have stabilised around that level. Approximately 60,000 tonnes, from a total P input of some 140,000 tonnes a year, is artificial. Application of artificial P has remained fairly constant in Ireland in the past ten years. Apart from the environmental costs of excessive soil enrichment, there is also an economic cost where money is being expended unnecessarily on mineral fertilisers. Teagasc has estimated that savings in excess of £25 million nationally could be achieved annually if fertiliser applications were tailored more closely to crop requirements.

A study by Teagasc/TCD on agricultural soil phosphorus losses to water has been commissioned under the *Operational Programme for Environmental Services, 1994-1999*. The aim of the study is to develop a model to predict soil P losses given soil type, soil P level and precipitation amounts so as to facilitate better targeting of pollution control resources.

Table 17 **Consumption of nitrogenous fertilisers**

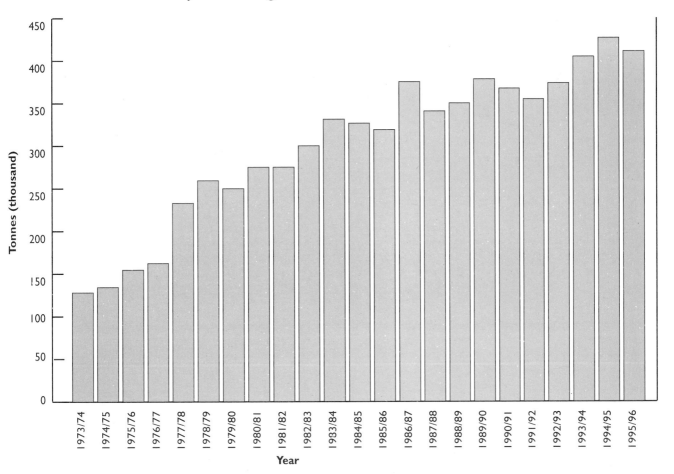

Note: Feritiliser year calculated on a July to June basis for the period 1973/74 to 1991/92; thereafter it is calculated on an October to September basis.

Sources: Department of Agriculture, Food and Forestry;
N. Culleton et al, "Sustainability in Irish Agriculture" in *Irish Geography* 27(1), (Dublin: Geographical Society of Ireland, 1994), pp. 36-37; and
M. Sherwood and H. Tunney, "Land application of manure and nutrient loading: the legislation in Ireland and Europe", proceedings of the *Environmental Impact Conference*, (Teagasc/The Institution of Engineers of Ireland, Johnstown Castle, Wexford, 1991).

As illustrated in the above table, consumption of nitrogenous fertilisers has exhibited a continuously increasing trend over the past twenty years reflecting increased agricultural production. As environmental awareness has increased, questions have been raised on the role of nitrogen as a pollutant of water and air. Losses of nitrogen to water and air in Ireland have been estimated at over 70% of nitrogen input used. These losses can have significant environmental effects and represent a financial loss to farmers. Despite a close relationship between agricultural output and nitrogen inputs, studies by Teagasc have indicated that efficiency in usage of nitrogen is decreasing as quantities used increase.

Good farm management responses can reduce and prevent water pollution from agricultural sources. The *Code of Good Agricultural Practice to Protect Waters from Pollution by Nitrates*, launched in 1996, includes recommended nitrogen application rates to grasslands to prevent the pollution of groundwaters and surface waters by nitrates from agricultural sources. The Code also addresses existing pollution problems from organic and chemical fertilisers containing nitrogen. Preventing build-up of nitrates in waters will maintain and improve the quality of waters for a range of uses including drinking water supply.

Table 18 **Afforestation**

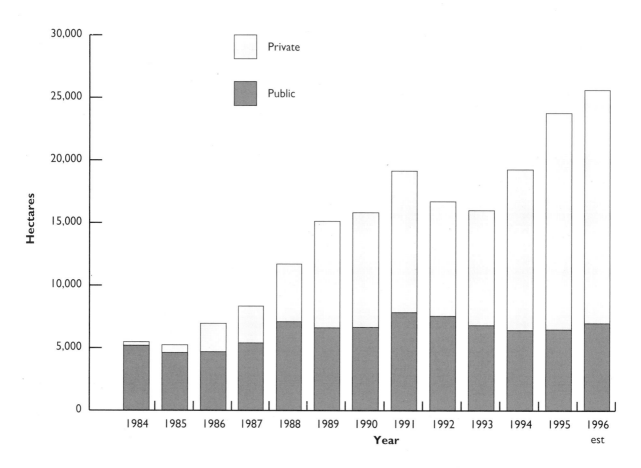

Sources: Department of Agriculture, Food and Forestry, *Growing for the Future: A Strategic Plan for the Development of the Forestry Sector in Ireland,* p. 27 and Department of Agriculture, Food and Forestry.

Afforestation levels in Ireland are now estimated at over 25,000 hectares (ha) *per annum.* The most dramatic change in relation to planting has been in private sector planting which has increased from 300 ha *per annum* in the early 1980s to over 17,000 ha in the mid-1990s. Tree planting *per capita* is now higher in Ireland than in many other developed countries. Forest cover as a percentage of total land area is presently increasing at a rate of 0.33% *per annum,* a reflection of Ireland's comparative advantage in Europe in respect of the rate of tree growth. Planting targets of 25,000 ha/*per annum* were set under the current afforestation programme.

A target of 17% of total land cover has been set for forestry by the year 2035. Annual planting by private operators (including farmers) reached 73% of total planting in 1995 with 85% of all private afforestation being undertaken by farmers.

Planning permission/Environmental Impact Assessment requirements allow for the protection of sensitive environments from over-afforestation.

It is estimated that up to 7,000 are employed directly in forestry with a further 9,000 employed in related sectors.

Table 19 **Broadleaves and Conifers in EU National Forest Estates**

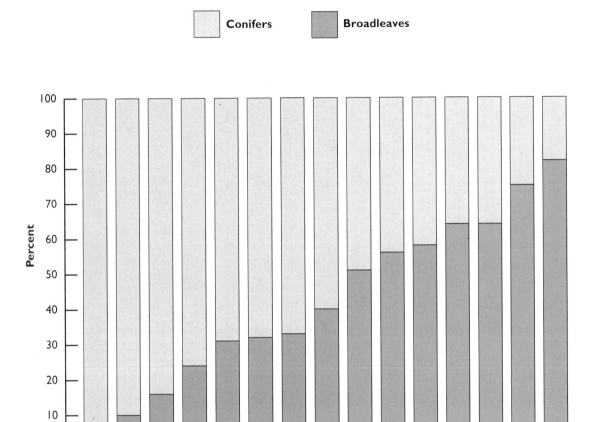

☐ **Conifers**   ■ **Broadleaves**

Source: Department of Agriculture, Food and Forestry, *Growing for the Future: A Strategic Plan for the Development of the Forestry Sector in Ireland*, p. 10.

The predominant species in Ireland is the Sitka spruce, representing 60% of the forest estate and 65% of current annual afforestation. Broadleaves account for an estimated 16% of the forest estate and 20% of the current annual afforestation compared to 3-4% in the late 1980s. The predominance of Sitka spruce afforestation is due to the high growth rate of this species of tree in Ireland in comparison with EU growth rates. A considerable amount of research has been carried out on the genetic, silvicultural and wood quality aspects of the Sitka spruce whereas knowledge of broadleaf establishment and management has been limited because of the scarcity, until recently, of suitable sites for broadleaf afforestation.

Table 20 **Broadleaf Afforestation**

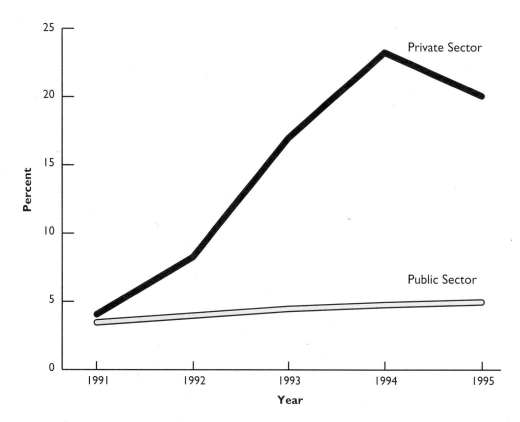

Source: Department of Agriculture, Food and Forestry

Trends in past afforestation have seen the predominant planting of coniferous rather than native and broad-leaved species, to the extent that 84% of forests comprise coniferous species. The 16% of the Irish forest estate which is made up of broadleaves is considerably less than in practically all other EU Member States, where the average proportion of broad-leaved forestry is 40% of the total. The emphasis on quick-growing softwoods reflected the exceptionally suitable conditions of the Irish climate for such species, supporting rapid growth and providing quick returns on investment.

Current policy places greater emphasis on the planting of broad-leaved species, with the target for annual broadleaf afforestation set at 20% of total annual afforestation. This has particular value in terms of landscape, heritage, amenity and habitats. In economic terms, it also offers long-term opportunities for the production of hardwood timber, allowing greater diversity of associated industries and products.

Table 21 **Timber Production**

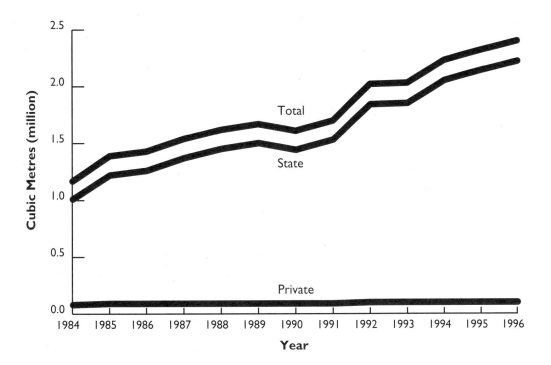

Source: Department of Agriculture, Food and Forestry

Annual timber production in 1996 was 2.3 million cubic metres and supported some 100 sawmills and three panel board mills. The value of the contribution of the sawnwood and panel board processing sectors to the national economy was estimated in 1993 at £87 million. The value added to industrial input timber and wooden furniture was estimated at £166 million. Irish forests supply around 60% of domestic requirements for structural and construction grade timber, while exports, comprising some 250,000 cubic metres, consist mainly of pallet-wood destined for the UK market.

Table 22 **Bathing Water Quality Monitoring Results for Sea Water Bathing Areas**

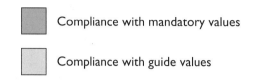

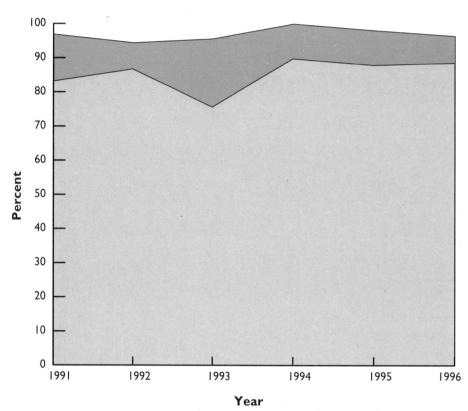

Note: For 1991-95, the parameters for which the compliance rate is calculated are total coliforms and faecal coliforms. For 1996, the parameters for which the compliance is calculated are total coliforms, faecal coliforms, mineral oils, surface active substances and phenols.

Source: Environmental Protection Agency, *Report to the European Commission on the Quality of Bathing Waters in Ireland for the 1996 Bathing Season,* p. 5.

The quality of bathing water in Ireland is generally very high, with most designated bathing areas (96%) complying with statutory quality requirements. The bathing season runs from 1 June to 31 August each year. The number of sea water bathing areas sampled in 1996 was 115, an increase of 7 on 1995. 114 of the 115 sampling points (99.13%) had sufficient sampling frequency and of these, 110 (96.5%) complied with mandatory values for total coliforms, faecal coliforms, mineral oils, surface active substances and phenols. In addition, 101 of the 114 sampling points (88.6%) complied with the guide values specified in Directive 76/160/EEC for these parameters.

Table 23 **Total Allowable Catch**

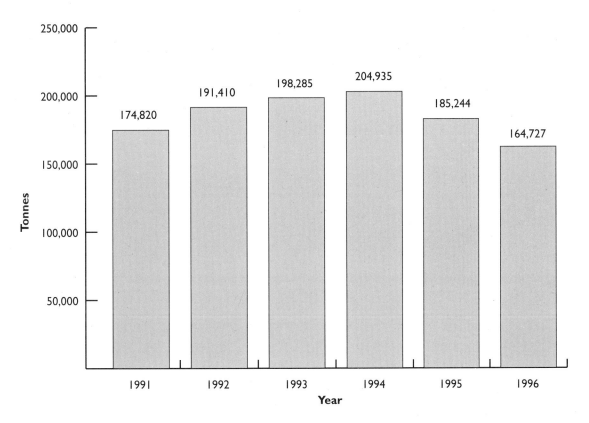

While the global fish catch increased five fold between 1950 and 1990, it has not increased since. The UN Commission on Sustainable Development, at its fourth session in 1996, agreed that significant fish stocks at global level are depleted or overexploited, and noted that urgent corrective action is necessary to rebuild depleted stocks and to ensure their sustainable use. Long term preservation and improvement of stocks, through careful management and responsible fishing practices, is vital for the future of the industry.

At EU level, the Common Fisheries Policy (CFP) already takes account of sustainability requirements in respect of stocks, and imposes quotas on certain traditionally fished key economic species. Total Allowable Catches (TACs) for certain key economic stocks such as Mackerel,

Herring, Cod and Haddock are set each year by the EU Council of Fisheries Ministers. TACs are essentially based on the results of analysis carried out by international fisheries scientists and are indicators of the health of stocks of the species concerned. Setting sustainable overall TACs to allow stocks to replenish is at the core of the conservation principles of the EU Common Fisheries Policy.

In order to maximise fishing possibilities while ensuring that conservation objectives are met, there has been significant diversification into non-TAC species in recent years. Consequently, there has been a significant growth in the level of Irish fish landings from 249,533 tonnes (valued at £95 million) in 1991 to 395,853 tonnes (valued at £129 million) in 1995.

Table 24 **Growth in Aquaculture Production**

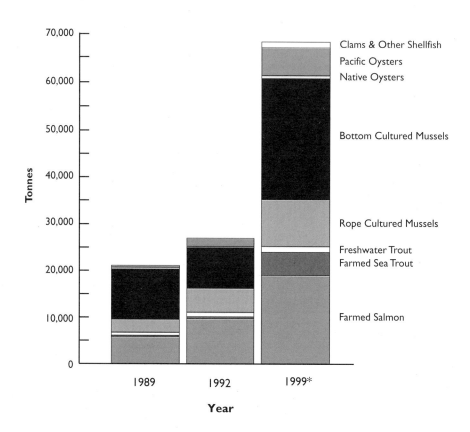

* 1999 projected figures

Source: *Operational Programme for Fisheries, 1994-1999.*

Aquaculture, including finfish and shellfish, is a growing sector of Irish marine industry. It now accounts for 25% of Ireland's fish production, and provides employment for over 2,500 people, mainly in remote coastal communities. The estimated value of the output from the sector in 1995 was £49 million. This represents a doubling of the value of aquaculture production since 1989.

The *Operational Programme for Fisheries, 1994-1999,* targets aquaculture as a key growth area, and the Government is committed to supporting the sustainable development of the industry as a source of jobs and economic activity.

Table 25 **Energy Demand and Economic Growth (GDP)**

Total Primary Energy
Requirement (TPER)

GDP (constant 1985 market prices)

IR£ million

TOE* (million)

Year

* TOE = Tonnes of Oil Equivalent

Source: Alison Myers, *Energy in Ireland, 1980-1993 - A Statistical Bulletin.*

This table shows the relationship between growth in energy demand and growth in the economy (GDP). Trends in Total Primary Energy Requirement (TPER) illustrate the relationship between energy and economic growth. As the national output of goods and services increased in this period, energy consumption also increased to meet the demands. While there are other factors which affect the level of energy consumption (i.e. weather patterns, energy price movements, etc.) economic growth is the strongest influence of all such factors. Ireland's energy intensity has been improving over recent years with more units of GDP being produced for fewer units of energy input at the margin. Average annual GDP growth over the period 1980-1993 was almost 3.6% while average annual growth in TPER was 1.7%. However, in the five years from 1988 to 1993, TPER grew relatively more quickly, probably because the stimulus of the huge price rises of 1973 and 1979 had worn off. Overall, this indicates a move towards the decoupling of economic growth from increased energy usage.

Table 26 (1) **Energy Consumption**

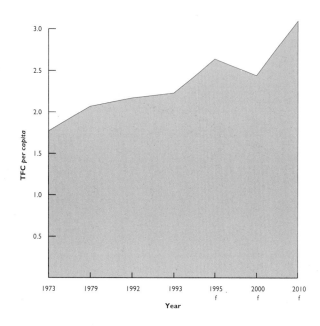

Total Final Consumption (TFC) is the measure of the amounts of various fuels used after usage in electricity production and other intermediary processes have been accounted for - in other words, the amounts which are used by end-users as final energy.

Ireland's energy intensity rating or TFC *per capita* of 2.23 compares with a European average of 2.37. The trend indicates that TFC is growing faster than the population growth rate. The trend of increasing energy consumption *per capita* is in contrast with the European average which has remained steady since 1980.

Table 26 (2) **Energy Intensity**

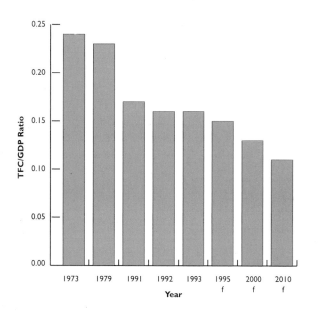

TFC/GDP is a measure of Ireland's energy intensity. Ireland's rate is on a par with the European average, has been improving in recent years and is forecast to decline further in the next century to a level of 0.11 in the year 2010. This is a firm indication illustrating the de-linking of economic growth with increased energy usage. (As TFC/GDP is declining over time, the growth in TFC is slower than the growth rate in GDP).

TFC is measured in Metric Ton of Oil Equivalent (TOE) per thousand US Dollars at 1990 prices and Exchange Rates.

Source: International Energy Agency, *Energy Policies of International Energy Agency (IEA) Countries, 1994 Review*, p. 304.

Table 27 **Fuel Mix in Total Primary Energy Requirement**

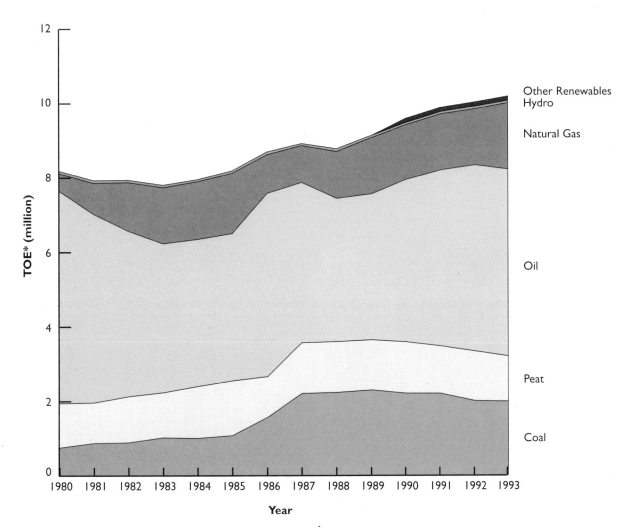

* TOE= Tonnes of Oil Equivalent

Source: Alison Myers, *Energy in Ireland, 1980-1993 - A Statistical Bulletin*, pp. 5-6.

Total Primary Energy Requirement (TPER) is a measure of all energy consumed including that lost in the transformation and distribution process. These processes include oil refining and the generation, transmission and distribution of electricity. Overall, TPER was 24% higher in 1993 than in 1980. The above graph illustrates significant trends within primary energy consumption over the last 15 years. These include:

- The discovery of natural gas and its use as a natural energy source. Gas did not play any role in TPER in 1978. By 1993 it represented 18% of TPER.
- Ireland's oil dependence declined from 75% in 1978 to 49% in 1993.
- Coal increased from 9% in 1980 to 19% in 1993 as a source of primary energy requirement.

Table 28 **Total Final Energy Consumption by Sector**

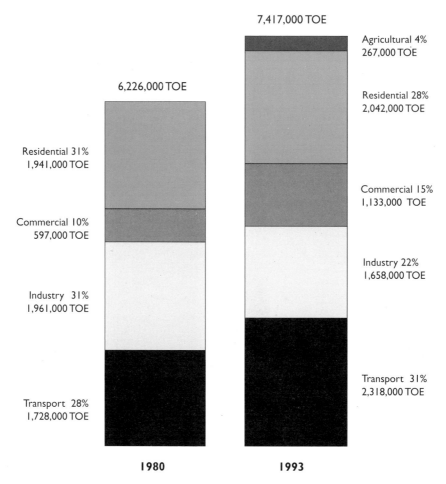

7,417,000 TOE

6,226,000 TOE

Residential 31%
1,941,000 TOE

Commercial 10%
597,000 TOE

Industry 31%
1,961,000 TOE

Transport 28%
1,728,000 TOE

Agricultural 4%
267,000 TOE

Residential 28%
2,042,000 TOE

Commercial 15%
1,133,000 TOE

Industry 22%
1,658,000 TOE

Transport 31%
2,318,000 TOE

1980   **1993**

Source: Alison Myers, *Energy in Ireland, 1980-1993 - A Statistical Bulletin.*

Total Final Consumption of energy represented by volume of Tonnes of Oil Equivalent (TOE), increased by 19% between 1980 and 1993, an annual increase of 1.35% on average over the period. (TFC in 1980 totalled 6,226,000 TOE; TFC in 1993 totalled 7,417,000 TOE). This compares with growth in GDP of 58% over the period or almost 3.6% *per annum*. The agricultural sector has only been identified as a separate consuming sector since 1990. Previously, the agriculture figure was contained partially in the domestic and commercial sector numbers. It is estimated that the combined residential, commercial and agri-

cultural sectors accounted for 41% of TFC in 1980 and for 47% in 1993. Growth in consumption has been driven principally by marked increases in energy use in the transport, residential and commercial sectors. On the other hand, there were significant fluctuations in the percentage of TFC consumed in the industrial sector over the period, which exhibited a drop from 31% to 22% of sectoral consumption. Consumption in the transport sector increased from 28% of TFC in 1980 to 31% in 1993. Energy consumed in this sector at the end of the period was virtually all oil.

Table 29 **Vehicle Numbers**

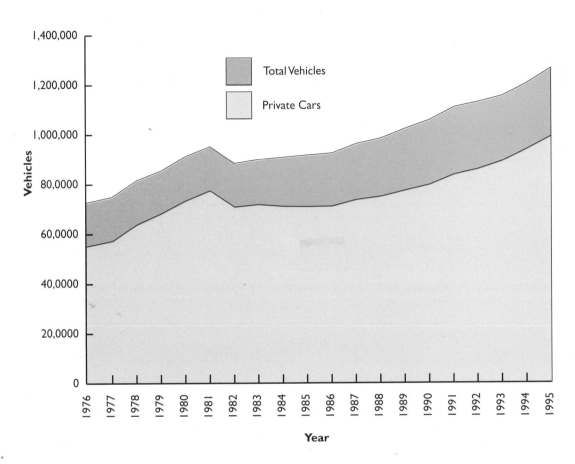

Source: Department of the Environment, *Irish Bulletin of Vehicle and Driver Statistics 1995,* p. 4.

Per head of population, the Irish road network is extensive compared with other European countries at just over 26 km per thousand persons, 92,300 km in total. Public roads are classified into three broad categories; national primary and secondary roads, regional roads and local roads.

With the increases in economic growth in recent years, there has been a continuous increase in the total number of motorised vehicles using the road network. This has caused serious traffic congestion in certain urban areas and has contributed to noise and air pollution. Sustainable transport policies require that unnecessary movement is minimised with greater efficiency in transport arrangements. The challenge is to break the link between economic growth and increased transport requirements so that transport does not contribute inordinately to environmental problems.

Table 30 **Heavy Goods Vehicles**

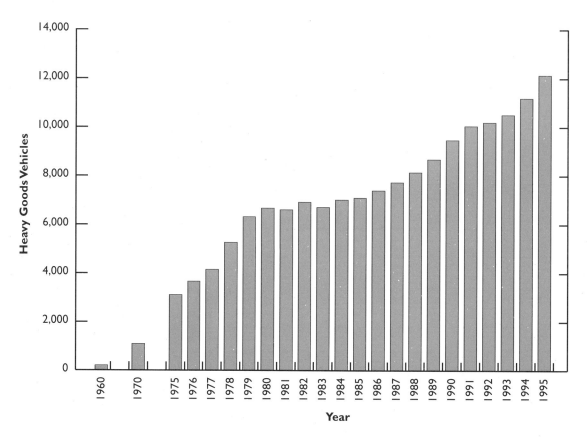

Source: Department of the Environment.

The number of Heavy Goods Vehicles (HGVs) on Irish roads has increased substantially over the last 35 years. From a low level of 195 in 1960, the number of HGVs has grown on average by over 12% *per annum* over the period 1960 to 1995 with a total fleet of some 12,116 in 1995.

89% of all freight traffic is carried on the road network. HGVs required for bulk freight transport impose major demands on road network. It has been estimated that the effect of one HGV on the road infrastructure is equivalent to 10,000 cars.

The age of the national goods vehicle fleet is relevant is considering pressure on the environment. At 31 December, 1995, 66% of all goods vehicles were 4 years old and over. Mandatory roadworthiness testing is now in force for commercial vehicles.

Table 31 **Ratio of Road Travel to Population**

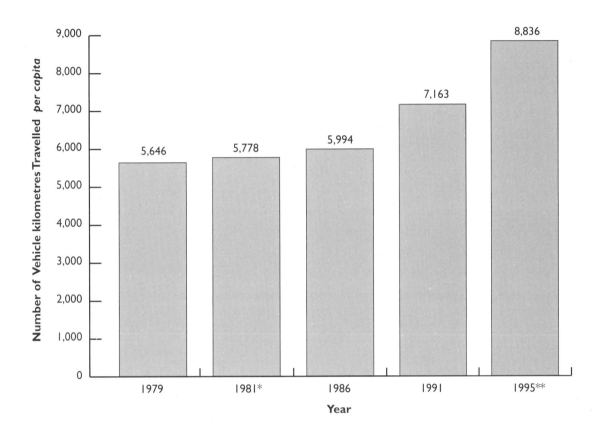

* 1981 ratio based on 1981 Census figure and 1980 road travel in million vehicle kilometres.
** 1995 ratio based on population estimate for 1995 contained in 1996 Labour Force Survey.

Source: National Roads Authority, *Traffic Station Counts and Road Travel for 1995*, p.12 and CSO, *Census 96 (Planning for the Ireland of tomorrow) - Preliminary Report.*

Transport growth in Ireland is concentrated on the roads. Economic growth, rising disposable incomes and an increased emphasis on personal mobility have all contributed to the increasing traffic. Irish car ownership is around 27 cars per 100 people, reflecting increases in private car numbers of over 5.3% in 1994 and 5.5% in 1995. While still below the EU average of 43 cars per 100 people, the Irish figure has increased from 22 cars per 100 people in 1989.

Growth in traffic volume is reflected in vehicle kilometres of road travel. Measured *per capita*, this increased from some 5,990 km in 1986 to over 8,800 km in 1995, an increase of 47%. Accelerating growth exacerbates transport pressures on the environment, making precautionary environmental measures more urgent.

Table 32 **Estimated Millions of Vehicle Kilometres* of Travel in Ireland, 1995**

Farm Tractors 1.4% (435)

Light Goods Vehicles 12.3% (3,906)

Miscellaneous 0.1% (38)

Trucks 6.2% (1,956)

Motor Cycle 0.9% (278)
Buses 1.1% (355)

Cars 78.1% (24,826)

Estimates of vehicle kilometres of travel in Ireland in 1995 are classified by vehicle type in the chart across. Car transport accounts for the largest percentage of vehicle kilometres travelled. In contrast, buses account for just over 1% of vehicle kilometres travelled. Roads account for 89% of all freight transport and 96% of all passenger transport.

* Rounded to nearest million kilometres.

Source: National Roads Authority, *Traffic Station Counts and Road Travel for 1995*.

Table 33(1) **Overseas Tourist Numbers**

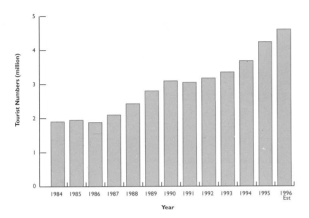

Trends in tourism revenue and numbers have been increasing significantly over recent years. Total earnings from both overseas and domestic tourism showed strong growth between 1985 and 1995, increasing at a rate of over 9% *per annum*. The high rate of growth continued in 1996; preliminary overseas visitor numbers are estimated to have increased by 10% to 4.6 million and earnings from overseas tourists are estimated to have reached £1.45 billion. Employment in the industry was forecast to rise to 107,000 in 1996, an increase of over 5,000 on the previous year. Tourism now employs over 8% of the total working population and is one of the most important sectors of the national economy.

Table 33(2) **Overseas Tourism Revenue**

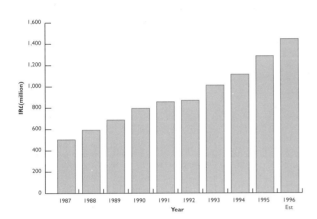

Tourism has been identified by the Government as a major source of continued economic growth for the coming years. To ensure sustainable tourism, Ireland must be able to develop the tourist sector while protecting, and where possible, enhancing the environment. With overseas tourist figures exceeding the resident population from 1994 on, policy now focuses on increasing the revenue value of tourism rather than the number of tourists.

Table 33(3) **Overseas Tourists by origin**

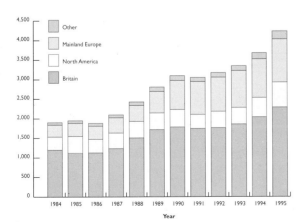

Source: Bord Fáilte, *Markets, 1991-1995, Perspectives on Irish Tourism.*

Table 34 **Employment Sustained by Tourism (full-time job equivalents)**

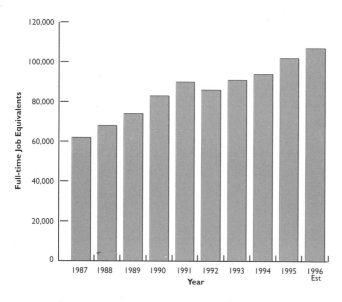

Source: Bord Fáilte, *Developing Sustainable Tourism, Tourism Development Plan, 1994–1999*, and Bord Fáilte, *Annual Report and Accounts*, 1994 and 1995.

Tourism provides around 8% of national employment, at some 102,000 full-time equivalent jobs in 1995, with 107,000 forecast for 1996 and 110,000 being forecast by end-1997. The *Operational Programme for Tourism, 1994-1999* is expected to deliver an additional 35,000 full-time job equivalents by 1999. It is likely, however, that these figures are an underestimation of the total employment impact of the tourism sector, as many jobs which are supported by tourism (e.g. in the retail and leisure sectors) are recorded elsewhere in the statistics. Tourism is a growing force for employment; the additional 30,000 tourism-related jobs created between 1987 and 1994 represented half of the net increase in employment in that period.

Table 35 **Domestic Tourism Numbers**

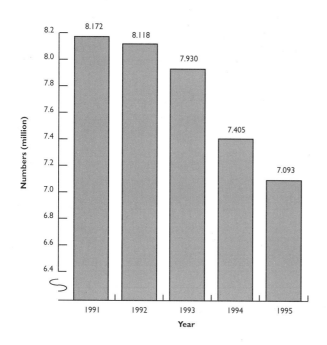

Source: Bord Fáilte, *Annual Report and Accounts, 1995.*

Over the last number of years, domestic tourism numbers have declined in terms of tourist trips. In 1995, domestic tourism numbers were just over 7 million, a drop of over 300,000 on 1994 figures. However, increases in overseas tourism numbers have more than offset the domestic decline and hence, a focus must be maintained on optimisation, taking account of environmental, social and economic considerations.

Table 36 **River Water Quality (recent trends)**

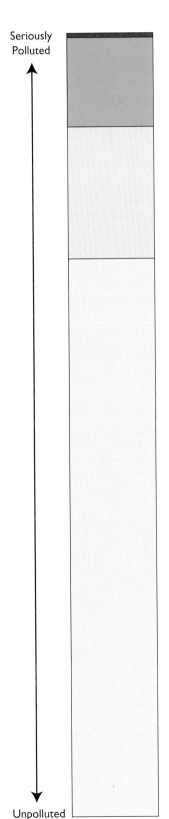

Seriously
Polluted

Unpolluted

Class D (seriously polluted)
77 Km (0.6%)

Class C (moderately polluted)
1,502 Km (11.4%)

Class B (slightly polluted)
2,222.5 Km (16.8%)

Class A (unpolluted)
9,396 Km (71.2%)

Detailed data on Irish water quality and trends are contained in *Water Quality in Ireland, 1991-1994*. These indicate that the bulk (71.2%) of river channel surveyed is unpolluted; 3724.5 km (28%) is slightly or moderately polluted and 77 km (0.6%) is seriously polluted. As might be anticipated, the most seriously polluted channels are located in the more densely populated and intensively farmed locations within the country. Serious pollution is most evident in the eastern region with more than half of the surveyed channel length slightly or moderately polluted. The Cavan/Monaghan area registered 44.1% of channel either slightly or moderately polluted whereas, in contrast, the Donegal/Sligo region (9.1%) and the southern region (13.1 %) show lower levels of pollution.

Note: Baseline survey of 13,200 kilometres of channel length, 1991-1994

Source: Environmental Protection Agency, *Water Quality in Ireland, 1991-1994.*

Table 37 **River Water Quality (long-term trends)**

Channel Length (percent)

Seriously Polluted

Unpolluted

	1971	1981	1986	1990	1994
Class D (seriously polluted)	6	4.1	2.7	1.9	1.2
Class C (moderately polluted)	4.6	7	8.4	13.1	14.5
Class B (slightly polluted)	5.1	11.1	19.8	19.5	26.8
Class A (unpolluted)	84.3	77.8	69.1	65.5	57.5

Class D (seriously polluted)

Class C (moderately polluted)

Class B (slightly polluted)

Class A (unpolluted)

Note: Long-term trend based on surveys carried out on 1971 baseline of 2,900 km (percentage of channel length in four biological quality classes)

Sources: 1971 data - Flanagan & Toner, 1972; 1981 data - Clabby et al, 1982; 1986 data - Toner et al, 1986; 1990 data - Clabby et al, 1992; 1994 data - Environmental Protection Agency, *Water Quality in Ireland, 1991-*

2,900 km of rivers/streams were surveyed in 1971 and this baseline has been re-examined at regular intervals since to assess the long term trend in river quality. There is a continuing decline in the length of Class A waters (unpolluted) from 84% of the total surveyed in 1971 to 57% in the most recent 4 year review undertaken by the EPA. There is also a significant decline in the length of channel which is affected by serious pollution; this has been reduced from 6% of surveyed channel in 1971 to less than 1% in the 1991-1994 survey. However, there is a five-fold increase in slightly polluted channel and a three-fold increase in moderately polluted channel over the period since 1971.

Table 38(1) **Lake Water Quality**

Table 38(2) **Lake Water Quality (by surface area)**

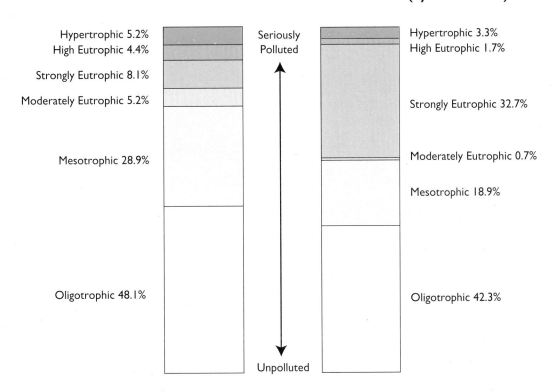

Table 38(1):
Hypertrophic 5.2%
High Eutrophic 4.4%
Strongly Eutrophic 8.1%
Moderately Eutrophic 5.2%
Mesotrophic 28.9%
Oligotrophic 48.1%

Seriously Polluted
Unpolluted

Table 38(2):
Hypertrophic 3.3%
High Eutrophic 1.7%
Strongly Eutrophic 32.7%
Moderately Eutrophic 0.7%
Mesotrophic 18.9%
Oligotrophic 42.3%

Source: Environmental Protection Agency, *Water Quality in Ireland, 1991-1994.*

Of 135 lakes examined in the EPA Water Quality Survey, 104 are classed oligotrophic or mesotrophic (i.e. unpolluted), 7 are moderately eutrophic, 11 are strongly eutrophic, 6 are highly eutrophic and 7 are hypertrophic (seriously polluted). The highest incidence of identified pollution was in the north-midlands where 16 of 47 lakes surveyed were polluted to some extent. In contrast, most lakes in the west and the majority elsewhere in the country (80%) were unpolluted. Non-point agricultural waste sources are of major significance in the pollution of lakes in Ireland but in several cases point source discharges of sewage or industrial waste waters are implicated. Water quality in Loughs Ennel, Leane and Muckno has been improved through phosphorus removal at sewage plants discharging into the lakes. An integrated catchment management initiative will now be implemented to reverse deteriorating water quality trends in selected catchments.

Table 39 **Bathing Water Quality Monitoring Results (Freshwater Bathing Areas)**

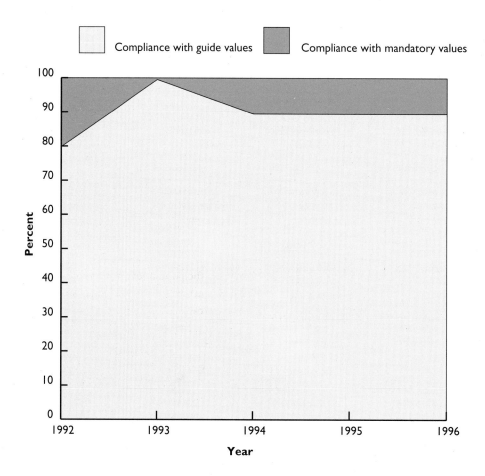

Note: For the 1991-1995 period, the parameters for which the compliance rate is calculated are total coliforms and faecal coliforms. For 1996, the parameters for which the compliance is calculated are total coliforms, faecal coliforms, mineral oils, surface active substances and phenols.

Source: Environmental Protection Agency, *Report to the European Commission on the Quality of Bathing Waters in Ireland for the 1996 Bathing Season*, p. 5.

The number of inland bathing areas designated and sampled in 1996 remained at nine. All inland water bathing areas complied with the mandatory values for total coliforms, faecal coliforms, mineral oils, surface active substances and phenols in the 1996 bathing season. Eight of the nine areas (88.9%) also complied with the guide values of Council Directive 76/160/EEC for these parameters.

Table 40(1)   **Household and Commercial Waste collected by, or on behalf of Local Authorities (Landfilled)**

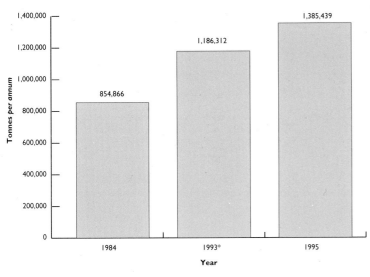

* The figure for 1993 is that reported by local authorities for household and commercial waste collected.

The table across indicates trends in household and commercial waste arisings, and suggests an increase of over 62% in eleven years, equivalent to just under 4.5% *per annum*. Trends in municipal waste arisings have been difficult to establish due to the differing methodologies used to gather waste statistics. Total municipal waste collected in 1995, including household and commercial waste collected for recycling as well as street cleansing waste, has been estimated at 1,549,962 tonnes. Actual household waste arisings are greater, however, than the volume collected as a collection service is not provided to 100% of the population. When adjusted in this regard, actual municipal waste arisings for 1995 are estimated at 1,848,232 tonnes. Apparent increases in municipal waste volumes are, to some extent, a function of better reporting methods over time. The *National Waste Database Report* suggests that the figure for actual household waste arisings (estimated to be 1,324,521 tonnes in 1995) should be considered as a benchmark for future comparisons.

Table 40(2)   **Quantities and Composition of Waste in 1995**

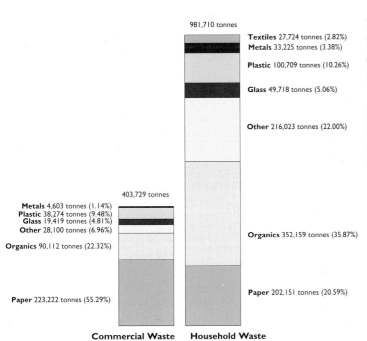

It is estimated that 403,729 tonnes of commercial waste were collected by, or on behalf of, local authorities in 1995. The table across illustrates the composition of this waste.

It is estimated that 981,710 tonnes of household waste were collected by, or on behalf of, local authorities in 1995. The table illustrates the composition of this waste.

Source: Environmental Protection Agency, *National Waste Database Report, 1995.*

Table 41 **Recycling Rates for Materials Recovered from the Household and Commercial Waste Stream**

*Scrap metal was excluded from commercial waste stream in 1995.

Source: Environmental Protection Agency, *National Waste Database Report, 1995*, p. 68.

In 1993, 92.6% of the household and commercial waste stream was landfilled and 7.4% was recycled. For household waste alone, 1.4% was recycled with the balance landfilled. The recycling rate for commercial waste was much higher at 14.5%. The figures for 1995 indicate that the overall recycling rate for household and commercial waste had risen to 10.4%, with 4.3% of household waste and 15.3% of commercial waste recycled. With regard to the 15.3% commercial recycling rate, it should be noted that tonnages for commercial waste recycled and landfilled in 1995 were lower than those reported for 1993 and that different methods were used to estimate commercial waste arisings and per cent recycled for the two years. Scrap metal was included as part of the commercial waste stream in 1993 and it is now considered that this material is better classified as part of the industrial waste stream. With scrap metals excluded from the commercial waste stream, the national recycling rate for the household and commercial waste stream for 1995 is 7.8%.

This Strategy includes among its objectives a stabilisation and reversal of the growth in waste production, and intensification of reuse and recycling activity so that 20% of municipal waste is diverted from landfill by recycling by 1999. Higher targets will be established for subsequent years, including an increase from 27% to at least 50% in the recovery rate for packaging waste by 2005.

Table 42 **Estimated Hazardous Industrial Waste Arisings**

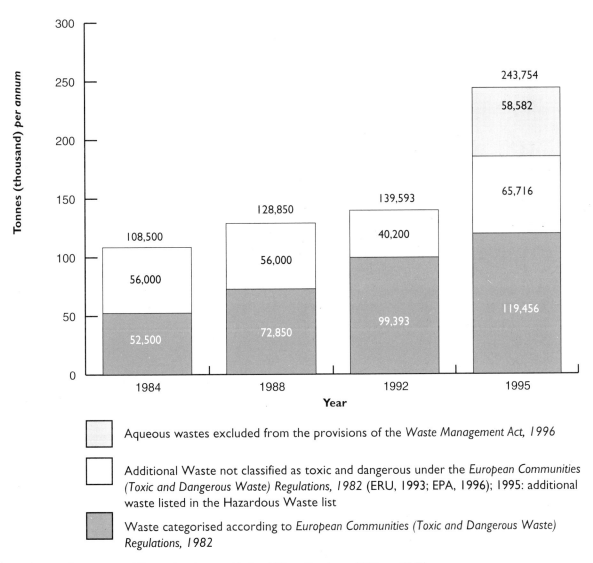

Aqueous wastes excluded from the provisions of the *Waste Management Act, 1996*

Additional Waste not classified as toxic and dangerous under the *European Communities (Toxic and Dangerous Waste) Regulations, 1982* (ERU, 1993; EPA, 1996); 1995: additional waste listed in the Hazardous Waste list

Waste categorised according to *European Communities (Toxic and Dangerous Waste) Regulations, 1982*

Source: Environmental Protection Agency, *National Waste Database, 1995*, pp. 70-71.

The above table illustrates estimated hazardous waste arisings. Surveys in 1984, 1988, and 1992 show a rising trend in waste regulated under the *European Communities (Toxic and Dangerous Waste) Regulations, 1982*. Figures for other wastes are not directly comparable due to changing definitions. The 1995 figures relate to wastes listed in the European Hazardous Waste List (94/904/EC). These figures cover wastes classifiable under the Toxic and Dangerous Waste Regulations, wastes not classifiable under the Regulations and aqueous wastes not included in the provisions of the *Waste Management Act, 1996*, as they are covered by other legislation.

Of reported hazardous waste arisings, 57.4% is disposed by various routes, with incineration and biological treatment being the main disposal routes. The recovery rate for reported hazardous waste arisings is 42.5%. Over 90% of hazardous waste is treated in Ireland with 78.2% treated on-site and 12% treated off-site. As a percentage of total reported industrial waste in 1995, hazardous industrial waste represents 3.79%. As a percentage of total waste in 1995, hazardous waste represents 3.18%. By far the greatest quantity of hazardous waste, as defined by the hazardous waste list, arose in the chemicals, chemical products and man-made fibre sector (88.4%).

Table 43 **CO$_2$ Emissions**

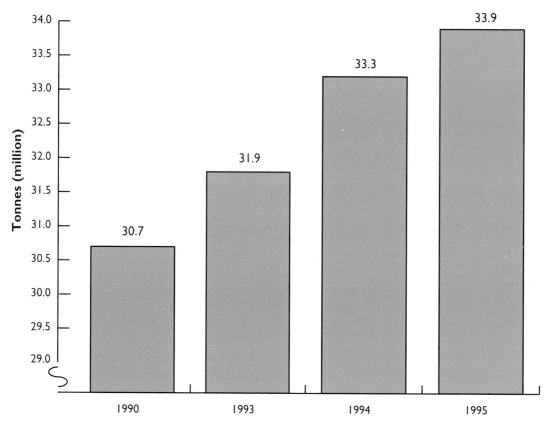

Source: Department of the Environment/Environmental Protection Agency

Carbon dioxide (CO$_2$) is the main gas generated by human activity which contributes to climate change. CO$_2$ arises principally as a result of the burning of fossil fuels in the energy and transport sectors. The above chart represents the increase in CO$_2$ emissions in the 1990s. A national climate change/CO$_2$ abatement strategy was published by the Department of the Environment in 1993. It sets the objective of limiting the growth in CO$_2$ emissions to 20% above their 1990 levels (a net increase of 11% when the estimated growth in carbon fixation by expanded afforestation is taken into account). It is now projected that CO$_2$ emissions in the year 2000 will be less than this target.

Negotiations are currently taking place under the auspices of the Framework Convention on Climate Change to strengthen the Convention commitments in respect of greenhouse gases, including CO$_2$, in the post-2000 period.

Table 44 **SO₂ Emissions**

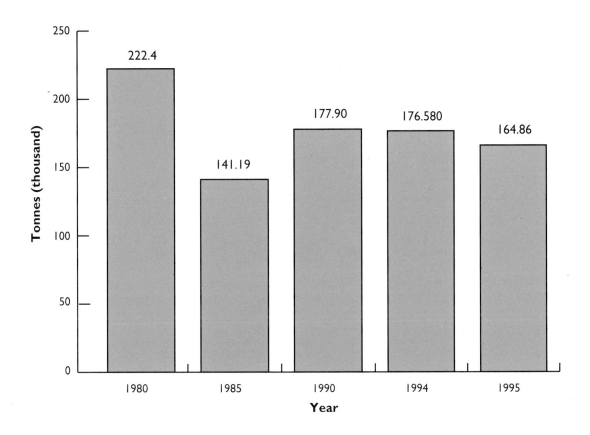

Source: Environmental Protection Agency

Sulphur dioxide (SO₂) can have adverse effects on human health, vegetation, materials and cultural heritage. Emissions of SO₂ are produced when fossil fuels containing sulphur are burnt. Electricity generation is the principal source of SO₂. Coal and oil produce varying amounts of SO₂ while gas produces little. Emissions of SO₂ decreased by approximately 25% over the period 1980 to 1995. This has mainly been achieved as a result of a switch to low sulphur fuels in the energy and industrial sectors, the reduction in fuel oil combustion in industry and the conversion of solid fuel heating systems in private dwellings to gas or oil fired systems.

Under the *Second Sulphur Protocol to the Convention on Long Range Transboundary Air Pollution*, which Ireland has signed, national emissions of SO₂ should be reduced to 157,000 tonnes from the year 2000 onwards (i.e. a reduction of 30% on 1980 levels). Ireland will ratify the Second Sulphur Protocol in 1997.

Table 45 **NO$_X$ Emissions**

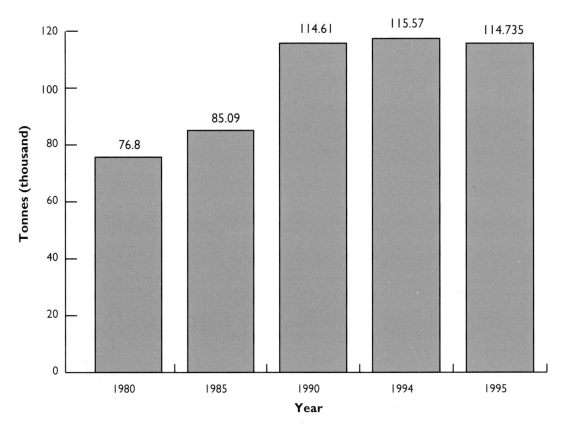

Source: Environmental Protection Agency

Nitrogen Oxides (NO$_x$) include two gases - nitric oxide (NO) and nitrogen dioxide (NO$_2$). Electricity generation and transport are the main sources of NO$_x$ through high temperature combustion. Short term exposure to very high concentrations of NO$_2$ can result in adverse affects on the respiratory system while both NO and NO$_2$ contribute to acid rain and the formation of ground level ozone. NO$_x$ emissions have increased by some 49% between 1980 and 1995, but abatement strategies are now starting to show results. Under the Sofia Protocol, signed in 1988, Ireland was required to stabilise NO$_x$ emissions at 105,400 tonnes from 1994 onwards. A revised protocol based on the critical loads approach is under negotiation and will require further NO$_x$ reductions after 2000. Ireland will work towards the achievement of the emission standards now being developed at UN ECE and EU level.

Table 46 **VOC Emissions**

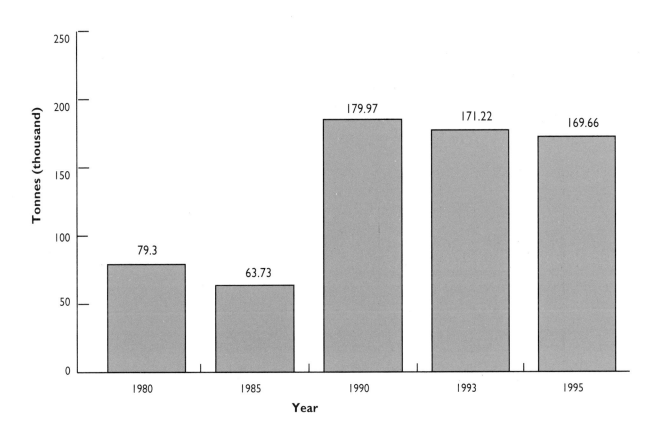

Source: Environmental Protection Agency

Volatile Organic Compounds (VOCs) are a primary air pollutant. The term VOC encompasses a wide range of reactive hydrocarbons and analogous compounds. VOCs include the aromatics, such as benzene, which is added to high octane unleaded petrol. The principal sources of VOCs have been identified as road traffic, petroleum distribution and the evaporation of solvents, emissions which principally have local or regional effects. Existing information indicates that industry emits limited quantities of VOCs mainly from the use of solvents. However, the Environmental Protection Agency has noted that emissions of VOCs from a range of industrial processes have not yet been reliably quantified. Combined with NO_x, VOCs form low level ozone which is damaging to both human and crop health. An investigation of VOC and PM_{10} in Dublin is being funded under the R&D Sub-programme of the *Operational Programme for Environmental Services, 1994-1999.*

Table 47 **CO Emissions**

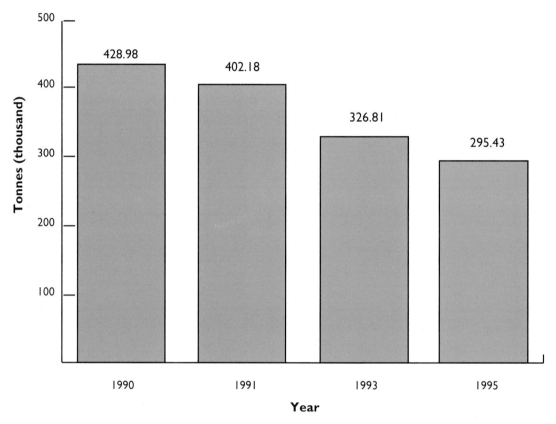

Carbon monoxide (CO), one of the major air pollutants, is a threat to human health. Emissions arise mainly as a result of the use of motor vehicles, with lesser amounts arising from residential and commercial combustion. Existing data indicate that industry emits limited quantities of this pollutant. The effects of CO are principally local and regional. An EU Framework Directive on air quality has been adopted; it will be followed by subsidiary Directives which will specify air quality standards for a number of pollutants, including CO.

Table 48 **Smoke Emissions**

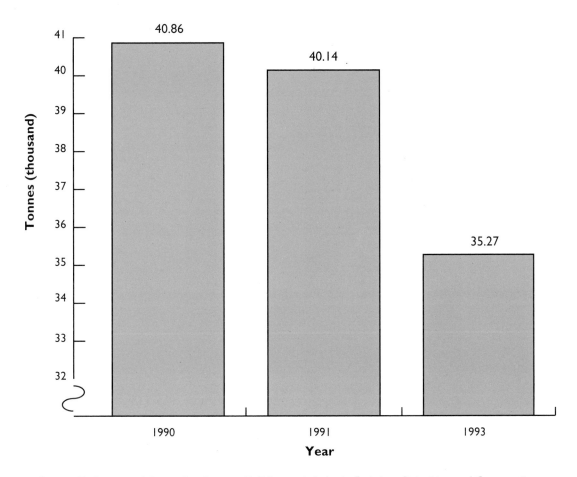

Source: Environmental Protection Agency, *Air Pollutants in Ireland - Emissions, Depositions and Concentrations, 1984-1994.*

Smoke emissions have been reduced in the course of the 1990s. Apart from transport, the major threat to urban air quality has been the burning of coal for domestic heating purposes. Serious smoke pollution in Dublin led to the ban of the sale, marketing and distribution of bituminous coal in the built up area of Dublin. A similar ban was extended to the Cork City area when it became clear that smoke emissions were approaching, though not exceeding, air quality standards. Concentrations of smoke have declined with the introductions of the bans in each city.

Appendix II

List of those who made submissions as part of the Public Consultation Process on the Strategy

Animal and Plant Health Association

An Taisce Economic Policy and International Group

An Taisce West Cork

Association of Consulting Engineers of Ireland

Bahá'í Information Office, Dublin 4

Ballylickey Tourist and Development Association, Co Cork

Mr Noel J Brady, Architect, Dublin 6

Mr Tony Carey, Enniskerry, Co Wicklow

Ms Maeve Clarke, Douglas, Cork

Clean Technology Centre, Regional Technical College, Cork

Conference of Religious of Ireland Justice Office

Cork Environmental Alliance Ltd

Mr R V Cortlandt Herbst, Castlegregory, Co Kerry

K T Cullen and Co Ltd, Dublin 4

Mr Thomas Cummins, Department of Environmental Resource Management, UCD

Cunnane Stratton Reynolds, Dublin 2

Mr Rory Donegan, Dublin 7

Dublin Regional Authority

Earthwatch/Friends of the Earth Ireland

Fehily Timoney Weston, Cork

Mr Tom Finn, Tralee, Co Kerry

Ms Kathleen Gibbons, Portumna, Co Galway

Global Action Plan Ireland

Greenpeace Ireland

IBEC - Irish Mining and Exploration Group

The Inland Waterways Association of Ireland

Irish Hydro Power Association

Irish Landscape Institute

Irish Wildbird Conservancy

Irish Women's Environmental Network

Irish Woodworkers for Africa

Keep Ireland Open

Mr Donal Lamont, Dublin 18

Landscape Alliance Ireland

Mr Paul Leech, Gaia Associates, Dublin 2

Leopardstown and Brewery Road Residents
Association Roads Committee, Co Dublin

Mr Brendan McGrath, Phibsborough, Dublin 7

Mr Ciarán Mannion, Minnesota Environmental
Initiative, USA

Mr John Markham, Greystones, Co Wicklow

Mayo Regional Game Council

Mr Michael Newman, Kilbeggan, Co Westmeath

Northern Regional Fisheries Board

Professor Dermot O'Connell, School of
Architecture, UCD

Mr Gerry O'Leary, Tralee, Co Kerry

Dr Jim Parkes, Faraday Centre, Carlow

Ms Anne Pender, Environmental Resource
Consultants, Dublin 9

Mr Nigel Pratt, Wicklow

Mr John Sheils, John Barnett & Associates, Dublin 4

Solid Fuel Industry Association

South-East Regional Authority

Mr Chris Southgate, Environment 2000 Ltd,
Dublin 4

Ms Hilary Tovey/Mr James Wickham, Department
of Sociology, TCD

Ulster Wildlife Trust

Appendix III

References: PART II - Strategic Framework
Chapter 2 Overview

1. *A Government of Renewal: Policy Agreement between Fine Gael, Labour Party, Democratic Left,* (Dublin: Stationery Office, 1994), p. 25.

2. Larry Stapleton (ed.),*State of the Environment in Ireland,*(Wexford: Environmental Protection Agency, 1996); additional information from Department of the Environment.

3. The World Commission on Environment and Development, *Our Common Future,*(Oxford University Press, 1987), p. 8. ["by permission of Oxford University Press"]

4. *Agenda 21: Programme of Action for Sustainable Development - The final text of agreements negotiated by Governments at the United Nations Conference on Environment and Development (UNCED), 3-14 June, 1992, Rio de Janeiro, Brazil,* (New York: United Nations Publications, 1993).

5. The Treaty on European Union, as signed in Maastricht on 7 February, 1992, published as, Council of the European Communities & Commission of the European Communities, *Treaty on European Union,* (Luxembourg: Office for Official Publications of the European Communities, 1992).

6. Commission of the European Communities Directorate-General XI - Environment, Nuclear Safety and Civil Protection, *Towards Sustainability: A European Community Programme of Policy and Action in Relation to the Environment and Sustainable Development,* (Luxembourg: Office for Official Publications of the European Communities, 1993).

7. *Agenda 21,* p. 15.

8. European Environment Agency, *Environment in the European Union, 1995: Report for the Review of the Fifth Environmental Action Programme,* edited by Keimpe Wieringa, (Luxembourg: Office for Official Publications of the European Communities, 1995).

9. *ibid.*

10. *An Environment Action Programme,* (Dublin: Department of the Environment, 1990).

11. *An Environment Action Programme: 1st Progress Report,* (Dublin: Department of the Environment, 1991).

12. *Moving Towards Sustainability: A Review of Recent Environmental Policy and Developments,* (Dublin: Department of the Environment, 1995).

13. Report of the Industrial Policy Review Group, *A Time for Change: Industrial Policy for the 1990s,* (Dublin: Stationery Office, 1992).

14. *Green 2000 Advisory Group Report,* (Dublin: Stationery Office, 1993).

15. *EU Structural Funds: A Practical Guide,* (Brussels: Irish Business Bureau, 1995), p. 4.

16. Council of the European Communities, "Council Regulation No. 792/93 of 13 March, 1993" in *Official Journal of the European Communities,* No. L79/74, 1 April, 1993; and Council of the European Communities, "Council Regulation No. 1164/94 of 16 May, 1994" in *Official Journal of the European Communities,* No. L130/1, 25 May, 1994.

17. *Ireland: National Development Plan 1994-1999,* (Dublin: Stationery Office, 1993).

18. *Ireland Community Support Framework, 1994-99,* (Luxembourg: Office for Official Publications of the European Communities, 1994).

19. European Commission, *Growth, Competitiveness, Employment: The Challenges and Ways Forward into the 21st Century* (White Paper), (Luxembourg: Office for Official Publications of the European Communities, 1994), pp. 161-167.

Chapter 3
Overall Goals and Priorities

1. cf. *State of the Environment in Ireland*, p. 33.

2. David Stanners and Phillippe Bourdeau (eds.), *Europe's Environment: The Dobris Assessment*, (Copenhagen: European Environment Agency, 1995).

3. United Nations Environment Programme, *Global Environmental Outlook*, (New York: Oxford University Press, 1997).

4. William E. Rees, "Revisiting Carrying Capacity: Area-Based Indicators of Sustainability" in *Population and Environment: A Journal of Interdisciplinary Studies*, Vol. 17, Number 3, (Human Sciences Press, Inc., 1996), p. 205.

5. *ibid.*, p. 210.

6. Further work remains to be done to more accurately define Ireland's ecological footprint. This is particularly so in the light of a revised methodology incorporating additional factors and calculations, published in March 1997 [see Mathis Wackernagel *et al.*, *Ecological Footprints of Nations: How Much Nature Do They Use? – How Much Nature Do They Have?*, (Mexico: Centro de Estudios para la Sustentabilidad, 1997], which suggests that all previous calculations significantly underestimated the size of ecological footprints.

7. As set out in *Moving Towards Sustainability*.

8. *Agenda 21*, p. 9.

9. cf. OECD, *Integrating Environment and Economy: Progress in the 1990s*, (Paris: OECD, 1996), pp. 21-23.

Chapter 4
Environment and Development

1. Central Statistics Office, *Census of Population of Ireland, 1996: Preliminary Report*, (Dublin: Stationery Office, 1996); Central Statistics Office, *1991 Census of Population - Detailed Report (Volume 2)*, (Dublin: Stationery Office, 1994); and Central Statistics Office, *Population & Labour Force Projections, 1996-2026*, (Dublin: Stationery Office, 1995).

2. Central Statistics Office, *1991 Census of Population - Detailed Report (Volume 1)*, (Dublin: Stationery Office, 1993).

3. *State of the Environment in Ireland*, pp. 146-159; Department of Agriculture, Food and Forestry, *Growing for the Future: A Strategic Plan for the Development of the Forestry Sector in Ireland*, (Dublin: Stationery Office, 1996), pp. 7-10.

4. *State of the Environment in Ireland*, p. 146.

5. *ibid.*, p. 147.

6. G. O'Sullivan, *A summary of uses of the CORINE land cover (Ireland) database* (Draft Report), (Dublin: Natural Resources Development Centre, Trinity College, 1995) cited in *State of the Environment in Ireland*, p. 146.

7. Figures supplied by CSO Data Service; see also *Shaping Our Future*, pp. 25-26, and *Economic Background to the Budget, 1997*, (Dublin: Department of Finance, 1997).

8. Forfás, *Shaping Our Future: A Strategy for Enterprise in Ireland in the 21st Century* (Summary Report), (Dublin: Forfás, 1996), p. 52.

9. Commission of the European Communities, *Economic Growth and the Environment: Some Implications for Economic Policy Making*, (Brussels: Communication from the Commission to the European Parliament and the Council, COM(94)465, 3 November, 1994); and European Commission, *Employment in Europe, 1995* [COM(95)361], (Brussels: Directorate-General for Employment, Industrial Relations and Social Affairs, 1995).

10. *Shaping Our Future*, p. 25.

11. *Economic Background to the Budget, 1997,* (Dublin: Department of Finance, 1997).

note: The seasonally adjusted standardised unemployment rate (live register) was 11.9% (281,700) at April 1996 [CSO, *Statistical Bulletin (December, 1996),* (Dublin: Stationery Office, 1996)]. Pending a review of the methodology for estimating unemployment rates on a monthly basis, revised estimates have not been made for the period after April 1996. The seasonally adjusted live register figure was 259,500 for February 1997.

12. *Green 2000 Advisory Group Report,* pp. 45-52.

13. *Employment in Europe,* pp. 155-157.

14. *Prosperity through Competitiveness: IBEC's Strategic Policy Framework, 1996-2005,* (Dublin: Irish Business and Employers Confederation, 1996), pp. 8-9.

15. *Integrating Environment and Economy: Progress in the 1990s,* p. 10.

16. *Employment in Europe,* p. 146

17. See, for example, OECD, *Environmental Policies and Industrial Competitiveness,* (Paris: OECD, 1993).

18. Brian Hutchinson and David Dowe, *Cleaner Manufacturing Technologies in Ireland,* (Dublin: Department of the Environment, 1993).

19. *A Time for Change: Industrial Policy for the 1990s,* p. 94.

20. *Shaping Our Future,* p. 51.

21. *Science, Technology and Innovation: The White Paper,* (Dublin: Stationery Office, 1996), p. 92.

22. *Report of the Joint Committee on Sustainable Development,* (Dublin: Stationery Office, 1997), p. iii.

23. Report of the Science Technology and Innovation Advisory Council, *Making Knowledge Work for Us: A Strategic View of Science Technology and Innovation in Ireland,* (Dublin: Stationery Office, 1995), pp. 34-36.

24. *Partnership 2000 for Inclusion, Employment and Competitiveness,* (Dublin: Stationery Office, 1996).

25. *Growth, Competitiveness, Employment: The Challenges and Ways Forward into the 21st Century,* pp. 164-167.

References: PART III - Strategic Sectors
Chapter 5 Agriculture

1. *Compendium of Irish Economic and Agricultural Statistics, 1996* [currently available on the website homepage of the Department of Agriculture, Food and Forestery - http://www.irlgov.ie/daff/index/htm].

2. Tony Leavy, "Use of Underutilised Resources in Irish Agriculture" in *Farm & Food,* (Dublin: Teagasc, 1996), p. 3.

3. Measure 1.1(d) on Farm Investment of *Operational Programme for Agriculture, Rural Development and Forestry, 1994-1999,* (Dublin: Stationery Office, 1994).

4. Measure 1.1(a) on Farm Investment of *OP for Agriculture, Rural Development and Forestry, 1994-1999.*

5. Information provided by the Department of Agriculture, Food and Forestry.

6. Council of the European Communities, "Regulation (EEC) No. 2078/92 of 30 June 1992 on agricultural production methods compatible with the protection of the environment and the maintenance of the country-side" in *Official Journal of the European Communities,* No. L 215/85, 30 July, 1992.

7. Information provided by the Department of Agriculture, Food and Forestry.

8. *State of the Environment in Ireland,* p. 84.

9. *1995 Annual Review & Outlook for Agriculture, the Food Industry and Forestry,* p. 40.

10. Central Statistics Office, *Statistical Abstract, 1996,* (Dublin: Stationery Office, 1996), p. 76.

11. Central Statistics Office, *June Survey,* (Dublin: Stationery Office, 1996).

12. Information provided under EU monitoring mechanism of Community CO_2 and other greenhouse gas emissions (as provided for in Council Decision 93/389/EEC, O.J. No. L 167, 9.3.1993).

13. *ibid.*

14. *Farm Wastes and Water Pollution: The Present Position,* (Dublin: Environmental Research Unit, 1989).

15. *ibid.,* p. 3.

16. *State of the Environment in Ireland,* p. 68; and John Lee, "Some Aspects of Sustainability in Relation to Agriculture in Ireland" in *Assessing Sustainability in Ireland,* p. 73.

17. John Lee, "Some Aspects of Sustainability in Relation to Agriculture in Ireland", p. 79.

18. *State of the Environment in Ireland,* p. 121.

19. B. Coulter and H. Tunney, "The Background to the P Debate"; papers for a Teagasc workshop, 1 November, 1996.

20. H. Tunney, "A Note on a Balance Sheet Approach to Estimating the Phosphorus Fertiliser Needs of Agriculture" in *Irish Journal of Agricultural Research 29(2),* pp. 149-154; also referred to in John Lee, "Some Aspects of Sustainability in Relation to Agriculture in Ireland", pp. 71-85.

21 H. Tunney, N. Culleton and O. Carton, "Phosphorus for Farming and the Environment" in *Farm & Food, July/December 1994,* (Dublin: Teagasc, 1994), p. 12.

22. *STRIDE Operational Programme for Ireland, 1991-93. Special Research Fund. Project 8: Eutrophication in the Inniscarra Reservoir, River Lee, Cork,* (Dublin: Department of the Environment, 1995).

23. H. Tunney, "Phosphorus for Farming and the Environment" in *Irish Journal of Agricultural Research,* (Dublin: Teagasc, 1990).

24. *OECD Environmental Data Compendium 1995,* (Paris: OECD, 1995), p. 265.

25. *State of the Environment in Ireland,* p. 157.

26. *ibid.,* pp. 118-121.

27. *The Quality of Drinking Water in Ireland - A Report for the Year 1995 with a Review of the Period 1993-1995,* (Wexford: Environmental Protection Agency, 1996), p. 15.

28. Donal Daly, "Chemical Pollutants in Groundwater: A review of the situation in Ireland", paper presented at Conference "Chemicals - A Cause for Concern?" in Cork, 3-4 November, 1994; and Michael O'Brien, "The Development of Groundwater Resources in North Cork", paper read at Spring Show Conference, 10 May, 1991.

29. O. T. Carton, M. Ryan and W. L. Magette, *Phosphorus Recommentations for Grassland - Good Agronomic Practice,* (Wexford: Teagasc, 1996).

30. *Code of Good Agricultural Practice to Protect Waters from Pollution by Nitrates,* (Dublin: Department of the Environment and Department of Agriculture, Food and Forestry, 1996).

31. *Operational Programme for Environmental Services, 1994-1999,* (Dublin: Stationery Office, 1994).

32. *Europe's Environment: The Dobris Assessment,* p. 146.

33. Central Statistics Office, *Land Utilisation and Number of Livestock - County Analysis Studies,* (Dublin: Stationery Office, 1996).

34. Information provided by the Department of Arts, Culture and the Gaeltacht.

35. C. O'Donnell, *Pesticides in Drinking Water: Results of a Preliminary Survey December 1994 - December 1995,* (Wexford: Environmental Protection Agency, 1996).

36. Council of the European Communities, "Council Directive 91/414/EEC of 15 July 1991 concerning the placing of plant protection products on the market" in *Official Journal of the European Communities,* No. L 230/1, 19 August, 1991.

37. *OECD Environmental Data Compendium 1995,* p. 271.

38. Information provided by the Department of Agriculture, Food and Forestry.

39. *ibid.*

40. *STRIDE Operational Programme for Ireland, 1991-1993. Special Research Fund. Project 6: Reuse and Recycling of Large Plastic Sheeting from the Agriculture, Horticulture, Building and Commercial Sectors,* (Dublin: Department of the Environment, 1995), p. 7.

41. *State of the Environment in Ireland,* p. 22.

42. *International Conference and Programme for Plant Genetic Resources: Country Report - Ireland,* (Dublin: Department of Agriculture, Food and Forestry, 1995).

43. Council of the European Communities, "Council Regulation (EC) No. 1467/94 of 20 June 1994 on the conservation, characterization, collection and utilization of genetic resources in agriculture" in *Official Journal of the European Communities,* No. L 159/1, 28 June, 1994.

44. *Shaping our Future,* p. 139.

45. *ibid.*

46. Council of the European Communities, "Council Directive (90/219/EEC) on the contained use of genetically modified micro-organisms" in *Official Journal of the European Communities,* No. L 117/1, 8 May, 1990.

47. Council of the European Communities, "Council Directive (90/220/EEC) of 23 April 1990 on the deliberate release into the environment of genetically modified organisms" in *Official Journal of the European Communities,* No. L 117/17, 8 May, 1990.

48. Council of the European Communities, "Council Regulation (EC) No. 258/97 of the European Parliament and of the Council of 27 January 1997 concerning novel foods and novel food ingredients" in *Official Journal of the European Communities,* No. L 43/1-7, 14 February, 1997.

Chapter 6
Forestry

1. *Growing for the Future,* p. 19.

2. *ibid.,* p. 15.

3. *ibid.,* p. 7.

4. Department of the Environment, *Ireland: Climate Change/CO$_2$ Abatement Strategy,* (Dublin: Stationery Office, 1993).

5. *State of the Environment in Ireland,* p. 242.

6. *Forestry and the Landscape Guidelines* and *Forestry and Archaeology Guidelines,* (Dublin: Department of Agriculture, Food and Forestry, 1993); *Forestry and Fisheries Guidelines,* (Dublin: Department of Agriculture, Food and Forestry, 1992).

7. *Forestry Development: Consultation draft of Guidelines for Planning Authorities,* (Dublin: Department of the Environment, 1997).

8. *Growing for the Future,* p. 10; data relate to 1985-91 except for Germany and Italy (data from Eurostat, 1976-86) and Ireland (1995 figures).

9. E.P. Farrell, "Sustainability of the Forest Resource" in *Assessing Sustainability in Ireland,* p. 135.

10. J. J. Bowman, *Acid Sensitive Surface Waters in Ireland,* (Dublin: Environmental Research Unit, 1991), cited in *State of the Environment in Ireland,* pp. 124-125.

11. Council of the European Communities, "Council Directive (79/409/EEC) of 2 April 1979 on the conservation of wild birds" ("the Birds Directive") in *Official Journal of the European Communities,* No. L 103/1, 25 April, 1979.

12. Council of the European Communities, "Council Directive (92/43/EEC) of 21 May 1992 on the conservation of natural habitats and of wild fauna and flora" ("the Habitats Directive") in *Official Journal of the European Communities,* No. L 206/35, 22 July, 1992.

13. Summary of criteria resulting from the Helsinki Conference follow-up process, provided by the Department of Agriculture, Food and Forestry.

14. "Resolution No. 1 of the 1993 Ministerial Conference on the Protection of Forests in Europe", *General Guidelines for the Sustainable Management of Forests in Europe,* (Helsinki: Ministry for Agriculture and Forestry, 1993).

15. "Statement of Forest Principles" in *Agenda 21,* pp. 291-294.

Chapter 7
Marine Resources

1. *Towards a Marine Policy for Ireland: Proceedings of the Consultative Process*, (Dublin: Marine Institute, 1996).

2. *New Directions for Agriculture, Forestry and Fisheries*, (Rome: United Nations Food and Agriculture Organisation, 1994), p. 16.

3. see *Operational Programme for Fisheries, 1994-1999*, (Dublin: Stationery Office, 1995), pp. 13, 29, data also provided by An Bord Iascaigh Mhara.

4. *Operational Programme for Fisheries, 1994-1999*, pp. 13, 29.

5. *International Convention for the Prevention of Pollution from Ships, 1973 done at London on the 2nd day of November, 1973, as amended by the protocol done at London on the 17th day of February, 1978 (MARPOL 73/78)*, (London: International Maritime Organisation).

6. *Code on the Safe Carriage of Irradiated Nuclear Fuel, Plutonium and High-Level Radioactive Wastes in Flasks on Board Ships (the INF Code)*, [IMO Assembly Resolution A18/Res.748], (London: International Maritime Organisation, 1993).

7. Papers from *Washington Global Programme of Action for the Protection of the Marine Environment from Land-based Activities*.

8. *ibid.*

9. *The International Convention for the Regulation of Whaling*, opened for signature in Washington DC on 2 December, 1946, and ratified by Ireland on 2 January, 1985, [International Whaling Commission, Cambridge, UK].

Chapter 8
Energy

1. International Energy Agency, *Energy Policies of IEA Countries: 1994 Review*, (Paris: OECD/IEA, 1995), p. 274.

2. Alison Myers, *Energy in Ireland 1980-1993: A Statistical Bulletin*, (Dublin: Department of Transport, Energy and Communications, 1994), p. 5.

3. *Energy Policies of IEA Countries: 1994 Review*, p. 278.

4. International Energy Agency, *Energy Policies of IEA Countries: Ireland 1994 Review*, (Paris: OECD/IEA, 1995), p. 31.

5. *Energy in Ireland 1980-1993*, p. 15.

6. *Energy Policies of IEA Countries: 1994 Review*, p. 275.

7. *ibid.*, p. 276.

8. Department of the Environment/ Environmental Protection Agency data (1994 figures).

9. Environmental Protection Agency information provided under the UN Framework Convention on Climate Change.

10. Intergovernmental Panel on Climate Change, *Climate Change 1995 - The Science of Climate Change: Contribution of Working Group 1 to the Second Assessment Report of the Intergovernmental Panel on Climate Change*, (Cambridge: University Press, 1996), p. 4.

11. Information provided by the Environmental Protection Agency.

12. *ibid.*

13. *State of the Environment in Ireland*, p. 57.

14. *Our Common Future*, p. 54.

15. *The European Auto Oil Programme: A Report by the European Commission Directorate-Generals for: Industry; Environment, Civil Protection and Nuclear Safety; and Energy*, (Brussels: European Commission, 1996).

16. *Renewable Energy: A Strategy for the Future,* (Dublin: Department of Transport, Energy and Communications, 1996), p. 13.

17. see *Environment Bulletin No. 26,* (Dublin: Department of the Environment, 1995), p. 7.

18. *Renewable Energy: A Strategy for the Future,* pp. 8-9.

19. Council of the European Communities, "Council Directive (96/16/EC) of 24 September 1991 concerning integrated pollution prevention and control" in *Official Journal of the European Communities,* No. L 257/26 of 10 October, 1996.

20. Department of Foreign Affairs, *Challenges and Opportunities Abroad: White Paper on Foreign Policy,* (Dublin: Stationery Office, 1996), p. 307.

Chapter 9
Industry

1. *Operational Programme for Industrial Development, 1994-1999,* (Dublin: Stationery Office, 1994).

2. *Task Force on Small Business,* (Dublin: Stationery Office, 1994), p. ii.

3. Central Statistics Office, *Statistical Abstract, 1996,* (Dublin: Stationery Office, 1997), p. 101.

4. *Ireland: National Development Plan, 1994-1999,* pp. 23, 53-61.

5. *Our Common Future,* p. 220.

6. M. F. McGettigan and C. O'Donnell, *Air Pollutants in Ireland: Emissions, Depositions and Concentrations 1984-1994,* (Wexford: Environmental Protection Agency, 1995), p. 9, as revised by EPA (see Fig 8.4).

7. Calculated from figures for 1994 provided by EPA (see Fig 8.4).

8. Calculated from figures for 1990 cited in *OECD Environmental Data Compendium 1995,* p. 21.

9. Calculated from figures for 1994 provided by EPA (see Fig 8.4).

10. *Air Pollutants in Ireland,* p. 19.

11. *State of the Environment in Ireland,* p. 116.

12. *ibid.,* p. 118.

13. *ibid.,* p. 156.

14. Colman Concannon, *Dioxins in the Irish Environment: An Assessment Based on Levels in Cow's Milk,* (Wexford: Environmental Protection Agency, 1996).

15. S. Scott and J. Lawlor, *Waste Water Services: Charging Industry the Capital Cost,* (Dublin: ESRI, 1994).

16. *Convention on the Prohibition of the Development, Production, Stockpiling and Use of Chemical Weapons and on their Destruction,* adopted on 3 September, 1992, at the Conference on Disarmament at Geneva.

17. Council of the European Communities, "Council Directive (82/501/EEC) of 24 June 1982 on the major-accident hazards of certain industrial activities" in *Official Journal of the European Communities*, No. L 230/1, 5 August, 1982.

18. P. Carey, G. Carty, J. Clarke, M. F. Crowe and P. J. Rudden, *National Waste Database Report 1995*, (Wexford: Environmental Protection Agency, 1996).

19. Council of the European Communities, "Council Directive (91/689/EEC) of 12 December 1991 on hazardous waste" in *Official Journal of the European Communities*, No. L 377/20, 31 December, 1991.

20. "Declaration and Resolution on Risk Reduction for Lead", adopted at Meeting of OECD Environment Policy Committee at Ministerial Level, Paris, 19-20 February, 1996.

21. *A Government of Renewal: Policy Agreement between Fine Gael, Labour Party, Democratic Left*, p. 25.

22. *Summary of Issues Raised at the Symposium on Sustainable Consumption*, 19-20 January, 1994, Oslo, Norway, cited in *OECD Workshop on Sustainable Consumption and Production: Clarifying the Concepts*, Rosendal, Norway, 2-4 July, 1995, (Paris: OECD, 1995), p. A7.

23. Commission of the European Communities, *Progress Report on Implementation of the European Community Programme of Policy and Action in Relation to the Environment and Sustainable Development "Towards Sustainability"*, (Brussels: Communication from the Commission, 10 January, 1996 - COM(95)624).

24. *Towards Sustainable Europe: The Study*, (Brussels: Friends of the Earth, 1995).

25. Repak, *Working Together on Waste: Report by IBEC's Industry Task Force on Recycling*, (Dublin: Irish Business and Employers Confederation, 1996).

26. Business Council for Sustainable Development, in association with UNEP, IEO, and CEC, *Getting Eco-Efficient: Report of the First Antwerp Eco-Efficiency Workshop*, November 1993, cited in *OECD Workshop on Sustainable Consumption and Production: Clarifying the Concepts*, p. A29.

27. *Industry and Environment, Vol. 17 No. 4*, (Geneva: UNEP IE, 1994), p. 4.

28. The first phase of *LIFE* (1992-95) has been completed; the legal basis for the second phase (1996-99) is Regulation (EC) No. 1404/96 adopted by the Council of Ministers on 15 July, 1996, (see *Official Journal of the European Communities*, No. L 181, 20 July, 1996).

29. Council of the European Communities, "Council Regulation (EEC) No. 1836/93 of 29 June 1993 allowing voluntary participation by companies in the industrial sector in a Community eco-management and audit scheme" in *Official Journal of the European Communities*, No. L 168/1, 10 July, 1993.

30. Adapted from *Guide to Environmental Self-Auditing*, (Dublin: The Chambers of Commerce of Ireland, 1993), p. 5.

31. "Launch of Environmental Training Programme for Irish Industry", IBEC Press Release, 15 January, 1997.

32. Council of the European Communities, "Council Regulation (EEC) No. 880/92, of 23 March 1992, on a Community eco-label award scheme" in *Official Journal of the European Communities*, No. L 99, 11 April, 1992.

33. Council of the European Communities, "European Parliament and Council Directive 94/62/EC of 20 December 1994 on packaging and packaging waste" in *Official Journal of the European Communities*, No. L 365/10, 31 December, 1994.

34. cf. *Shaping Our Future*, p. 247.

35. *Environmental Technologies from Ireland*, (Dublin: An Bord Tráchtála, 1995).

36. *Report of the Joint Committee on Sustainable Development*, p. 10.

Chapter 10
Transport

37. *Making Knowledge Work for Us: A Strategic View of Science Technology and Innovation in Ireland (Vol. 1),* (Dublin: Stationery Office, 1995), p. 107.

38 *Task Force on the Implementation of the Report of the Science, Technology and Innovation Advisory Council,* (Dublin: Department of Enterprise and Employment, 1996), pp. 103-108.

39. Loraine Fegan, *Environmental Research: Discussion Document on a National Programme and Priorities,* (Wexford: Environmental Protection Agency, 1995).

40. *Europe's Environment: The Dobris Assessment,* p. 421.

41. *Guidelines for Good Environmental Practice in Mineral Exploration,* (Dublin: Department of Transport, Energy and Communications, 1995).

42. *A New Minerals Policy: Report of the National Minerals Policy Review Group,* (Dublin: Stationery Office, 1995).

1. *Operational Programme for Transport, 1994-1999,* (Dublin: Stationery Office, 1994), p. 5.

2. *ibid.*

3. European Commission, *The Future Development of the Common Transport Policy: A Global Approach to the Construction of a Community Framework for Sustainable Mobility,* (Brussels: Directorate-General for Transport, 1992).

4. *Common Transport Policy Action Programme, 1995-2000,* (Luxembourg: Office for Official Publications of the European Communities, 1996).

5. European Commission, *Towards Fair and Efficient Pricing in Transport: Policy Options for Internalising the External Costs of Transport in the European Union,* (Brussels: Directorate-General for Transport, 1995).

6. European Commission, *The Citizens' Network: Fulfilling the potential of public passenger transport in Europe, Green Paper,* (Luxembourg: Office for Official Publications of the European Communities, 1996).

7. Based on an analysis of road travel in million vehicle-kilometres *per annum* in *Traffic Station Counts and Road Travel for 1995,* (Dublin: National Roads Authority, 1996), p. 11-12.

8. Information provided by the Dublin Transportation Office.

9. *Irish Bulletin of Vehicle and Driver Statistics, 1995,* (Dublin: Department of the Environment, 1996), p. 3.

10. Calculated from *World Road Statistics, 1997 Edition,* (Geneva: International Road Federation, 1997).

11. *Irish Bulletin of Vehicle and Driver Statistics, 1995,* p. 3.

12. *ibid.,* p. 26.

13. *Energy in Ireland 1980-1993: A Statistical Bulletin,* p. 19.

14. Figures extracted from *Irish Bulletin of Vehicle and Driver Statistics* [various years].

15. *Transport OP, 1994-1999,* p. 21.

16. *State of the Environment in Ireland,* p. 109.

17. Council of the European Communities, "Council Directive 96/62/EC of 27 September 1996 on ambient air quality assessment and management" in *Official Journal of the European Communities,* No. L 296/55, 21 November, 1996.

18. Calculated from figures supplied by the Environmental Protection Agency (see Fig 8.4).

19. Environmental Protection Agency information provided under the UN Framework Convention on Climate Change.

20. Information from European Commission Directorate-General XVII.

21. Calculated from figures supplied by the Environmental Protection Agency (see Fig 8.4).

22. *State of the Environment in Ireland,* p. 110.

23. *Irish Bulletin of Vehicle and Driver Statistics, 1995,* p. 3.

24. Information from European Commission Directorate-General for Environment, Nuclear Safety and Civil Protection. (DG-XI)

25. *Budget 1996,* (Dublin: Stationery Office, 1996), p. 27.

26. Information from European Commission DG XI.

27. *Irish Bulletin of Vehicle and Driver Statistics, 1995,* p. 3.

28. *Environment Bulletin No. 26,* p. 12; more recent data from Department of the Environment.

29. *Irish Bulletin of Vehicle and Driver Statistics, 1995,* p. 3.

30. *Ireland: Climate Change/CO$_2$ Abatement Strategy,* p. 13.

31. see *Environment Bulletin No. 31,* p. 40.

32. *White Paper: An Energy Policy for the European Union,* (Brussels: European Commission, 1995 - COM(95)682).

33. *Dublin Transportation Initiative: Final Report,* (Dublin: Stationery Office, 1995), pp. 150-151.

34. Michael Keating, *The Earth Summit's Agenda for Change: A plain language version of Agenda 21 and the other Rio Agreements,* (Geneva: Centre for Our Common Future, 1993), p. 12.

35. *Europe's Environment: The Dobris Assessment,* p. 362.

36. *State of the Environment in Ireland,* p. 193.

Chapter 11
Tourism

1. *Operational Programme for Tourism, 1994-1999*, (Dublin: Stationery Office, 1994).

2. See *Developing Sustainable Tourism*; *OP for Tourism, 1994-1999*; 1996 figures provided by the Department of Tourism and Trade.

3. *Developing Sustainable Tourism*, p. 12.

4. *Bord Fáilte Report and Accounts, 1995*, (Dublin: Bord Fáilte, 1996), p. 14.

5. See *Environment Bulletin No. 29*, pp. 31-32.

6. See *Environment Bulletin No. 30*, p. 4.

7. See supplement to *Environment Bulletin No. 29*.

8. Sinéad Ní Mhainnín, "Tourism Eco-Labelling" in Dave Hogan and Adrian Phillips (eds.), *Seeking a Partnership Towards Managing Ireland's Uplands*, (Dublin: Irish Uplands Forum, 1996), pp. 124-128; see also *Environment Bulletin No. 27*, pp. 29-30.

9. Information provided by Bord Fáilte.

10. *Developing Sustainable Tourism*, p. 13.

11. *State of the Environment in Ireland*, p. 223.

12. Information provided by the Department of Tourism and Trade.

13. *State of the Environment in Ireland*, p. 178.

14. *Developing Sustainable Tourism*, p. 30.

15. *ibid.*, p. 15.

16. *ibid.*, pp. 55-58.

17. Jeanne Meldon and Conor Skehan, *Tourism and the Landscape: Landscape Management by Consensus*, (Dublin: Bord Fáilte/An Taisce, 1996), p. iii.

18. Adapted from *Tourism and the Landscape: Landscape Management by Consensus*, p. 20.

19. *Developing Sustainable Tourism*, p. 54.

20. See *Environment Bulletin No. 26*, p. 21.

21. See *Environment Bulletin No. 31*, p. 11.

22. Extract from "Principles of Sustainable Development", the Irish Hotel and Catering Institute policy on Sustainable Development in the Hospitality Industry.

Chapter 12
Trade

1. *Statistical Bulletin* (December 1996), (Dublin: Central Statistics Office, 1996), p. 723.

2. *Shaping Our Future*, p. 90.

3. "Rio Declaration on Environment and Development" in *Agenda 21*, p. 10.

4. Commission of the European Communities, *Communication from the Commission to the Council and the European Parliament on Trade and Environment*, [Brussels: COM(96)54 final, Brussels, 28 February, 1996].

5. *Agenda 21*, p. 19.

6. *Challenges and Opportunities Abroad: White Paper on Foreign Policy*.

7. *Growing for the Future*, p. 35.

8. *Convention on International Trade in Endangered Species of Wild Fauna and Flora, 1973*, [CITES]; also being implemented in the European Community in "Council Regulation (EEC) No. 3626/82 of 3 December 1982 on the implementation in the Community of the Convention on International Trade in Endangered Species of Wild Fauna and Flora" in *Official Journal of the European Communities*, No. L 384, 31 December, 1982.

References: PART IV - Supporting the Strategy

Chapter 13 Environmental Quality

1. *State of the Environment in Ireland,* p. xxvi.

2. *Europe's Environment: The Dobris Assessment,* p. 13.

3. cited in *State of the Environment in Ireland,* pp. 113-117.

4. Council of the European Communities, "Council Directive (91/271/EEC) of 21 May, 1991 concerning urban waste water treatment" in *Official Journal of the European Communities,* No. L 135/40, 30 May, 1991.

5. Generale Des Eaux/M. C. O'Sullivan & Co. Ltd., *Greater Dublin Water Supply Strategy: Strategic Development Plan,* (Dublin: Department of the Environment, 1996).

6. *State of the Environment in Ireland,* pp. 10, 49.

7. *Irish Wildbird Conservancy Annual Report, 1995,* (Dublin: IWC/BirdWatch Ireland, 1996), p. 3.

8. *OP for Environmental Services, 1994-1999,* pp. 46-49, 78-81.

9. K. Dubsky, "Pressures on the Coastal Zone", in *Assessing Sustainability in Ireland,* pp. 113-117.

10. See *Environment Bulletin No. 28, p. 16.*

11. *State of the Environment in Ireland,* p. 179.

12. See *Dáil Debates* 6 March, 1996, pp. 1481-1507.

13. *State of the Environment in Ireland,* p. 72.

14. *Recycling for Ireland: A Strategy for Recycling Domestic and Commercial Waste,* (Dublin: Department of the Environment, 1994).

15. *Working Together on Waste: Report by IBEC's Industry Task Force on Recycling.*

16. *OP for Environmental Services, 1994-1999,* pp. 42-45, 72-77.

17. Alan Barrett and John Lawlor, *The Economics of Solid Waste Management,* (Dublin: The Economic and Social Research Institute, 1995).

18. John Dunne, Director-General, IBEC, in the foreword to *Working Together on Waste.*

19. *State of the Environment in Ireland,* p. 59.

20. *ibid.,* p. 98; see also *Environment Bulletin No. 26,* p. 11.

Chapter 14 Spatial Planning and Land Use

1. *Europe's Environment: The Dobris Assessment,* p. 24.

2. *Windfarms Development: Guidelines for Planning Authorities,* (Dublin: Department of the Environment, 1996).

3. *Telecommunications Antennae and Support Structures: Guidelines for Planning Authorities,* (Dublin: Department of the Environment, 1996).

4. *Forestry Development: Consultation draft of Guidelines for Planning Authorities,* (Dublin: Department of the Environment, 1997).

5. Department of the Environment, *Better Local Government - A Programme for Change,* (Dublin: Stationery Office, 1996).

6. Council of the European Communities, "Council Directive (85/337/EEC) of 27 June 1985 on the assessment of the effects of certain public and private projects on the environment" in *Official Journal of the European Communities,* No. L 175/40, 5 July, 1985.

7. *Draft Guidelines on the Information to be Contained in Environmental Impact Statements* and *Advice Notes on Current Practice,* (Wexford: Environmental Protection Agency, 1995).

8. United Nations Economic Commission for Europe, *Convention on Environmental Impact Assessment in a Transboundary Context done at Espoo (Finland), on 25 February, 1991,* (New York & Geneva: United Nations, 1994).

Chapter 15
The Built Environment

1. *Agenda 21*, pp. 52-54.

2. *Europe and Architecture Tomorrow*, (Brussels: Architects' Council of Europe, 1995), p. 6.

3. *Report of the United Nations Conference on Human Settlements (HABITAT II) (Istanbul, 3-14 June, 1996)* ["HABITAT Agenda"], (New York: United Nations, 1996), p. 57 [note: preliminary version of Report, reference A/CONF.165/14].

4. *Dublin Transportation Initiative: Final Report*, p. 129.

5. European Commission, *European Sustainable Cities: Report by the Expert Group on the Urban Environment*, (Brussels: European Commission - DG XI - Environment, Nuclear Safety and Civil Protection, 1996), p. 242.

6. *Operational Programme for Local Urban and Rural Development, 1994-1999*, (Dublin: Stationery Office, 1994).

7. *Guidelines on Residential Development in Designated Tax Incentive Areas*, (Dublin: Department of the Environment, 1996).

8. *A Study on the Urban Renewal Schemes: A Study Prepared by KPMG in association with Murray O'Laoire Associates, Architects and Urban Designers and the Northern Ireland Economic Research Centre*, (Dublin: Stationery Office, 1994).

9. *Strengthening the Protection of the Architectural Heritage*, (Dublin: Stationery Office, 1996).

10. Ann McNicholl and J. Owen Lewis (eds.), *Green Design: Sustainable Building for Ireland*, (Dublin: Stationery Office, 1996), p. 3.

11. Information provided by the Department of the Environment.

12. Information provided by the Irish Energy Centre.

13. *Green Design: Sustainable Building for Ireland*, p. 17.

14. *HABITAT Agenda*, p. 69.

15. *Annual Housing Statistics Bulletin, 1996*, (Dublin: Stationery Office, 1997).

16. *A Plan for Social Housing*, (Dublin: Department of the Environment, 1991).

17. *Social Housing - The Way Ahead*, (Dublin: Department of the Environment, 1995).

18. *Housing Management Group*: First Report, (Dublin: Department of the Environment, 1996).

Chapter 16
Public Action and Awareness

1. *Shaping Our Future*, p. 245.

2. INRA (Europe) - E.C.O., *Europeans and the Environment in 1995*, (Brussels: European Commission Directorate-General XI - Environment, Nuclear Safety and Civil Protection, 1995).

3. From submission made by An Taisce West Cork under the public consultation process for the preparation of this Strategy.

4. Erna Witoelar, "Sustainable consumption, our common challenge" in *Industry and Environment*, (UNEP IE, Oct-Dec 1995), p. 25.

5. *Europeans and the Environment in 1995*.

6. *Energy in Ireland 1980-1993: A Statistical Bulletin*, p. 15.

7. See *Environment Bulletin No. 28*.

8. S. Scott, "Energy Conservation in the Home - Are We Contrary?" in John FitzGerald and Daniel McCoy (eds.), *Issues in Irish Energy Policy*, (Dublin: Economic and Social Research Institute, 1993).

9. An Foras Forbartha, *Domestic Energy Use 1985-86: Results of a Survey*, (Dublin: An Foras Forbartha, 1988) as referred to in S. Scott, "Energy Conservation in the Home - Are We Contrary?".

10. *State of the Environment in Ireland*, p. 65.

11. *Greater Dublin Water Supply Strategy: Strategic Development Plan*, p. 14.

12. *Global Action Plan's Ecoteam Workbook*, (Dublin: GAP Ireland, 1996), p. 55.

13. *State of the Environment in Ireland*, p. 92.

14. *ibid.*, p. 90.

15. See *Environment Bulletin No. 29*, for *Action Against Litter* policy statement.

16. *Agenda 21*, p. 267.

17. See *Environment Bulletin No. 27*, pp. 18-19.

18. From submission made by An Taisce West Cork under the public consultation process for the preparation of this Strategy.

19. From submission made by Earthwatch/Friends of the Earth Ireland under the public consultation process for the preparation of this Strategy.

20. Up to and including December 1996; see also *Environment Bulletin No. 30,* p. 12 and *Environment Bulletin No. 29,* p. 4.

21. *Our Common Future,* p. 113.

22. *The Report of the Inter-Departmental Working Group on Environmental Awareness,* (Dublin: An Roinn Oideachais, 1994), p. 9.

Chapter 17
Ireland in the International Community

1. *Challenges and Opportunities Abroad: White Paper on Foreign Policy,* pp. 297-307.

2. *The Environmental Imperative,* Declaration by the European Council, Dublin, 25-26 June, 1990.

3. *Challenges and Opportunities Abroad: White Paper on Foreign Policy,* pp. 232-233.

4. *ibid.,* p. 230.

5. Information from the Department of Foreign Affairs.

6. Patrick D. McGuckian (ed.), *Irish Aid and Agriculture: A Report to the Minister for Foreign Affairs,* (Dublin: Irish Aid Advisory Council, 1996), p. 12.

7. See *Environment Bulletin No. 33.*

References: PART V - Implementing and Monitoring the Strategy

Chapter 18
Monitoring and Indicators

1. F. J. Convery, "Assessing Sustainability in Ireland - a Synthesis" in *Assessing Sustainability in Ireland,* p. 8.

2. *Agenda 21,* p. 284.

3. *ibid.,* p. 286.

4. *IRELAND Community Support Framework, 1994-99,* p. 62.

5. *ibid.*

6. *ibid.,* p. 63.

7. *ibid.,* p. 65.

8. *ibid.*

9. *ibid.,* p. 66.

10. S. Scott, B. Nolan and T. Fahey, *Formulating Environmental and Social Indicators for Sustainable Development,* (Dublin: ESRI, 1996).

11. *Environment Indicators:* OECD Core Set, (Paris: OECD, 1994).

12. *The OECD List of Social Indicators,* (Paris: OECD, 1982).

13. Published in *Assessing Sustainability in Ireland.*

14. *State of the Environment in Ireland,* p. xxv.

Chapter 19
Implementation and Review

1. *Strategic Management Initiative - Delivering Better Government, Second Report to Government of the Co-ordinating Group of Secretaries: A Programme of Change for the Irish Civil Service,* (Dublin: Government of Ireland, 1996), p. 14.

2. See *Environment Bulletin No. 24.*

3. *A Government of Renewal: Policy Agreement between Fine Gael, Labour Party, Democratic Left,* p. 25.

4. *ibid.*

5. *The Green Government Guide: Promoting Environmental Management & Practice in Government,* (Dublin: Department of the Environment, 1996).

6. *Energy Conservation Programme for State Buildings,* (Dublin: Office of Public Works, Department of Transport, Energy and Communications and Irish Energy Centre, 1995); see also Kevin O'Rourke (ed.), *Energy Officers Guidebook,* (Dublin: Irish Energy Centre, 1995).

7. *Better Local Government: A Programme for Change,* p. 11.

8. Submissions in this regard were made by the South-East Regional Authority and the Dublin Regional Authority as part of the public consultation process in the preparation of this Strategy.

9. *Local Authorities and Sustainable Development: Guidelines on Local Agenda 21,* (Dublin: Department of the Environment, 1996), Minister's Foreword.

10. *Agenda 21,* p. 230.

11. *Integrating Environment and Economy: Progress in the 1990s,* p. 23.